Microsoft® Office Excel® 2016: Part 2

About This Course

Whether you need to crunch numbers for sales, inventory, information technology, human resources, or other organizational purposes and departments, the ability to get the right information to the right people at the right time can create a powerful competitive advantage. After all, the world runs on data more than ever before and that's a trend not likely to change, or even slow down, any time soon. But with so much data available and being created on a nearly constant basis, the ability to make sense of that data becomes more critical and challenging with every passing day. You already know how to get Excel to perform simple calculations and how to modify your workbooks and worksheets to make them easier to read, interpret, and present to others. But, Excel is capable of doing so much more. To gain a truly competitive edge, you need to be able to extract actionable organizational intelligence from your raw data. In other words, when you have questions about your data, you need to know how to get Excel to provide the answers for you. And that's exactly what this course aims to help you do.

This course builds upon the foundational knowledge presented in the *Microsoft® Office Excel® 2016: Part 1* course and will help start you down the road to creating advanced workbooks and worksheets that can help deepen your understanding of organizational intelligence. The ability to analyze massive amounts of data, extract actionable information from it, and present that information to decision makers is at the foundation of a successful organization that is able to compete at a high level.

This course covers Microsoft Office Specialist exam objectives to help students prepare for the Excel 2016 Exam and the Excel 2016 Expert Exam.

Course Description

Target Student

This course is designed for students who already have foundational knowledge and skills in Excel 2016 and who wish to begin taking advantage of some of the higher-level functionality in Excel to analyze and present data.

Course Prerequisites

To ensure success, students should have completed Logical Operations' *Microsoft® Office Excel® 2016: Part 1* or have the equivalent knowledge and experience.

Course Objectives

Upon successful completion of this course, you will be able to leverage the power of data analysis and presentation in order to make informed, intelligent organizational decisions.

You will:

- Work with functions.

- Work with lists.
- Analyze data.
- Visualize data with charts.
- Use PivotTables and PivotCharts.

The CHOICE Home Screen

Logon and access information for your CHOICE environment will be provided with your class experience. The CHOICE platform is your entry point to the CHOICE learning experience, of which this course manual is only one part.

On the CHOICE Home screen, you can access the CHOICE Course screens for your specific courses. Visit the CHOICE Course screen both during and after class to make use of the world of support and instructional resources that make up the CHOICE experience.

Each CHOICE Course screen will give you access to the following resources:

- **Classroom**: A link to your training provider's classroom environment.
- **eBook**: An interactive electronic version of the printed book for your course.
- **Files**: Any course files available to download.
- **Checklists**: Step-by-step procedures and general guidelines you can use as a reference during and after class.
- **LearnTOs**: Brief animated videos that enhance and extend the classroom learning experience.
- **Assessment**: A course assessment for your self-assessment of the course content.
- Social media resources that enable you to collaborate with others in the learning community using professional communications sites such as LinkedIn or microblogging tools such as Twitter.

Depending on the nature of your course and the components chosen by your learning provider, the CHOICE Course screen may also include access to elements such as:

- LogicalLABS, a virtual technical environment for your course.
- Various partner resources related to the courseware.
- Related certifications or credentials.
- A link to your training provider's website.
- Notices from the CHOICE administrator.
- Newsletters and other communications from your learning provider.
- Mentoring services.

Visit your CHOICE Home screen often to connect, communicate, and extend your learning experience!

How to Use This Book

As You Learn

This book is divided into lessons and topics, covering a subject or a set of related subjects. In most cases, lessons are arranged in order of increasing proficiency.

The results-oriented topics include relevant and supporting information you need to master the content. Each topic has various types of activities designed to enable you to solidify your understanding of the informational material presented in the course. Information is provided for reference and reflection to facilitate understanding and practice.

Data files for various activities as well as other supporting files for the course are available by download from the CHOICE Course screen. In addition to sample data for the course exercises, the course files may contain media components to enhance your learning and additional reference materials for use both during and after the course.

Checklists of procedures and guidelines can be used during class and as after-class references when you're back on the job and need to refresh your understanding.

At the back of the book, you will find a glossary of the definitions of the terms and concepts used throughout the course. You will also find an index to assist in locating information within the instructional components of the book.

As You Review

Any method of instruction is only as effective as the time and effort you, the student, are willing to invest in it. In addition, some of the information that you learn in class may not be important to you immediately, but it may become important later. For this reason, we encourage you to spend some time reviewing the content of the course after your time in the classroom.

As a Reference

The organization and layout of this book make it an easy-to-use resource for future reference. Taking advantage of the glossary, index, and table of contents, you can use this book as a first source of definitions, background information, and summaries.

Course Icons

Watch throughout the material for the following visual cues.

Icon	Description
	A **Note** provides additional information, guidance, or hints about a topic or task.
	A **Caution** note makes you aware of places where you need to be particularly careful with your actions, settings, or decisions so that you can be sure to get the desired results of an activity or task.
	LearnTO notes show you where an associated LearnTO is particularly relevant to the content. Access LearnTOs from your CHOICE Course screen.
	Checklists provide job aids you can use after class as a reference to perform skills back on the job. Access checklists from your CHOICE Course screen.
	Social notes remind you to check your CHOICE Course screen for opportunities to interact with the CHOICE community using social media.

1 | Working with Functions

Lesson Time: 1 hour, 30 minutes

Lesson Objectives

In this lesson, you will work with functions. You will:

*   Use range names in formulas.

*   Learn function syntax.

*   Analyze data with logical functions.

*   Work with data & time functions.

*   Work with text functions.

Lesson Introduction

You already know how to get Microsoft® Office Excel® 2016 to perform simple calculations to make your job easier. However, manually entering formulas will take you only so far. The most commonly used functions in Excel may not be enough to handle complex data analysis needs. As you progress with Excel, and as you are called upon to provide a deeper understanding of your organization's data to decision makers, you'll need to know how to ask Excel more complex questions about your data and to get the answers you expect.

Of course, the more complex your data analysis tasks are, the more complexity you're likely to need in your formulas and functions. This means that you'll need to know how to "talk" to Excel at a higher level to get the most out of your data. As with mathematics in general, and all forms of computer programming, understating the language Excel speaks is the key to having productive conversations with Excel and getting the answers you need.

TOPIC A

Work with Ranges

Working with formulas and functions that calculate results from cells within one worksheet can be difficult enough; working with multiple worksheets and workbooks can seem downright impossible. To make it easier for you and others that utilize the work you do, Excel 2016 enables you to name ranges for use in functions and formulas. This provides a way for you to read a formula or function more naturally because these names are often based on existing titles used in the worksheet. In addition, with very large worksheets, navigation can take some time and cell and range names give you a way to navigate the worksheet much faster.

Cell and Range Names

Cell names and *range names* are exactly what they sound like. They are meaningful names you assign to a given cell or range to make it easier to both understand what calculations are being performed in a formula and to reuse the references for a number of purposes. Take a look at the following image, which shows two versions of the same formula: one using cell references and one using names.

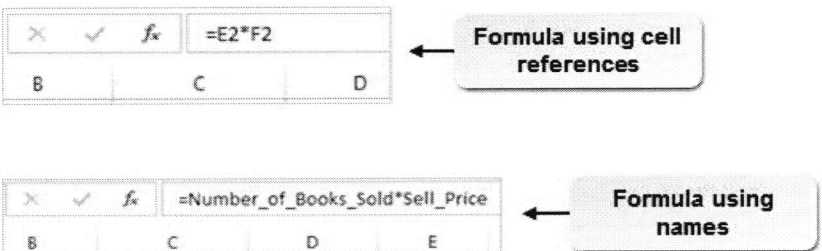

Figure 1–1: The same formula using cell references and names.

Now, imagine that you open this workbook months, or even years, after you created it. At first glance, which formula is easier to interpret? And, if you share this workbook with a colleague, which would make it clearer to the workbook recipient what he or she is looking at? It's pretty clear how powerful a feature this is.

 Note: Cell and range references aren't the only items you can name in Excel. You can name other objects, such as tables and even formulas themselves. Collectively, the names you assign to all of these items are known as *defined names*.

In short, cell and range names are concise, descriptive names you can assign to cells or ranges for the purpose of making formulas easier to read and maintain. You can assign a name to both contiguous ranges and noncontiguous ranges. Names refer to absolute references by default, but you can change those to relative references to facilitate the reuse of formulas.

 Note: It may be a good idea to indicate in a name whether the reference is absolute or relative, as the name will be displayed precisely as you created it, regardless of which type of reference it contains.

Although you can come up with an incredible array of different names, there are some rules you must follow:

- Names must begin with a letter, an underscore, or a backslash.
- After the first character, names can contain letters, numbers, periods, and underscores.
- Names cannot contain spaces.
- Names cannot be the same as a cell or a range reference. For example, you cannot use *A1* as a name.

- Names have a defined scope, either to a worksheet or a workbook, and must be unique within that scope.
- Names can contain up to 255 total characters.
- Excel does not recognize casing differences for names. So, within the same scope, you cannot, for example, create both *SalesTotals* and *salestotals* as names.
- You can use a single letter as a name, but you cannot use either *C* or *R*, either uppercase or lowercase, as these are used as shorthand for selecting an entire row or an entire column in other Excel features.

Names and the Name Box

There are several methods you can use to create names in Excel 2016. The most direct of these is to use the **Name Box**. To name a cell or a range, you can simply select the desired cell or range and then type the desired name in the **Name Box**. Once you've created named cells and ranges, you can access those cells and ranges from the **Name Box** drop-down menu. This is a quick way to select a cell or range that you've already named. Additionally, if you manually select a named cell or range on a worksheet, the name, not the cell reference, appears in the **Name Box**. Names created in the **Name Box**, by default, have "Workbook" as their scope.

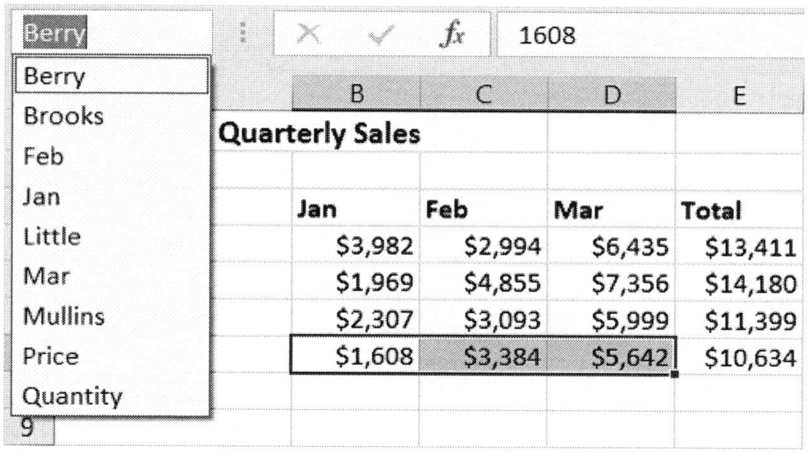

Berry				
Berry				
Brooks		B	C	D	E
Feb	Quarterly Sales			
Jan				
Little		Jan	Feb	Mar	Total
Mar		$3,982	$2,994	$6,435	$13,411
Mullins		$1,969	$4,855	$7,356	$14,180
Price		$2,307	$3,093	$5,999	$11,399
Quantity		$1,608	$3,384	$5,642	$10,634
9				

Figure 1–2: Named ranges in the Name Box.

The New Name Dialog Box

You can also name cells or ranges by using the **New Name** dialog box. The advantage here is that you have greater control over configuring precisely what the name refers to. You can access the **New Name** dialog box by selecting **Formulas→Defined Names→Define Name**.

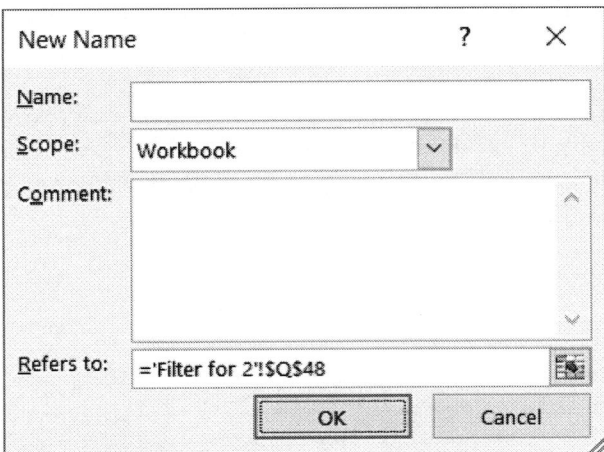

Figure 1-3: The New Name dialog box gives you greater control over naming cells and ranges.

The following table describes the various elements of the **New Name** dialog box.

New Name Dialog Box Element	Enables You To
Name field	Enter a name for the cell or range.
Scope drop-down menu	Assign a scope to the name. This can be either the entire workbook or a particular worksheet. You cannot create two identical names within the same scope. You can, however, create identical names for both a worksheet and the workbook containing that worksheet. On the worksheet, the name that has the worksheet as its scope will take precedence. On all other worksheets, the name that has the workbook as its scope will take precedence.
Comment field	Enter a brief description of the named cell or range to help clarify its purpose.
Refers to field	View or edit the name's reference. Whatever cell or range is selected when you open the **New Name** dialog box will be displayed as an absolute reference in the **Refers to** field by default.

The Create from Selection Command

Another method you can use to name ranges is the **Create from Selection** command. This command enables you to quickly and easily create a single range name or multiple range names at once, based on the range you currently have selected. The **Create from Selection** command does not work for naming individual cells. By default, named ranges you create by using this command have "Workbook" as their scope.

When you select a range and then select the **Create from Selection** command, Excel opens the **Create Names from Selection** dialog box, which enables you to select the cells from which Excel will create the names. This feature works best for ranges with clearly defined content types and appropriately labeled rows and columns. You may get unexpected results or error messages if labels don't align with Excel's naming conventions. If you use the **Create from Selection** command when a range in a single row or column is selected, Excel will create a single named range. If a range that covers multiple rows and columns is selected, Excel will create a series of named ranges based on the cell selection and the option you check in the **Create Names from Selection** dialog box. The cells from which Excel creates the names are not included in the range reference for the named ranges. The **Create from Selection** command is available in the **Defined Names** group on the

Formulas tab. You can also use the **Ctrl+Shift+F3** keyboard shortcut to open the **Create Names from Selection** dialog box.

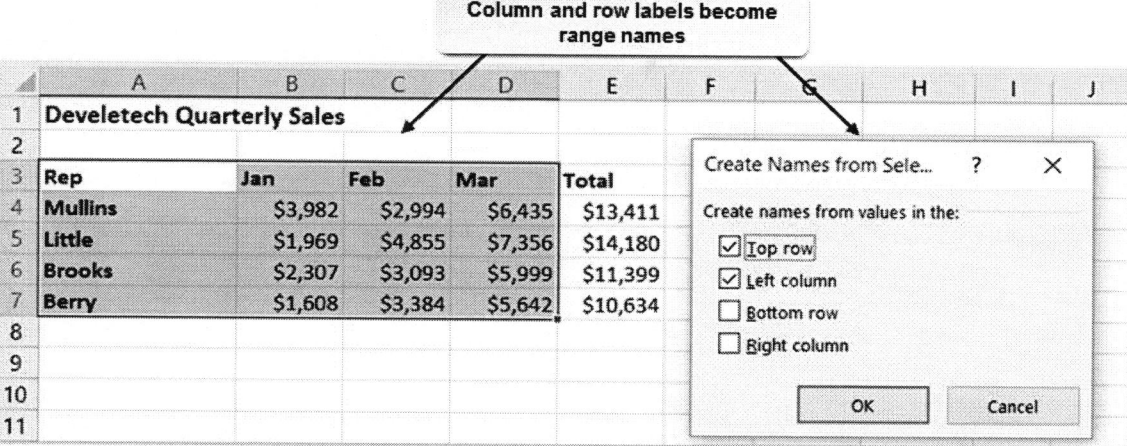

Figure 1-4: Use the Create from Selection command to quickly create multiple named ranges.

The Name Manager Dialog Box

As most workbooks are dynamic, changing documents, it stands to reason that you will likely have to edit named cells and ranges from time to time. For example, if you need to add rows to a range of data, you will likely want your named ranges to include the new rows. As such, Excel 2016 includes the **Name Manager** dialog box, a tool you can use to view and manage all of the named objects in your workbooks. From here, you can rename, edit, and delete existing defined names, and access the **New Name** dialog box to create new named cells or ranges. You cannot, however, change the scope of an existing cell or range name by using the **Name Manager** dialog box. To do this, you can delete the existing name and create a new one with the desired scope. The **Name Manager** dialog box also displays a **Filter** command, which you can use to filter the display of existing names. Use the **Filter** command, for example, to view only those names that have the entire workbook as their scope, names that have a particular worksheet as their scope, or names containing errors. You can access the **Name Manager** dialog box by selecting **Formulas→Defined Names→Name Manager**.

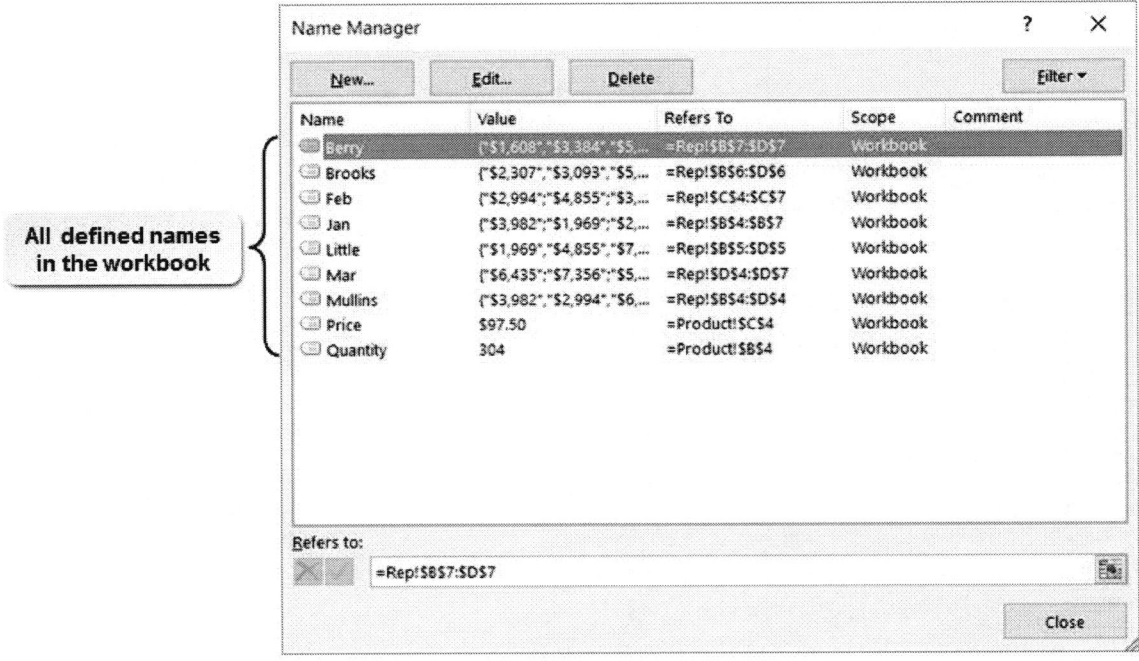

Figure 1-5: The Name Manager dialog box.

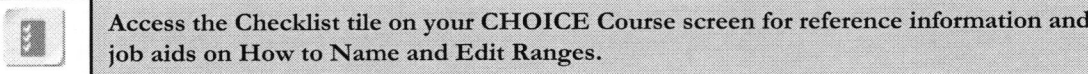
Access the Checklist tile on your CHOICE Course screen for reference information and job aids on How to Name and Edit Ranges.

ACTIVITY 1-1
Naming and Editing Ranges

Data File

C:\091056Data\Working with Functions\Current Projects.xlsx

Before You Begin

You are on the Windows 10 desktop.

Scenario

You are a Regional Sales Manager at Develetech Industries, a manufacturer of home electronics based in the fictitious city and state of Greene City, Richland (RL). Develetech is known as an innovative designer and producer of high-end televisions, video game consoles, laptop and tablet computers, and mobile phones. Develetech is a mid-sized company, employing approximately 2,000 residents of Greene City and the surrounding area. Develetech also contracts with a number of offshore organizations for manufacturing and supply-chain support. You have been asked to total regional data by quarter. To help yourself and others quickly identify the data being totaled, you decide to use range names in order to create the totals for each region and quarter.

 Note: Activities may vary slightly if the software vendor has issued digital updates. Your instructor will notify you of any changes.

1. Open Excel and the **Current Projects.xlsx** workbook.
   a) Open Excel 2016.
   b) From the **Start** screen, select **Open Other Workbooks**.
   c) Select **Browse**.
   d) Navigate to **C:\091056Data\Working with Functions** and open the file **Current Projects.xlsx**.

2. Use the **New Name** dialog box to create a named range in the **Quarter 1** column.
   a) Verify that you are on the **Region** worksheet.
   b) Select cell **B4** and then press **Ctrl+Shift+Down Arrow** to select the entire range in column **B**.
   c) Select **Formulas→Defined Names→Define Name**.
   d) In the **New Name** dialog box, in the **Name** field, verify **Quarter_1** is listed.
   e) From the **Scope** drop-down menu, ensure that **Workbook** is selected.
   f) Ensure that the **Refers to** field displays the following range reference: **=Region!$B$4:$B$7** and select **OK**.
   g) Select **Close**.

3. Use the **Name Box** to create a named range in the **Quarter 2** column.
   a) Select cell **C4:C7** and select the **Name Box**, type *Quarter_2* and press **Enter**.

b) Verify the new range name for Quarter_2 is listed in the **Name Box**.

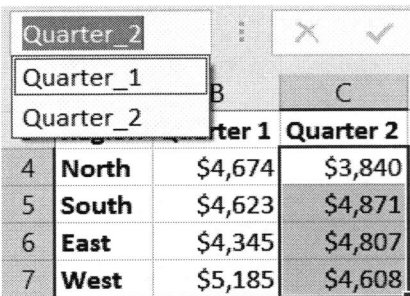

4. Use the **Create from Selection** command to create a named range in the **Quarter 3** and **Quarter 4** columns.

   a) Select the range D3:E7 and then select **Formulas→Defined Names→Create from Selection**.
   b) In the **Create Names from Selection** dialog box, ensure that the **Top row** check box is checked and then select **OK**.
   c) Select the **Name Box** drop-down arrow and verify that the two additional named ranges exist, confirming that the names appear as expected.

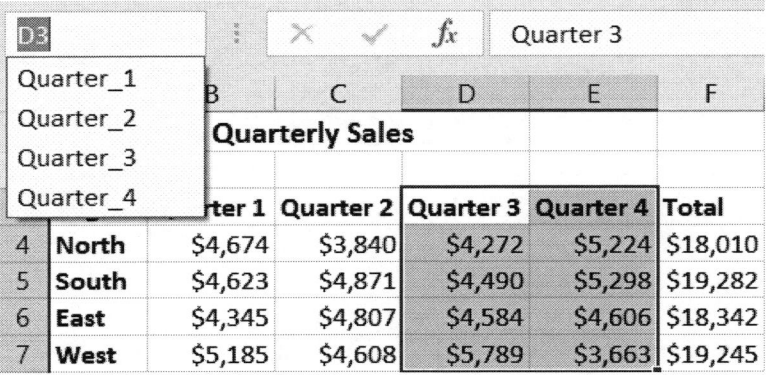

5. Use the **Create from Selection** command to create named ranges for the **Region** rows simultaneously.
   a) Select the range A4:E7.
   b) Select **Formulas→Defined Names→Create from Selection**.
   c) In the **Create Names from Selection** dialog box, ensure that the **Left column** check box is checked and then select **OK**.
   d) Verify that Excel created four unique named ranges for the **Region** rows.

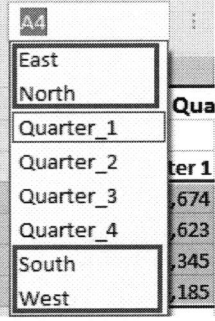

6. Navigate to a range and verify the correct total.

   a) From the **Name Box** drop-down list, select **South**.

   > **Note:** You may also use the **Go To** dialog box to navigate to ranges by pressing **F5**.

   b) Verify that Excel selected the quarterly values for the range **South** in **B5:E5**.

   c) With this range selected, note the **Total** for the range in cell **F5** and verify that the same total appears on the **Status Bar** for the **Sum** function.

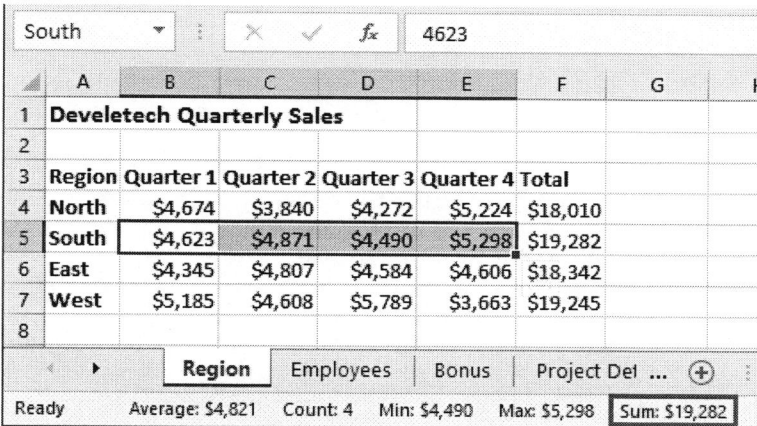

7. Edit the range names for the quarterly columns to make them a bit shorter.

   a) Select **Formulas→Defined Names→Name Manager**.

   b) In the **Name Manager** dialog box, select the **Quarter_1** named range and then select **Edit**.

   c) In the **Edit Name** dialog box, in the **Name** field, type *Qtr_1* and then select **OK**.

   d) Change the named range **Quarter_2** to *Qtr_2*.

   e) Edit the **Quarter_3** and **Quarter_4** named ranges to *Qtr_3* and *Qtr_4* respectively.

   f) Close the **Name Manager** dialog box.

   g) Examine the **Name Box** and verify that the names have changed as expected.

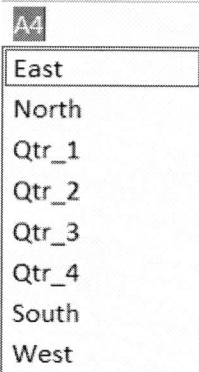

8. Save the workbook to the **C:\091056Data\Working with Functions** folder as *My Current Projects.xlsx*

Cell and Range Names in Formulas

Although it's certainly helpful to be able to name a range or a cell for easy navigation, the real power of this feature lies in the ability to easily identify references in formulas and to quickly and accurately insert references into multiple formulas. Once you've defined a name, you can simply use the name in place of a standard cell or range reference in any formula or function.

Figure 1-6: Named cells and ranges make it easy to identify the purpose of formulas and to enter cell and range references accurately.

As with many of the features and functions in Office applications, Excel provides several ways to perform a task. In Excel, inserting cell and range names in formulas and functions is one such task. The most common, though certainly not the only, methods for entering cell and range names are manually typing the name in a formula or function, using the **Use in Formula** command, and using the **Formula AutoComplete** feature. Let's look at each of these in some detail.

Manually Entering Cell or Range Names

The most direct method for including cell or range names instead of references in formulas or functions is to simply type them. Wherever you would normally enter a cell or range reference, you can type a defined name instead. The formula will reference the cell or range by name just as it would if you typed the cell or range reference, and your calculation results will be the same.

 Note: It is important to note that you can still type the cell or range references for a named cell or range in a formula, and they will still appear as cell or range references.

You can also manually select a cell or range that you've applied a name to directly on a worksheet to enter it into a formula just as you would with any unnamed range or cell. When you do this, Excel automatically displays the name, not the reference, though.

The Use in Formula Command Method

Excel 2016 includes a ribbon command you can use to insert cell and range names into formulas and functions: the **Use in Formula** command. As with manually typing a cell or a range name, you can use this method anywhere you would normally enter a range or cell reference in a formula. Instead of typing the name, you simply select the **Use in Formula** command, and then select the desired defined name from the drop-down menu. You can access the **Use in Formula** command by selecting **Formulas→Defined Names→Use in Formula**.

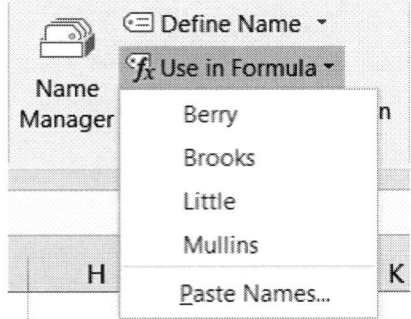

Figure 1-7: The Use in Formula command displays all valid defined names for use in formulas and functions.

From the **Use in Formula** drop-down menu, you can also select **Paste Names**, which opens the **Paste Name** dialog box. This provides you with yet another option for selecting a named cell or range. The added benefit here is that there is a keyboard shortcut, **F3**, that you can use to quickly open the **Paste Name** dialog box.

The Formula AutoComplete Method

You already know the Formula AutoComplete feature can help you enter functions into worksheet cells without having to type the full function name. Well, the Formula AutoComplete feature can also help you enter range and cell names into formulas and functions, and it works in the exact same way. As you type a formula or a function into a cell, whether directly into the cell or by using the **Formula Bar**, and you begin to type a cell or range name, the Formula AutoComplete feature automatically opens the same pop-up menu that appears when you type a function name. You can select any valid named cells or ranges from the pop-up menu to enter into the formula or function. The pop-up menu automatically filters the available defined names just as it would Excel functions. You can differentiate between functions and defined names in the Formula AutoComplete feature by viewing the icon next to each option. Functions will display the **Insert Function** icon, *fx* whereas defined names will display an icon that looks like a paper tag. Once you've entered the cell or range name, you simply continue entering the rest of the formula or function as you normally would.

⊿	A	B	C	D	E	F	G
1	**Develetech Quarterly Sales**						
2							
3	**Rep**	**Jan**	**Feb**	**Mar**	**Total**		
4	**Mullins**	$3,982	$2,994	$6,435	$13,411		
5	Little	$1,969	$4,855	$7,356	=SUM(li		
6	**Brooks**	$2,307	$3,093	$5,999	SUM(**number1**, [number2], …)		
7	**Berry**	$1,608	$3,384	$5,642	$10,(⨍ₓ LINEST		
8					Little		

Figure 1–8: Adding a range name by using the Formula AutoComplete feature.

 Access the Checklist tile on your CHOICE Course screen for reference information and job aids on How to Use Defined Names in Formulas and Functions.

ACTIVITY 1-2
Using Defined Names in a Formula

Before You Begin

The **My Current Projects.xlsx** workbook is open.

Scenario

Now that you have created named ranges for the various columns, you will use them to enter functions to provide your supervisor with the total sales by representative for the first quarter. This makes it easier for any person reviewing your work to identify where the values originate in the worksheet.

1. Use an existing range in a function.
   a) Verify that you are on the **Region** worksheet and select cell **F4** and type *=SUM(*
   b) Select **Formulas→Defined Names→Use in Formula→North**.
   c) Type *)* and press **Enter** to complete the function.
   d) Verify that the total for the North region is entered.

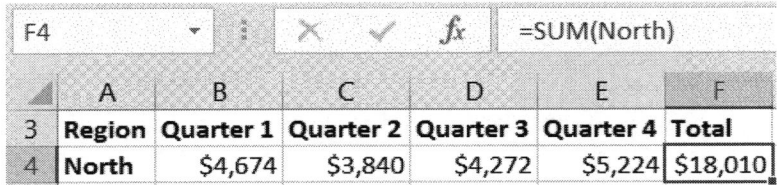

F4			f_x	=SUM(North)	
	A	B	C	D	E	F
3	Region	Quarter 1	Quarter 2	Quarter 3	Quarter 4	Total
4	North	$4,674	$3,840	$4,272	$5,224	$18,010

2. Enter a range name with the Formula AutoComplete method.
   a) Select cell **F5**, if necessary.
   b) Type *=SUM(so*
   c) From the **Formula AutoComplete** pop-up menu, double-click **South** or press **Tab**.

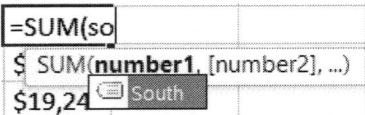

   =SUM(so
   $ SUM(**number1**, [number2], ...)
   $19,24   South

   d) Type *)* and press **Enter** to complete the function.

3. Replace cell references with range names.
   a) Select the range **F6:F7**.
   b) Select **Formulas→Defined Names→Define Name drop-down arrow→Apply Names**.
   c) Make sure that only **East** and **Wast** are selected and select **OK**.

   Note: The **Apply Names** dialog box has a built-in sticky function. This means that more than one range name may be selected. Simply deselect any range name not needed, or select all ranges and allow Excel to choose the correct range name.

d) Verify that the range names **East** and **West** are applied to cells **F6** and **F7**, respectively.

F7		⋮	×	✓	*fx*	=SUM(West)

◢	A	B	C	D	E	F
3	**Region**	**Quarter 1**	**Quarter 2**	**Quarter 3**	**Quarter 4**	**Total**
4	**North**	$4,674	$3,840	$4,272	$5,224	$18,010
5	**South**	$4,623	$4,871	$4,490	$5,298	$19,282
6	**East**	$4,345	$4,807	$4,584	$4,606	$18,342
7	**West**	$5,185	$4,608	$5,789	$3,663	$19,245

4. Save the workbook and keep the file open.

TOPIC B

Use Specialized Functions

You are already familiar with the most basic functions and formulas in Excel. You're also likely aware that there are far more complex tasks you can perform in Excel beyond adding up rows and columns and multiplying the sum by some other figure. To that end, you will need to use specialized functions to perform advanced calculations.

Excel contains a large set of built-in functions in several categories that will allow you to go beyond basic mathematics and perform operations on specialized types of data such as text, dates, and times. In this topic, you will learn the syntax of specialized functions to perform calculations on a variety of worksheet data.

Function Categories

You will find every built-in Excel function in the **Function Library** group on the **Formulas** tab. Here, the vast collection of available functions is organized into task-related categories. There are 13 standard categories of included functions, and this can be expanded by installing certain Excel add-ins.

 Note: You have to access several of these categories via the **More Functions** drop-down menu in the **Function Library** group, as well as by selecting the **Insert Function** command.

The Excel Function Reference

While it is certainly advantageous to be familiar with the purpose and syntax of functions you regularly work with, you will likely run into situations in which you need to use functions you are unfamiliar with or in which you need to identify which function serves a given purpose. In these cases, you'll want a fast, easy way to look up such information. Fortunately, Excel 2016 provides you with a powerful resource to do so: the *Excel function reference*. The function reference is not a separate, discrete tool; it is a Help resource available online. The function reference is basically a Help article that lists all Excel functions by category and describes each in detail. Each function's entry includes a general description of the function's task, any special considerations you should keep in mind regarding its use, a description of the function's syntax and arguments, and examples of the function in use. You can access the function reference by searching for ***Excel functions by category*** using either the **Tell me** field on the ribbon or the **Search** field in the **Excel 2016 Help** window. The **Excel 2016 Help** window is accessible by selecting the **File** tab and selecting the **Microsoft Excel**

Help button ? on the right side of the **Title bar** or by pressing **F1**.

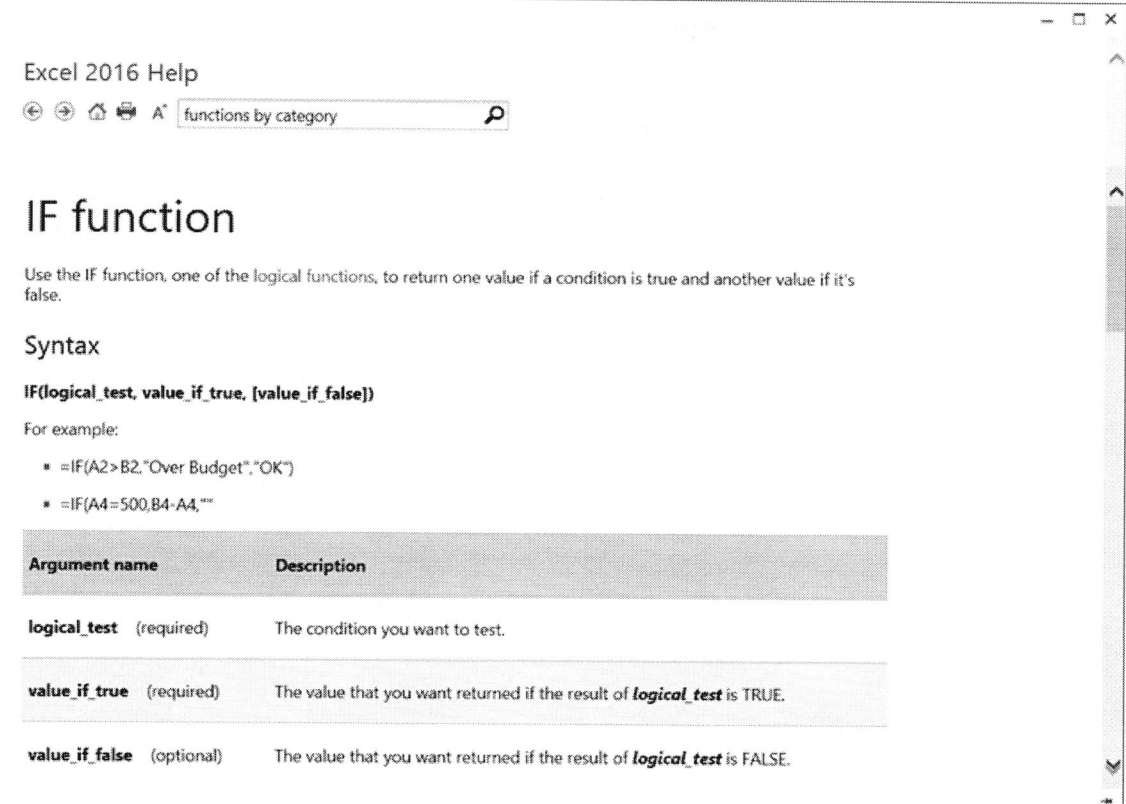

Figure 1-9: Use the Excel function reference to examine any function in detail.

Note: The **Insert Function** dialog box also provides some assistance for identifying the correct function to use for particular tasks, although it is much less detailed than what is available in the function reference. Because of this, you may find it helpful to use the **Insert Function** dialog box to identify the correct function and then look up that function in the function reference to see detailed information about it.

Access the Checklist tile on your CHOICE Course screen for reference information and job aids on How to Locate Functions by Using the Excel Function Reference.

Comparison Operator Basics

Before examining the syntax of more Excel functions, there is a group of operators you may not yet be familiar with in terms of Excel: comparison operators. You might, however, remember these as the mathematical symbols that indicate conditions such as one figure being greater than or less than another. As you advance in your understanding of Excel functions, you will find that these comparison operators form the basis for using many of Excel's functions and take advantage of many of its features. For now, it will be enough to simply understand what these comparison operators mean. The following table briefly describes what each of the operators means in Excel functions.

Comparison Operator	Meaning
=	Equal to
<	Less than

Comparison Operator	Meaning
>	Greater than
<=	Less than or equal to
>=	Greater than or equal to
<>	Not equal to

Function Syntax

By now, you have likely familiarized yourself with the syntax for a number of basic Excel functions and have had some opportunity to use them regularly. You'll remember that a function's syntax defines the structure of the function and identifies the required and optional arguments you can use to complete it. As you advance in your Excel proficiency, you'll want to add to your lexicon of familiar functions so you don't have to frequently look up functions as you develop your workbooks. Here is an overview of some of the most commonly used Excel functions you may not already be familiar with.

Remember that, in Excel function syntax, arguments in bold are required and arguments within square brackets (**[ ]**) are optional. In addition, remember that all arguments are separated by commas.

The COUNTIF Function

Syntax: =COUNTIF**(range,criteria)**

Use COUNTIF, one of the statistical functions, to count the number of cells that meet a criterion. For example, suppose you have a list of customers and one of the columns included the city where each customer is located. With the COUNTIF function, you can count the number of times a particular city appears in the list.

$$\times \quad \checkmark \quad f_x \quad | \quad =\text{COUNTIF(A1:E59,"Greene City")}$$

Figure 1–10: The COUNTIF function calculating the number of times Greene City appears in the customers list.

 Note: The **criteria** argument must be enclosed in quotation marks (" ") if it contains text, mathematical operators, or comparison operators. This is common among the various functions that contain the **criteria** argument.

The TODAY Function

Syntax: =TODAY()

This function enters the current date in a cell. Unlike other functions, the TODAY function does not have any arguments. This functions result is termed volatile, which means that it changes every time the worksheet recalculates. For example, you may need to calculate the difference between a given date (order date, shipping date, or hire date) and today's date. Each time the workbook is opened, the function updates to the current date, thus updating the difference between the dates.

Automatic Workbook Calculation

By default, Excel 2016 automatically recalculates the values returned by a formula or function if the data feeding the formula or function changes. In many cases, this functionality is preferred by users. However, in large workbooks with thousands of rows or columns of data and a large number of interdependent formulas, automatic recalculation can take anywhere from a few seconds to more than a minute. If you need to update multiple values in such a workbook, the automatic calculation functionality can actually hinder your efforts; while Excel is recalculating, you are unable to work in your worksheets. In these cases, you may want to temporarily disable automatic workbook calculations, revise the necessary data, and then update the workbook calculations. You can also choose to keep automatic workbook calculations turned off and manually update calculations by using the **Calculate Now** command found on the ribbon in the **Calculation** group of the **Formulas** tab, when updates are necessary.

The following table describes Excel's calculation options.

Calculation Option	Description
Automatic	Recalculates all dependent formulas every time you make a change to a value, formula, or name. This is the default calculation setting.
Automatic Except for Data Tables	Recalculates all dependent formulas—except data tables—every time you make a change to a value, formula, or name.
Manual	Turns off automatic recalculation and recalculate open workbooks only when you explicitly do so.
Calculate Now	Manually recalculates all open worksheets, including data tables, and updates all open chart sheets when **Manual** calculation is selected.
Calculate Sheet	Manually recalculates the active worksheet and any charts and chart sheets linked to the active worksheet.

 Access the Checklist tile on your CHOICE Course screen for reference information and job aids on How to Use Specialized Functions.

ACTIVITY 1–3
Locating and Using Specialized Functions

Before You Begin

The **My Current Projects.xlsx** workbook is open.

Scenario

You are an HR Generalist for Develetech Industries. You have been provided with an Excel workbook containing the hire dates of various employees. Your manager has asked you to find out what functions to use in order to determine which employees have a tenure of over 20 years with the company. You need to first find a function that will insert today's date, calculate the number of years an employee has been with the company based on that date, and count the number of employees that meet the 20 year criteria. To count the number of employees that meet the 20 year criteria, you will use the COUNTIF function using the **Insert Function** dialog box.

Find out how to:

- Insert today's date.
- Count the number of employees with 20 years of service.

---

1. Determine which function will insert the current date.
   a) Select the **Employees** worksheet and verify that cell **B3** is selected.
   b) On the ribbon, select the **Tell Me** search box and type *"insert current date"*
   c) Select **Get Help on "insert current date"**.
   d) Select the Help topic, **Insert the current date and time in a cell**.
   e) Read the Help topic on inserting the current date and close the **Excel 2016 Help** window.
   f) In cell **B3**, type *=TODAY()* and press **Enter**.

2. Calculate the years of service values for each employee.
   a) Select cell **C8**.
   b) Enter the formula, *=($B$3-B8)/365* and press **Enter**.
   c) Select cell **C8** and double-click the **AutoFill** handle to fill in the remaining years of service through cell **C37**.

    Note: Remember the AutoFill handle is the black square in the bottom-right corner of any cell or range, and when you place your mouse on it, it turns into a black plus sign.

3. Determine the number of employees with over 20 years of service.
   a) Select cell **B5**.
   b) Select **Formulas→Function Library→Insert Function**.
   c) Select the **Or select a category** drop-down arrow and select **Statistical**.
   d) From the **Select a function** list box select **COUNTIF** and select **OK**.
   e) In the **Function Arguments** dialog box, verify that your cursor is in the **Range** text box. Select the range **C8:C37** and then press **Tab**.
   f) In the **Criteria** text box, type *>=20* and select **OK**.

    Note: Note that Excel will enclose your criteria in double quotes.

g) Verify that five employees have a tenure over 20 years.

| B5 | ▾ | ⋮ | × | ✓ | *fx* | =COUNTIF(C8:C37,">=20") |

◢	A	B	C	D	E
1	**Develetech Employee Tenure**				
2					
3	**Current Date**	8/26/2015			
4					
5	**Over 20 Years Tenure**	5			
6					

 Note: Because the current date changes there may be more than five employees with a tenure over 20 years.

4. Save the workbook and keep the file open.

TOPIC C

Work with Logical Functions

Comparing and testing values, whether numbers, text, dates, or times can be a useful tool to analyze data. The logical functions in Excel provide a method for testing various conditions to calculate a result of a value, text, or a calculation which enable you to ask questions of your data. In this topic, you will analyze data with logical functions.

Logical Functions

One of the keys to data analysis is the ability to ask Excel questions about your data and get the answers you need. Perhaps the most foundational set of tools to do this is the collection of logical functions available in Excel. Logical functions enable you to ask questions of your data, for which Excel can return one of two values: TRUE or FALSE. Logical functions also enable you to perform calculations when certain conditions are met or to perform different calculations based on a variety of criteria.

By adding simple logic decision making to your formulas and functions, you can begin to gain a whole new perspective on the information available in your raw data. Before diving into the operators and syntax associated with logical functions, you'll need to look at a new type of cell data: logical values.

Logical Values

You are already familiar with the four basic types of data that can be entered into Excel cells: numeric values, text/labels, formulas/functions, and dates and times. When working with logical functions and comparison operators in Excel, you will encounter a new type of data: *logical values*. The only values that Excel can return when you apply a logical test to your data are TRUE or FALSE. This actually forms the basis for all logic used in computer programming and why the binary numbering system is so critical to how computers operate. In Excel, these logical values serve the same purpose as they do for programmers, establishing whether or not given criteria have been met.

Logical values may look like text, but they are quite different in both appearance (for the most part) and behavior. First, logical values are always displayed in capital letters, which distinguishes them from standard text strings. In fact, if you enter "true," "false," "True," or "False" in a cell, Excel automatically converts the text to logical values and displays them in uppercase letters. In order to even be able to enter these as standalone text strings, you must format the cell for text only, or use text functions/formulas to enter the text.

Second, logical values behave similarly to numeric values in functions and formulas, and in some cases are treated as either a 1 or a 0. And, logical values can be used as arguments in certain functions, as well as be returned by Excel as the result of a function performing a logical test.

> **Note:** The IF, AND, and OR functions discussed later in this topic all perform logical tests and can result in either TRUE or FALSE.

Comparison Operators

One other key component of working with logical functions that you need to examine before diving into specific logical functions and their syntax is *comparison operators*. Comparison operators behave similarly to mathematical and reference operators in that they tell Excel which specific task to perform. You use comparison operators to examine two values to see if they meet a specific logical condition. If the values meet the logical condition, the operation returns a logical value of TRUE; if the values do not meet the logical condition, the operation returns a logical value of FALSE. For example, say you have the value 10 in cell **A1**, and the value in **B1** is 15. If you use comparison operators to ask Excel if the value in cell **A1** is greater than the value in cell **B1**, Excel would return the logical value FALSE.

The following table describes the syntax and purpose of the comparison operators in Excel.

Name	Comparison Operator	This Comparison Operator Determines Whether or Not
Equal to	=	The specified values are the same.
Greater than	>	The first value is greater than the second value.
Less than	<	The first value is less than the second value.
Greater than or equal to	>=	The first value is greater than or equal to the second value.
Less than or equal to	<=	The first value is less than or equal to the second value.
Not equal to	<>	The specified values are different.

IF Function

Syntax: =IF(**logical_test**,value_if_true,value_if_false)

The IF function returns one value if the logical test you enter as an argument is true, and it returns a different value if the logical test is not true. You would use this function, for example, to determine a sales rep's commission if, and only if, he or she met a particular sales goal.

In the function's syntax, **logical_test** is the condition you would like to test; for example, are employee X's sales more than $1 million? You can use any item that returns a logical value for this argument: cells, ranges, or arrays populated with logical values; simple logical statements; or even other logical functions. Excel returns the result of the **value_if_true** argument if the logical condition is met. It returns the result of the **value_if_false** argument if the logical condition is not met. Either of these arguments can contain numeric values, references, text, or even formulas and functions. Text strings in either the **value_if_true** or the **value_if_false** argument must be enclosed in double quotation marks. (" "). If you do not enter a value in these arguments, they return the numeric value zero (0).

Let's take a look at a couple of examples of the IF function in worksheets. In this first example, sales reps will receive a 9-percent commission on their annual sales if those sales meet or exceed the $6,500 threshold. Otherwise, they will not receive a commission.

G7			f_x	=IF(F7>=$B$3,F7*$B$4,"No Commission")			

⊿	A	B	C	D	E	F	G
1	**Sales Rep Commissions**						
2							
3	**Sales Goal**	$6,500					
4	**Commission Rate**	9.0%					
5							
6	**Sales Rep**	**Q1**	**Q2**	**Q3**	**Q4**	**Total**	**Commission**
7	**Barbara**	$1,871	$1,950	$1,891	$1,419	$7,131	$641.79
8	**Thomas**	$1,342	$1,400	$1,518	$1,082	$5,342	
9	**Robert**	$1,618	$1,691	$1,700	$1,250	$6,259	

Figure 1-11: The IF function performing a calculation as a result of the test.

> **Note:** Note the use of absolute cell references for both the Sales Goal and Commission Rate. If you do not use absolute cell references for these cells when the formula is copied from one row to the next, they will shift to the next row as well. You should also be aware that you can use cell and range names instead, as they act as absolute cell references as well.

In this example, the **logical_test** argument asks Excel to examine the value in cell **F7** to determine if it is greater than or equal to the sales goal in **B3**. If it is, Excel should multiply the value in cell **F7** by the commission rate in cell **B4**. If it is not, Excel should display the text "No commission." As the logical test returns a value of TRUE, Excel performs the calculation in the **value_if_true** argument and returns the result in the cell. Now let's see what happens when the formula is copied to the next rep's row. In this case, as the value in cell **F8** is less than the sales goal, meaning the logical test returns a value of FALSE, Excel displays the text, "No Commission".

G8			×	✓	f_x	=IF(F8>=$B$3,F8*$B$4,"No Commission")	

	A	B	C	D	E	F	G
1	**Sales Rep Commissions**						
2							
3	**Sales Goal**	$6,500					
4	**Commission Rate**	9.0%					
5							
6	**Sales Rep**	**Q1**	**Q2**	**Q3**	**Q4**	**Total**	**Commission**
7	**Barbara**	$1,871	$1,950	$1,891	$1,419	$7,131	$641.79
8	**Thomas**	$1,342	$1,400	$1,518	$1,082	$5,342	No Commission
9	**Robert**	$1,618	$1,691	$1,700	$1,250	$6,259	

Figure 1–12: The IF function displaying text as a result of a false test.

Keep in mind that you don't always need an IF function to perform a calculation. You could simply use it to answer the question "Does each sales rep get a commission?" Here's what you would enter.

G8			×	✓	f_x	=IF(F8>=$B$3,"Yes","No")	

	A	B	C	D	E	F	G
1	**Sales Rep Commissions**						
2							
3	**Sales Goal**	$6,500					
4	**Commission Rate**	9.0%					
5							
6	**Sales Rep**	**Q1**	**Q2**	**Q3**	**Q4**	**Total**	**Commission**
7	**Barbara**	$1,871	$1,950	$1,891	$1,419	$7,131	Yes
8	**Thomas**	$1,342	$1,400	$1,518	$1,082	$5,342	No
9	**Robert**	$1,618	$1,691	$1,700	$1,250	$6,259	

Figure 1–13: The IF function displaying text answering a yes/no question.

Or, you can simply ask the IF function to return the value in a particular cell if the condition is met. In this last example, assume the sales reps get a flat $500 commission only if their sales exceed $6,500.

G9			$\times$ $\checkmark$ f_x	=IF(F9>$B$3,$B$4,)		

▲	A	B	C	D	E	F	G
1	**Sales Rep Commissions**						
2							
3	Sales Goal	$6,500					
4	Commission	$500					
5							
6	Sales Rep	Q1	Q2	Q3	Q4	Total	Commission
7	Barbara	$1,871	$1,950	$1,891	$1,419	$7,131	$500.00
8	Thomas	$1,342	$1,400	$1,518	$1,082	$5,342	$0.00
9	Robert	$1,618	$1,691	$1,700	$1,250	$6,259	$0.00

Figure 1-14: The IF function displaying a value as a result.

Here, because the **value_if_true** argument contains a cell reference, the function returns the value in cell **B4** when the logical test returns the value TRUE. Also, as the **value_if_false** argument has been left off, the function returns a value of zero (0) in cases where the logical condition was not met.

 Note: You must include the second comma in the IF function arguments if you want the function to return 0 when the logical condition isn't met. Otherwise, it will return a value of FALSE.

Functions Similar to the IF Function

There are several other useful functions that can perform calculations based on the logical comparisons.

Function Name	Function Definition	Function Arguments
SUMIF	You use the SUMIF function to sum the values in a range that meet criteria that you specify.	SUMIF(**range,criteria**, [sum_range])
SUMIFS	The SUMIFS function, one of the math and trig functions, adds all of its arguments that meet multiple criteria.	SUMIFS(**sum_range,criteria_range1, criteria1,**[criteria_range2,criteria2], ...)
COUNTIF	Use COUNTIF, one of the statistical functions, to count the number of cells that meet a criterion.	COUNTIF(**range,criteria**)
COUNTIFS	Use COUNTIFS to count cells using multiple criteria.	COUNTIFS(**criteria_range1,criteria1,** [criteria_range2,criteria2]...)
AVERAGEIF	Use the AVERAGEIF function to return the average of all the cells in a range that meet a given criterion.	AVERAGEIF(**range,criteria**, [average_range])
AVERAGEIFS	Use the AVERAGEIFS function to return the average of all the cells that meet multiple criteria.	AVERAGEIFS(**average_range,criteria_range1,criteria1,** [criteria_range2,criteria2], ...)

In the function's syntax, **range** is the range of cells to which the criteria is applied, **criteria** is the condition that must be met, and **sum_range** or **average_range** is the range of cells from which to add or average values if you want that range to differ from the one specified in the **range** argument.

If you do not specify a range for the optional **sum_range** or **average_range** argument, the function sums or averages the qualifying values from the cells specified in the **range** argument.

AND Function

Syntax: =AND(**logical1**, [logical2], ..., [logical30])

The AND function returns the logical value TRUE when all arguments entered in the function are true and returns the logical value FALSE if any one or more of the arguments are not true. You would use this function, for example, to determine if a sales rep has fulfilled all requirements to receive a commission bonus or to determine if an applicant has met all requirements to qualify for a loan.

In the function's syntax, **logical1** is the first logical test you wish to apply. Technically, only one argument is required in the AND function, but typically more than one is used; if you only wish to perform a single logical test, you could simply enter a formula containing the single logical test. The AND function can contain up to 30 arguments, all of which must either return a logical value, or be a cell or range reference or an array containing logical values. In addition to using comparison operators to return a logical value, you can also use mathematical statements as arguments. For example, 1+1=2 would return a logical value of TRUE.

For the following examples, assume cell **A1** contains the value 10, cell **A2** contains the value 15, and cell **A3** contains the value 20.

	A	B	C	D
1	10		**AND Function Examples**	**Formula Result**
2	15		=AND(A1<A2,A2<A3)	TRUE
3	20		=AND(A1<A2,A1>A3)	FALSE
4			=AND(A1<>A2,1+1=2)	TRUE
5			=AND(A3>A2,A4)	FALSE

Figure 1–15: Various AND function examples.

OR Function

Syntax: =OR(**logical1**, [logical2], ..., [logical30])

The only difference between the OR function and the AND function is that the OR function will return a logical value of TRUE if any one of the arguments evaluates to TRUE. It contains the same arguments, can support the same number of arguments, and the arguments can be the same items as with the AND function. If all of the arguments in an OR function are not true, the function will return the logical value FALSE. You would use this function, for example, if you wanted to identify sales reps who achieved at least one out of a set of multiple sales targets.

For the following examples, assume cell **A1** contains the value 10, cell **A2** contains the value 15, and cell **A3** contains the value 20.

	A	B	C	D
1	10		**OR Function Examples**	**Formula Result**
2	15		=OR(A1<A2,A2>A3)	TRUE
3	20		=OR(A1>A2,A2>A3)	FALSE
4			=OR(A1=A2,1+1=2)	TRUE
5			=OR(A3>A2,A4)	FALSE

Figure 1–16: Various OR function examples.

NOT Function

Syntax: =NOT(**logical1**)The NOT function is a logical function used to reverse the value determined by a logical comparison. If the comparison within the NOT function is determined to be true, the NOT function returns a value of FALSE. If the comparison is determined to be false, the function returns a value of TRUE. A common example of the NOT function is to reverse the behavior of another function.

For the following example, assume cell **A1** contains the value 10, cell **A2** contains the value 15, and cell **A3** contains the value 20.

	A	B	C	D
1	10		**NOT Function Examples**	**Formula Result**
2	15		=NOT(A1>0)	FALSE
3	20		=NOT(AND(A1<A2,A2<A3))	FALSE
4			=NOT(OR(A1>A2,A2>A3))	TRUE

Figure 1-17: Various NOT function examples.

ACTIVITY 1-4
Working with Logical Functions

Before You Begin

The **My Current Projects.xlsx** workbook is open.

Scenario

Heading the sales team at Develetech, you have recommended a compensation structure such that a 4 percent bonus will be given to all salespersons who meet their targets. Additionally, a bonus of 1 percent will be given for each business with sales greater than $85,000. You also want to count the number of times an employee achieves the category goal. You will use logical functions to quickly and easily calculate these bonuses.

1. Enter a function to calculate the 1 percent goal bonus for employees.
   a) Select the **Bonus** worksheet.
   b) Verify that cell **J8** is selected and type *=IF(*
   c) On the **Formula Bar**, select **Insert Function**.
   d) In the **Logical_test** text box, type *G8>=H8* and press **Tab**.
   e) In the **Value_if_true** text box, type *G8*$C$4* and press **Tab**.
   f) In the **Value_if_false** text box, type *0* and select **OK**.
   g) **AutoFill** the formula in cells **J9:J11** to calculate the goal bonus for the remaining employees.
   h) Verify a goal bonus has been earned by all but one employee.

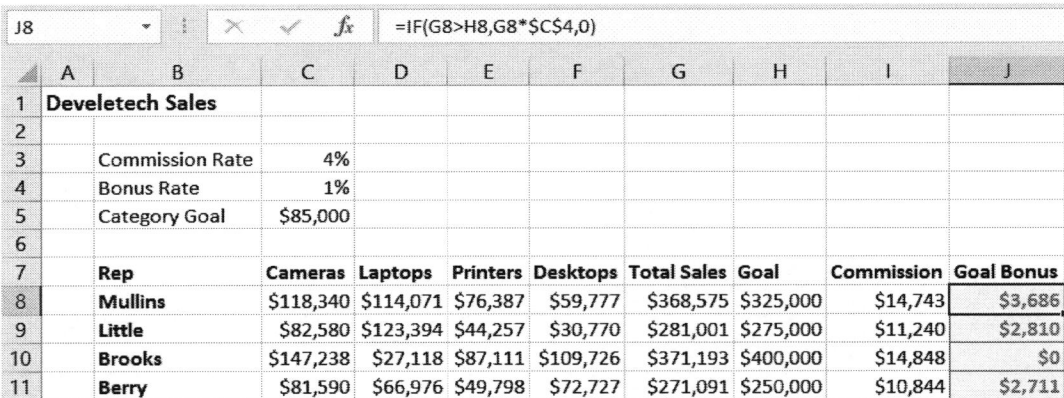

2. Enter a formula to calculate the category bonus, 1 percent of the sum of any category above the category goal, for the employees.
   a) Select cell **K8** and type *=$C$4*SUMIF(*
   b) On the **Formula Bar**, select **Insert Function**.
   c) In the **Function Arguments** dialog box, in the **Range** text box, type *C8:F8* and press **Tab**.
   d) In the **Criteria** text box, type *>85,000* and select **OK**.
   e) **AutoFill** the formula in cells **K9:K11** to calculate the category bonus for the remaining employees.

f) Verify all employees except one received a category bonus.

| Cell K11 | =$C$4*SUMIF(C11:F11,">85000") |

	A	B	C	D	E	F	G	H	I	J	K
1	Develetech Sales										
2											
3		Commission Rate	4%								
4		Bonus Rate	1%								
5		Category Goal	$85,000								
6											
7		Rep	Cameras	Laptops	Printers	Desktops	Total Sales	Goal	Commission	Goal Bonus	Category Bonus
8		Mullins	$118,340	$114,071	$76,387	$59,777	$368,575	$325,000	$14,743	$3,686	$2,324.11
9		Little	$82,580	$123,394	$44,257	$30,770	$281,001	$275,000	$11,240	$2,810	$1,233.94
10		Brooks	$147,238	$27,118	$87,111	$109,726	$371,193	$400,000	$14,848	$0	$3,440.75
11		Berry	$81,590	$66,976	$49,798	$72,727	$271,091	$250,000	$10,844	$2,711	$0.00

3. Enter a function to calculate the number of times each employee received a category bonus.

   a) In cell **L8**, type *=COUNTIF(C8:F8,">"&$C$5)* and press **Enter**.

    **Note:** The ampersand (&) character used here concatenates the greater than (>) operator enclosed in quotes and the cell reference together, joining the criteria argument for Excel to evaluate as >85,000. The ampersand character is discussed in text functions later in this lesson.

   b) AutoFill the formula in cells **L9:L11** to calculate the number of category bonuses for the remaining employees.

   c) Verify counts of each category bonus.

| Cell L11 | =COUNTIF(C11:F11,">"&$C$5) |

	A	B	C	D	E	F	G	H	I	J	K	L
1	Develetech Sales											
2												
3		Commission Rate	4%									
4		Bonus Rate	1%									
5		Category Goal	$85,000									
6												
7		Rep	Cameras	Laptops	Printers	Desktops	Total Sales	Goal	Commission	Goal Bonus	Category Bonus	Bonus Count
8		Mullins	$118,340	$114,071	$76,387	$59,777	$368,575	$325,000	$14,743	$3,686	$2,324.11	2
9		Little	$82,580	$123,394	$44,257	$30,770	$281,001	$275,000	$11,240	$2,810	$1,233.94	1
10		Brooks	$147,238	$27,118	$87,111	$109,726	$371,193	$400,000	$14,848	$0	$3,440.75	3
11		Berry	$81,590	$66,976	$49,798	$72,727	$271,091	$250,000	$10,844	$2,711	$0.00	0

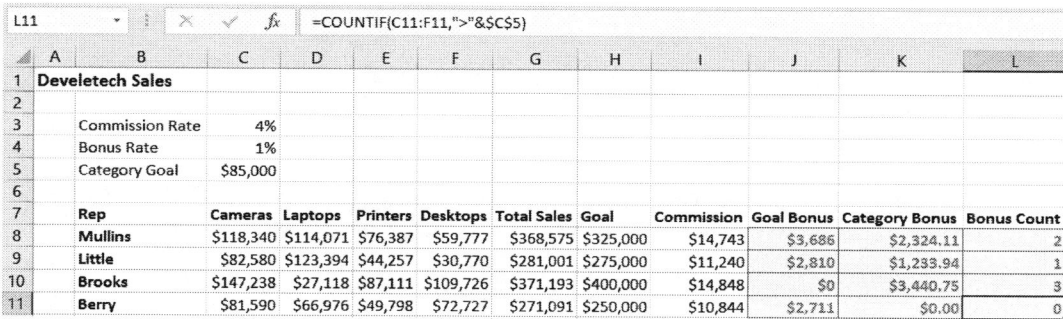

4. Save the workbook and keep the file open.

Nesting

The key to combining multiple calculations into a function in a single cell is *nesting*. Nesting is, simply, using a function as an argument within another function. Whatever value the nested function returns becomes the value the main function uses for the argument. This works much like including a reference to the value in a cell in a formula or function. Nesting enables you to craft highly complex functions that perform a wide variety of calculations or perform multiple logical tests in order to achieve a single result in a single cell.

Excel enables you to nest more than one function within the same larger function, and you can nest functions within nested functions. In fact, Excel 2016 supports up to 64 levels of nesting. A function nested within another function is referred to as a second-level function. A function nested within the nested function is called a third-level function, and so on.

Main Function

=IF(AND(I8>0,K8>1),"President's Club","")

Nested Function

Figure 1-18: Nesting enables you to use the value returned by one function as an argument in another function.

Nested Function Syntax

As is the case with all other Excel functions, the key to understanding nested functions is understanding nested function syntax. Because the particular syntax of any one nested function depends on the particular syntax of the first-level function and all of the other functions you wish to nest, this section will mainly focus on presenting a couple of examples of nested functions and then breaking down the syntax into chunks to examine the specific calculation.

Before looking at a few examples, however, there are some important points to keep in mind regarding nested functions in general:

- Any function used as an argument must return a value of the same data type as is required for the argument.
- You do not include the equal sign (=) before a nested function, but all remaining function syntax is the same as it usually is for the function. You still must include the equal sign before the first-level function.
- Each function, both the first-level function and all nested functions, must have a complete set of parentheses. These can become tricky to track, but they must all be present.

Now, let's take a look at two examples.

In this first example, the user is trying to determine if members of a group of sales reps qualify for a bonus. The bonus is based on meeting two criteria: having sales greater than $3,000 and having sold more than 2,000 units of product. It's easy to use an IF function to determine whether or not someone qualifies for a bonus based on a single criterion, but what about two criteria? For this, you can nest an AND function within an IF function.

D2	▼	× ✓ *fx*	=IF(AND(B2>3000,C2>2000),"Bonus", "No Bonus")					
	A	B	C	D	E	F	G	H	I
1	**Rep**	**Total Sales**	**Unit Sales**	**Bonus**					
2	Jack	$4,133	1818	No Bonus					
3	Constance	$3,168	1293						
4	Victor	$2,417	1756						
5	Cedric	$3,459	2200						
6	Timmy	$3,186	2413						
7									

Figure 1-19: Two AND logical tests nested within an IF function.

Here, we are simply using the AND function as the **logical_test** argument in the IF function. So the logical test includes both conditions stipulated by the AND function. As Jack has met only one of the conditions set out in the AND function, the IF function returns a value of FALSE. Remember that the **logical_test** argument can be either a logical test or a logical value. As the argument evaluates to the logical value FALSE, the IF function returns the **value_if_false** value, which in this case is "No Bonus."

 Note: Note that the AND function contains a complete set of parentheses and is fully contained within the space between the IF function's opening parenthesis and the IF function's first comma. This makes sense, as the entire AND function is the IF function's first argument. The IF function ignores the comma within the AND function's parentheses, as it is only looking for the value returned by the AND function.

In this second example, the user is calculating commission payments for a group of sales reps. But the particular commission rate depends on the sales volume generated by each rep. If the rep's sales are less than $2,000, he or she receives a 5-percent commission. If sales are between $2,000 and $4,999, the commission rate is 7 percent. If sales are $5,000 or more, the rep receives a 9-percent commission. If this were only a matter of two different rates, a simple IF function would suffice. But how do you add the second logical test? You nest one IF function within another.

C2			f_x	=IF(B2<2000,B2*0.05,IF(B2<5000,B2*0.07,B2*0.09))					
	A	**B**	**C**	**D**	**E**	**F**	**G**	**H**	**I**
1	**Rep**	**Sales**	**Commission**	**Total**					
2	Jack	$4,133	289.31	$4,422					
3	Constance	$3,168		$3,168					
4	Victor	$2,417		$2,417					
5	Cedric	$3,459		$3,459					
6	Timmy	$3,186		$3,186					
7									

Figure 1–20: An example of a nested IF function in the value_if_false argument.

Let's break down the function's syntax. If this had been a case of applying one of two commission rates, say either 5 or 7 percent, the function would have looked like this:

=IF(B2<2000,B2*0.05,B2*0.07)

But there is a third condition. Instead of telling Excel to multiply any value greater than $2,000 by a single value, you have to specify a second logical test. This second logical test, on its own, would typically look something like this:

=IF(B2<5000,B2*0.07,B2*0.09)

This function should be included as the third argument in the original function, without the leading equal sign, to get this:

=IF(B2<2000,B2*0.05,IF(B2<5000,B2*0.07,B2*0.09))

If you were to read this function aloud, it would sound something like, "If the value in cell B2 is less than 2,000, then multiply it by 5 percent; else, if the value is less than 5,000, multiply it by 7 percent; otherwise, multiply it by 9 percent." You do not need to include a logical argument for the value being greater than or equal to 5,000 as the first two logical arguments already include all values that don't match that description.

It is easy to see how nesting can quickly become highly complex. If you break the first-level function and all nested functions down into chunks and carefully think about what each function's syntax is asking Excel to do, you can read or write nearly any combination of nested functions.

 Note: To explore other methods of writing powerful formulas and functions, access the LearnTO **Use Wildcard Characters in References and Formulas** presentation from the **LearnTO** tile on the CHOICE course screen.

Guidelines for Combining Functions

 Note: All of the Guidelines for this lesson are available as checklists from the **Checklist** tile on the CHOICE Course screen.

As long as you understand the syntax of all functions you wish to nest, you can combine up to 64 levels of functions within a single first-level function. But you must carefully follow/understand these guidelines:

- To nest a function within another, include the nested function as an argument in the first-level function. Subsequent, lower-level functions can be nested within the nested function(s).
- You must include the equal sign (=) for the first-level function.
- Do not include an equal sign for any of the nested functions. The rest of the syntax for all nested functions remains the same.
- All functions, nested or otherwise, must include a full set of parentheses.
- Higher-level functions ignore the commas within the parentheses of nested functions. Those commas separate only the arguments for the associated function.
- Any function used as an argument must return a value of the same data type required for the argument.
- You can combine nested functions and other calculations within a single argument. For example, an argument that needs to be a numeric value can be made up of a function multiplied by a constant or by the value in a cell.
- You can include more than one nested function within a single argument.

ACTIVITY 1-5
Combining Functions

Before You Begin
The **My Current Projects.xlsx** workbook is open.

Scenario
You are pleased with the progress of your bonus worksheet. Now that you have calculated the goal and category bonuses, as well as counted the number of category bonuses, you want to test to see which employees will be awarded with a Winner's Club vacation. If employees exceed their targets and get a bonus in two or more business categories, they will be rewarded with a Winner's Circle vacation.

1. Enter a nested formula to test whether employees receive the Winner's Circle vacation.
   a) Verify that the Bonus worksheet is selected and select cell **N8**.
   b) Type *=IF(AND(* and then on the **Formula Bar**, select **Insert Function**.
   c) In the **Function Arguments** dialog box, in the **AND** function, verify that your cursor is in the **Logical1** text box.
   d) Type *J8>0* and press **Tab**.
   e) In the **Logical2** text box, type *L8>1*
   f) On the **Formula Bar**, select the **IF** function.

    Note: The **Function Arguments** dialog box will change from the **AND** function arguments to the **IF** function arguments.

   g) In the **Function Arguments** dialog box, select the **Value_if_true** text box, type *"Winner's Circle"* and press **Tab**.
   h) In the **Value_if_false** text box, type *""* and select **OK**.

    Note: There are no spaces between the double quotes.

   i) **AutoFill** the formula in cells **M9:M11** to calculate the honor for the remaining employees.

2. Verify that only Mullins is awarded the Winner's Circle achievement.

N11			fx	=IF(AND(J11>0,L11>1),"Winners Circle","")									
	A	B	C	D	E	F	G	H	I	J	K	L	M	N
1	Develetech Sales													
2														
3		Commission Rate	4%											
4		Bonus Rate	1%											
5		Category Goal	$85,000											
6														
7		Rep	Cameras	Laptops	Printers	Desktops	Total Sales	Goal	Commission	Goal Bonus	Category Bonus	Bonus Count	Total Compensation	Honor
8		Mullins	$118,340	$114,071	$76,387	$59,777	$368,575	$325,000	$14,743	$3,636	$2,324.11	2	$389,328	Winners Circle
9		Little	$82,580	$123,394	$44,257	$30,770	$281,001	$275,000	$11,240	$2,810	$1,293.94	1	$296,285	
10		Brooks	$147,238	$27,118	$87,111	$109,726	$371,193	$400,000	$14,848	$0	$3,440.75	3	$389,481	
11		Berry	$81,590	$66,976	$49,798	$72,727	$271,091	$250,000	$10,844	$2,711	$0.00	0	$284,646	

3. Save the workbook and keep the file open.

TOPIC D

Work with Date & Time Functions

Excel's date and time functions are often used by business analysts, human resources professionals, and project managers, who all frequently deal with scheduling and analyzing data for particular periods of time. But there are also a couple of handy functions for simply entering the current date or time. In this topic, you will work with of some of the more commonly used date and time functions.

The TODAY Function

Syntax: =TODAY()

This function enters the current date in a cell. This function has no arguments. As such, this functions results are known as volatile. That means that whenever the workbook is opened and Excel calculates all formulas and functions within the workbook that the date will update to the current date. Simply enter it into a cell to return the current date in whatever date format you have applied to the cell. You can use the value returned by this function to perform other calculations related to durations of time.

Excel uses a serial number system to represent dates and times. January 1, 1900 is represented by the number 1. Each day after that increases by one whole number. So, January 12, 1900 is represented by the number 12. This is how Excel is able to display dates in a number of different formats as the underlying serial number is always the same.

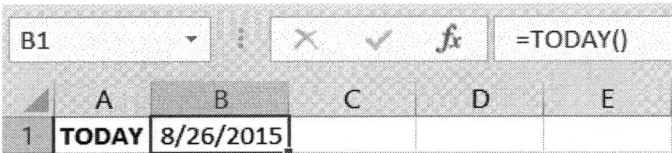

Figure 1-21: The TODAY function in cell B1.

 Note: If you do not wish the date to update when the workbook is opened simply enter a static date or press **CTRL+;** to insert the current date.

The NOW Function

Syntax: =NOW()

Like the TODAY function, this function has no arguments; it simply returns the current date and time in the cell you enter it into. You can use the value returned by this function to perform other calculations related to durations of time.

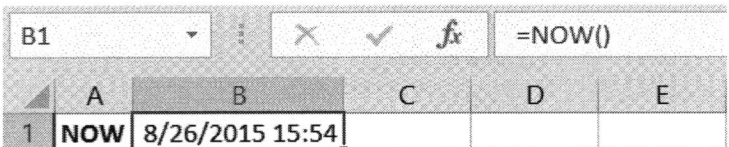

Figure 1-22: The NOW function is entered in cell B1.

Note: When you enter the NOW function in a cell, Excel automatically formats the cell with a custom cell format used to accommodate both the date and the time. Here is the format: m/d/yyyy h:mm. Although the format displays only a single *m* for month and a single *d* for day, dates will appear in cells with both numbers for months and dates that contain two digits. If you alter the format to a different date or time format, you will alter the value in the cell.

The DATE Function

Syntax: =DATE(**Year,Month,Day**)

A function similar to TODAY and NOW is the DATE function. The DATE function returns the serial number for the date entered in the arguments. Although the DATE function technically returns the specified date's serial number, it displays the date in whatever date format is applied to your worksheet cells.

In the DATE function's syntax, the **Year** argument is the four-digit year you wish to enter, the **Month** argument is the calendar month represented in numbers from 1 to 12, and the **Day** argument is the desired date. You use the DATE function largely to make calculations using other date and time functions, as using plain text or simply entering the date and time values can return errors.

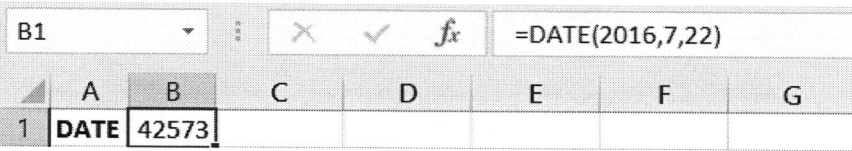

Figure 1–23: The serial number of the date 7/22/2016.

The NETWORKDAYS Function

Syntax: =NETWORKDAYS(**start_date,end_date**,[holidays])

The NETWORKDAYS function returns a count of the number of work days between two specific dates. You would use this function, for example, to determine how many working days you'll have to complete a project from now until a specific date in the future, or to calculate how much of a particular benefit employees have accrued. In the function's syntax, the **start_date** argument is the first date of the range for which you wish to count the number of work days. The **end_date** argument is the last day of the range. The optional **holidays** argument enables you to exclude known holidays so they are not counted as work days. The NETWORKDAYS function automatically excludes weekends from the calculation.

Note: In the United States, typical workdays are Monday-Friday and the weekend days are Saturday and Sunday. If you need to specify different working and weekend days use the NETWORKDAYS.INTL function.

In the following example,the number of working days are being counted in a project that starts on July 18, 2016 and ends on December 16, 2016. The project team will all be off every other Friday beginning at the end of July and running through August. The cells in the range B2:B6 have all been entered manually, but you can just as easily use the DATE function.

| B9 | ▼ | ⋮ | × | ✓ | fx | =NETWORKDAYS(B4,B5,B6:B8) |

	A	B	C	D	E
1	**Project Information**				
2					
3	**Description**	**Date**			
4	Start date of project	7/18/2016			
5	End date of project	12/16/2016			
6	Seassonal Shut Down Day	7/29/2016			
7	Seassonal Shut Down Day	8/12/2016			
8	Seassonal Shut Down Day	8/26/2016			
9	Total Work Days	107			
10					

Figure 1-24: The number of working days between the project start and end dates accounting for holidays.

The WEEKDAY Function

Syntax: =WEEKDAY(serial_number,[return_type])

Description: Returns the day of the week corresponding to a date. The day is given as an integer, ranging from 1 (Sunday) to 7 (Saturday), by default. You can specify what day of the week is assigned 1.

Required argument:

- **Serial_number**: A sequential number that represents the date of the day you are trying to find. Dates should be entered by using the DATE function, or as results of other formulas or functions. For example, use DATE(2016,5,23) for the 23rd day of May, 2016. Problems can occur if dates are entered as text.

Optional argument:

- **Return_type**: A number from 1 to 7 identifying the day of the week that is marked as day 1, the day of the week marked as day 2, and so on. The first three return types are listed in the following; the remaining return types are 11, 12, 13, 14, 15, 16, and 17. Each change the designated first day of the week.
  - 1 or omitted returns the numbers 1 for Sunday through 7 for Saturday.
  - 2 returns the numbers 1 for Monday through 7 for Sunday.
  - 3 returns the numbers 0 for Monday through 6 for Sunday.

In the following example, the date (8/26/2016), which is a Friday, is entered into cell **B1**. What day of the week is this date assuming you count from Sunday? The answer would be 6, as seen in cell **B3**. This is the default action of Excel; however, you can change the day of the week that you begin counting from by adding a return type. For example, the return type of 2 begins counting on Monday instead of the default Sunday. In this example, the day of the week would be 5, as seen in cell **B4**.

| B4 | ▼ | ⋮ | × | ✓ | fx | =WEEKDAY(B1,2) |

	A	B	C	D
1	Date	8/26/2016		
2				
3	Weekday	6		
4	Weekday starts on Monday	5		

Figure 1-25: The WEEKDAY Function.

The WORKDAY Function

Syntax: =WORKDAY(start_date, days, [holidays])

Description: Returns a number that represents a date that is the indicated number of working days before or after a date (the starting date). Working days exclude weekends and any dates identified as holidays.

Required arguments:

- **Start_date**: A date that represents the start date.
- **Days**: The number of non-weekend and non-holiday days before or after **start_date**. A positive value for days yields a future date; a negative value yields a past date.

Optional argument:

- **Holidays**: An optional list of one or more dates to exclude from the working calendar, such as state and federal holidays and floating holidays. The list can be either a range of cells that contain the dates or an array constant of the serial numbers that represent the dates.

Use the WORKDAY function to exclude weekends or holidays when you calculate invoice due dates, expected delivery times, or the number of days of work performed. While most people will enter dates as text, this can cause problems, so it is recommended that you enter dates using the DATE function. In the following example, the start date of a project is entered in cell **B2** and the project length is 150 days, as entered in cell **B3**. Additional non-working days are entered in **B4:B6**. Excel uses the WORKDAY function to calculate the end date of the project (**B7**).

B7		⌄	⋮	✕	✓	*fx*	=WORKDAY(B2,B3,B4:B6)	

◢	A	B	C	D	E
1	**Description**	**Date**			
2	Start date of project	7/22/2016			
3	Length of project	150			
4	Seasonal shut down day	7/29/2016			
5	Seasonal shut down day	8/12/2016			
6	Seasonal shut down day	8/26/2016			
7	End date of project	2/22/2017			

Figure 1-26: The WORKDAY Function.

The ISOWEEKNUM Function

Syntax: =ISOWEEKNUM(**Date**)

The ISOWEEKNUM function returns the number of the week in the year for the date entered. All weeks begin on a Monday. Week one starts on Monday of the first week of the calendar year that contains a Thursday. Generally, this means that week 1 is the week that contains January 1st. If you are in a manufacturing industry you might use this function to know the week number or you might see it beside the weeks of a monthly calendar.

B2		⌄	⋮	✕	✓	*fx*	=ISOWEEKNUM(B1)	

◢	A	B	C	D	E
1	Date	7/22/2016			
2	ISOWEEKNUM	29			
3					

Figure 1-27: The ISOWEEKNUM of a date.

ACTIVITY 1-6
Work with Date & Time Functions

Before You Begin

The **My Current Projects.xlsx** workbook is open.

Scenario

Based on the excellent work you did to calculate employee bonuses, you have now been asked to calculate the number of work days between the start and end of a project taking into account several seasonal shut down days that will occur within the project dates. In order to do this you will use the NETWORKDAYS function.

---

1. Select the Project Details worksheet and verify the project dates are entered for the project.
   a) The project dates should match the following:

	A	B
1	**Project Information**	
2		
3	**Description**	**Date**
4	Start date of project	7/18/2016
5	End date of project	12/16/2016
6	Seasonal Shut Down Day	7/29/2016
7	Seasonal Shut Down Day	8/12/2016
8	Seasonal Shut Down Day	8/26/2016
9	**Total Work Days**	

2. Enter the NETWORKDAYS function to calculate the total work days for the project.
   a) Verify that cell **B9** is selected.
   b) On the **Formula Bar**, select **Insert function**.
   c) In the **Insert Function** dialog box, from the **Or select a category** drop-down list, select the **Date & Time** category.
   d) From the **Select a function** list box, select the **NETWORKDAYS** function.
   e) Select **OK**.
   f) In the **Start_date** text box, type or select cell *B4* and press **Tab**.
   g) In the **End_date** text box, select cell **B5** and press **Tab**.
   h) In the **Holidays** text box, select the range, **B6:B8** and select **OK**.

i) Verify the total work days for the project.

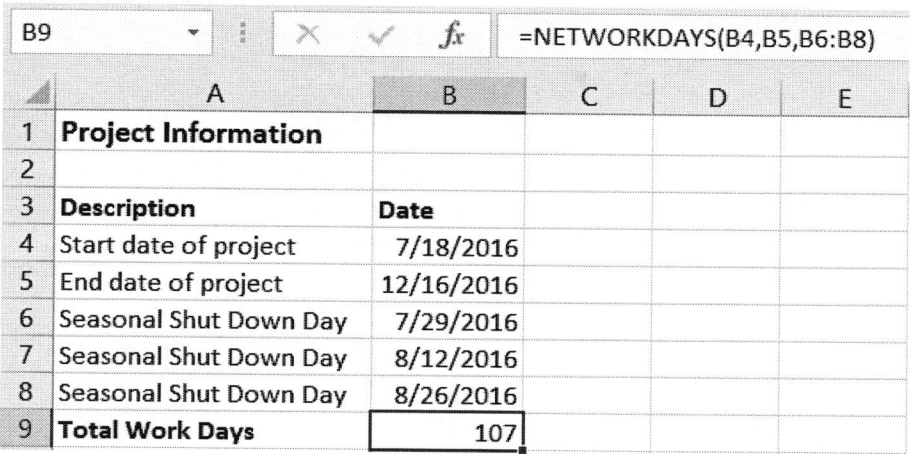

3. Save the workbook and keep the file open.

TOPIC E

Work with Text Functions

As you work with Excel, you will either enter data yourself or be provided with raw data from varied systems. You will be asked to perform calculations to produce the desired results for yourself or management. Excel's text functions let you manipulate text in cells to extract portions of text to other cells or combine them to produce full names or addresses.

The LEFT Function

Syntax: =LEFT(**text**,[num_chars])

The LEFT function returns the first character or characters in a text string, based on the number of characters you specify. For example, if the full name Mark Thompson was in cell A2, you could use the LEFT function in cell B2 to extract the first four characters of that text resulting in a cell with the first name Mark.

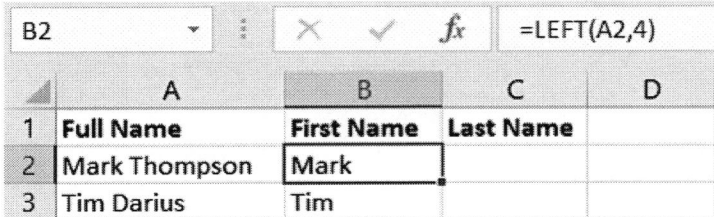

Figure 1–28: The LEFT Function returns the first four characters from cell A2.

The FIND Function

Syntax: =FIND(**find_text**,**within_text**,[start_num])

To extract text from cells that contain values of varying characters, Excel also includes the FIND function. The FIND function locates one text string within a second text string, and returns the number of the starting position of the first text string from the first character of the second text string. For example, if a cell contains a full name in the format, Last name, First name, with the FIND function nested within the [num_char] argument of the LEFT function you can locate the comma (,) separating each name and return the comma and all characters before the comma. Normally, you would want to remove the comma from the result, therefore, we modify the LEFT functions [num_char] by subtracting one character from the result (the comma) by entering, -1.

Figure 1–29: The FIND function locates the comma and returns the text before the comma.

The RIGHT Function

Syntax: =RIGHT(**text**,[num_chars])

The RIGHT function returns the first character or characters in a text string, based on the number of characters you specify. For example, if the full name Timothy Darius was in cell A3 you could use the RIGHT function in cell C3 to extract six characters from the right of that text resulting in a cell with the last name Darius.

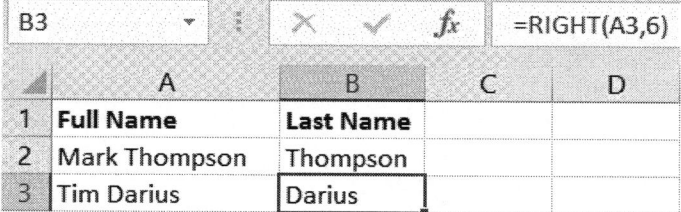

Figure 1-30: The RIGHT function displaying the result of the last six characters of text.

The Text to Columns Feature

The **Text to Columns** feature in the **Data Tools** group on the **Data** tab of the ribbon is another method of splitting text. This feature splits a single column of text into multiple columns. For example, you can create first and last name columns from one column of full names. When used, this feature starts the Convert Text to Columns Wizard. The wizard's three steps let you select how the text should be treated as a group, what character separates the text, and the destination of the text in other columns.

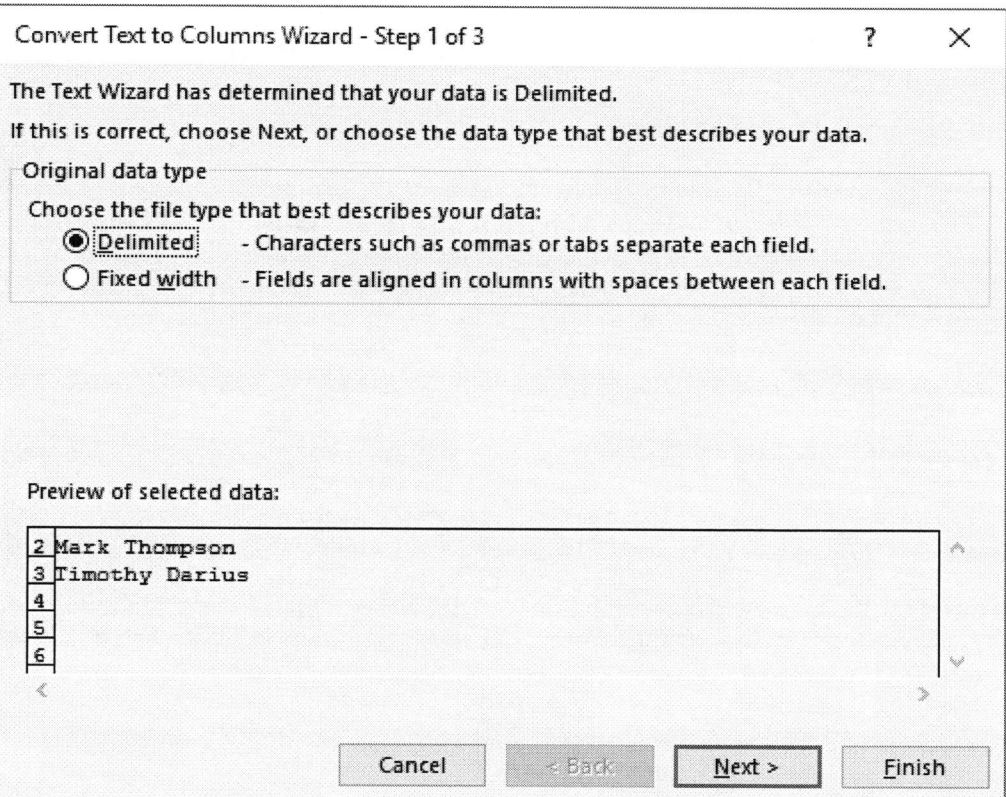

Figure 1-31: The Convert Text to Columns Wizard.

The MID Function

Syntax: =MID(**text,start_num,num_chars**)

The MID function returns the characters from the middle of a text string, starting at the position you specify, based on the number of characters you specify. For example, various man made acronyms or codes can be separated into their respective parts. Imagine your organization has multiple campuses and several, multi-floored buildings on each campus. A campus/building/floor code could be built, such as C1BAFL01, and you could be asked to extract the building identifier (BA) from a list of codes. The MID function can perform this operation by looking at the text in cell A2 starting at the third character, and returning the next two characters.

C2	▾	×	✓	f_x	=MID(A2,3,2)	

◢	A	B	C	D
1	**Campus/Building/Floor**	**Campus**	**Building**	**Floor**
2	C1BAFL01	C1	BA	
3	C1BBFL02	C1		
4	C1BAFL02	C1		
5	C1BBFL03	C1		
6	C1BAFL03	C1		
7	C1BCFL01	C1		
8	C1BCFL02	C1		
9	C1BCFL03	C1		
10				

Figure 1–32: The MID function extracting characters from the middle of text.

The CONCATENATE Function

Syntax: =CONCATENATE(**text1**,[text2], ...)

One of the most powerful text functions available in Excel 2016 is the CONCATENATE function. This function enables you to concatenate, or join together, text strings from multiple cells into a single cell. This function can save you massive amounts of time when you need to pull together data from multiple cells that already exists in your worksheets. Say you've been placed in charge of updating your organization's personnel records, which the human resources department saves in Excel workbooks. You've been asked by HR to change the format in which names are entered. Previously, first and last names were entered into separate columns within the worksheets, but now HR would prefer full names entered into a single column. The CONCATENATE function is perfect for tasks such as this.

In the function's syntax, **text1** is the only required argument, which represents the first string of text you wish to include in the new cell. You can add up to 254 other arguments for a total of 255 joined text strings. You can manually type text or numerical values as arguments, and you can use cell references to include text entered into cells. The CONCATENATE function will include empty spaces (leading spaces, trailing spaces, and spaces between words and values in cells) when it joins text strings together. If you wish to include spaces where none are present in the original data, you can use an empty space enclosed in double quotation marks (" ") as an argument.

The following examples illustrate several methods of using the CONCATENATE function.

D2	▾	⋮	×	✓	fx	=CONCATENATE(A2,B2)	

◢	A	B	C	D	E
1	**First Name**	**Last Name**	**Suffix**	**Full Name**	
2	John	Howell	Jr.	JohnHowell	
3					

Figure 1-33: The CONCATENATE function joining first and last name without spaces.

In this first example, notice the CONCATENATE function joined the text strings from cells **A2** and **B2** together in cell **C2**, and that there is no space between the first and the last name. This is because there are no leading or trailing spaces in either cell **A2** or **B2**, and because we didn't include one in the function. Now let's modify this function to include a space between the names.

D2	▾	⋮	×	✓	fx	=CONCATENATE(A2," ",B2)	

◢	A	B	C	D	E
1	**First Name**	**Last Name**	**Suffix**	**Full Name**	
2	John	Howell	Jr.	John Howell	
3					

Figure 1-34: The CONCATENATE function joining first and last name with a space.

Here, the CONCATENATE function placed a space between the first and the last name because the empty space has been included as an argument. In this last example, you see the CONCATENATE function used to join text from more than two cells and add a character manually.

D2	▾	⋮	×	✓	fx	=CONCATENATE(A2," ",B2,", ",C2)	

◢	A	B	C	D	E
1	**First Name**	**Last Name**	**Suffix**	**Full Name**	
2	John	Howell	Jr.	John Howell, Jr.	
3					

Figure 1-35: The CONCATENATE function joining first name, last name, and suffix with spaces and punctuation.

Text Concatenation with the Ampersand

Another way to concatenate text strings and numeric values from worksheet cells is to use the ampersand (&) operator in formulas. By using this method, you can still include either cell references or text and values entered in double quotation marks to join text strings. This is how the aforementioned first and the third examples would work if you used the ampersand operator in formulas instead of the CONCATENATE function.

C2	▾	⋮	×	✓	fx	=A2&" "&B2	

◢	A	B	C	D
1	**First Name**	**Last Name**	**Full Name**	
2	John	Howell	John Howell	
3				

Figure 1-36: The Ampersand character joining first and last name with a space.

D2	▼	:	×	✓	fx	=A2&" "&B2&", "&C2	

	A	B	C	D	E
1	**First Name**	**Last Name**	**Suffix**	**Full Name**	
2	John	Howell	Jr.	John Howell, Jr.	
3					

Figure 1-37: The Ampersand character joining first name, last name, and suffix with spaces and punctuation.

Other Text Functions

Many times, data that comes from sources such as text files, mainframes, or databases can store data in various formats. When this data is rendered in Excel it can often make reading the data difficult because the data can be combined with other text or simply displayed in uppercase or lowercase letters. Excel contains three text functions that are very useful for formatting text to display it in the desired format. The UPPER, LOWER, and PROPER functions are described below. These functions are all similar in that they only have a **text** argument. In addition, these functions are extremely helpful when nested in the CONCATENATE function.

The UPPER Function

Syntax: =UPPER(**text1**)

Description: The UPPER function converts a text string to uppercase or capitalizes all the text in a string.

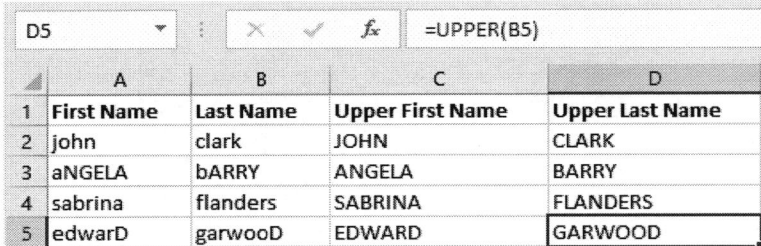

D5	▼	:	×	✓	fx	=UPPER(B5)	

	A	B	C	D
1	**First Name**	**Last Name**	**Upper First Name**	**Upper Last Name**
2	john	clark	JOHN	CLARK
3	aNGELA	bARRY	ANGELA	BARRY
4	sabrina	flanders	SABRINA	FLANDERS
5	edwarD	garwooD	EDWARD	GARWOOD

Figure 1-38: The UPPER function capitalizing all text.

The LOWER Function

Syntax: =LOWER(**text1**)

Description: The LOWER function converts a text string to lowercase or capitalizes all the text in a string. The LOWER function does not change characters in text that are not letters.

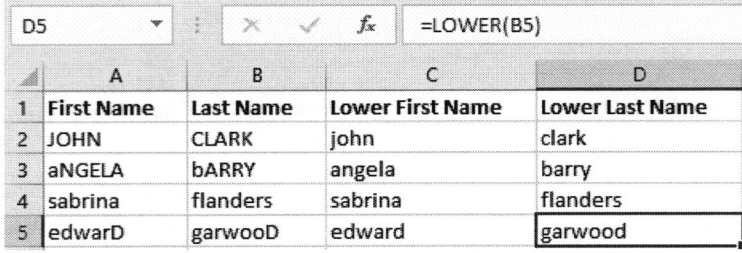

D5	▼	:	×	✓	fx	=LOWER(B5)	

	A	B	C	D
1	**First Name**	**Last Name**	**Lower First Name**	**Lower Last Name**
2	JOHN	CLARK	john	clark
3	aNGELA	bARRY	angela	barry
4	sabrina	flanders	sabrina	flanders
5	edwarD	garwooD	edward	garwood

Figure 1-39: The LOWER function displaying all text in lowercase.

The PROPER Function

Syntax: =PROPER(**text1**)

Description: The PROPER function converts a text string to proper case, meaning that the function capitalizes the first letter in a text string and converts the other letters to lowercase.

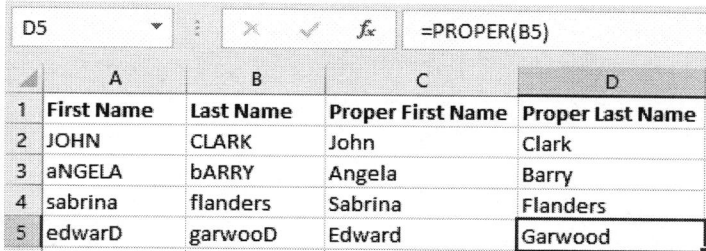

Figure 1–40: The PROPER function capitalizing the first letter of text and making all other letters lowercase.

ACTIVITY 1–7
Working with Text Functions

Before You Begin
The **My Current Projects.xlsx** workbook is open.

Scenario
You are an HR Generalist at Develetech Industries. Your company has a large campus with multi-floored buildings. In order to locate an employee in any building of the campus you have been asked to extract various parts of data from text provided to you by your manager. The first two characters of the code are campus notation, the next two characters represent the building code, and the last four characters comprise the floor location. In order to do this, you will use text functions.

1. Select the **Campus Information** worksheet.

2. Extract the campus code, the first two characters, from the combined field.
   a) Verify that cell **D2** is selected.
   b) Select **Formulas→Function Library→Text→LEFT**.
   c) In the **Text** text box, type or select cell *C2* and press **Tab**.
   d) In the **Num_chars** text box, type *2* and select **OK**.
   e) Verify that the campus code was extracted.

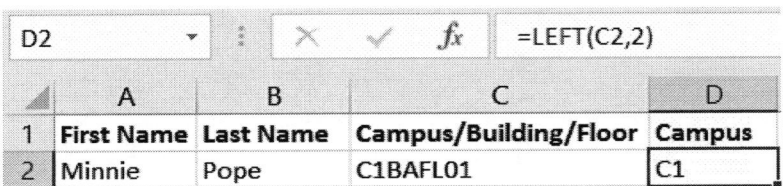

3. Extract the building code, the third and fourth characters, from the combined field.
   a) Select cell **E2**.
   b) Select **Formulas→Function Library→Text→MID**.
   c) In the **Text** text box, type or select cell *C2* and press **Tab**.
   d) In the **Start_num** text box, type *3* and press **Tab**.
   e) In the **Num_chars** text box, type *2* and select **OK**.
   f) Verify that the building code was extracted.

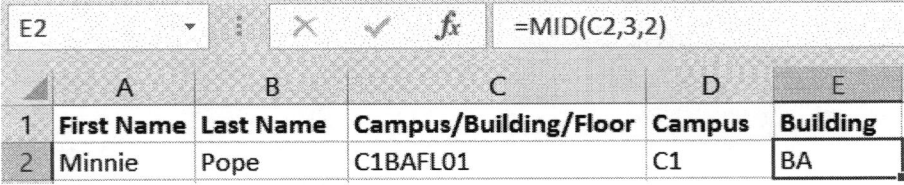

4. Extract the floor code, the last four characters, from the combined field.
   a) Select cell **F2**.

b) Select **Formulas→Function Library→Text→RIGHT**.

c) In the **Text** text box, type or select cell *C2* and press **Tab**.

d) In the **Num_chars** text box, type *4* and select **OK**.

e) Verify that the floor code was extracted.

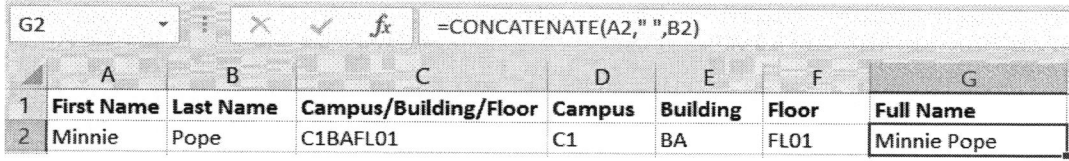

| F2 | | | ✕ | ✓ | *fx* | =RIGHT(C2,4) | |

⊿	A	B	C	D	E	F
1	**First Name**	**Last Name**	**Campus/Building/Floor**	**Campus**	**Building**	**Floor**
2	Minnie	Pope	C1BAFL01	C1	BA	FL01

5. Concatenate the personnel names in the first name, last name format.

a) Select cell **G2**.

b) Type *=CONC* and press **Tab** to use Formula AutoComplete.

c) In the **text1** argument, select or type *A2* and type a comma (**,**)

d) In the **[text2]** argument type *" "* and type a comma (**,**)

 Note: There is a space between the two quotation marks.

e) In the **[text3]** argument, select or type *B2* and type a right parenthesis *)* to complete the function and press **Ctrl+Enter**.

f) Verify the personnel name appears in the first name and last name format.

| G2 | | | ✕ | ✓ | *fx* | =CONCATENATE(A2," ",B2) | |

⊿	A	B	C	D	E	F	G
1	**First Name**	**Last Name**	**Campus/Building/Floor**	**Campus**	**Building**	**Floor**	**Full Name**
2	Minnie	Pope	C1BAFL01	C1	BA	FL01	Minnie Pope

6. AutoFill in the remaining rows of data.

a) Select cells **D2:G2** and double-click the **AutoFill** handle of cell **G2**.

b) Verify that the campus, building, floor, and full names are listed for all personnel.

⊿	A	B	C	D	E	F	G
1	**First Name**	**Last Name**	**Campus/Building/Floor**	**Campus**	**Building**	**Floor**	**Full Name**
2	Minnie	Pope	C1BAFL01	C1	BA	FL01	Minnie Pope
3	Terry	Hart	C1BBFL02	C1	BB	FL02	Terry Hart
4	Dianna	Watts	C1BAFL02	C1	BA	FL02	Dianna Watts
5	Martha	Fernandez	C1BBFL03	C1	BB	FL03	Martha Fernandez
6	Alyssa	Underwood	C1BAFL03	C1	BA	FL03	Alyssa Underwood
7	Dexter	Cox	C1BCFL01	C1	BC	FL01	Dexter Cox
8	Julius	Ferguson	C1BCFL02	C1	BC	FL02	Julius Ferguson
9	Hannah	Duncan	C1BCFL03	C1	BC	FL03	Hannah Duncan

7. Save the workbook and then close the file.

Summary

In this lesson, you created advanced formulas by using range and cell names instead of references, by examining the syntax of commonly used specialized functions, and by writing logical, date & time, and text functions. You are just beginning to unlock Excel's potential as a data analysis tool, which will take you far beyond using Excel as a mere calculator and data storage tool. By building this foundational knowledge of Excel formula syntax, you are taking the first steps to true Excel mastery.

How do you think using defined names will benefit you as you create future workbooks?

How do you plan to incorporate the use of varied functions in your workbooks?

 Note: Check your CHOICE Course screen for opportunities to interact with your classmates, peers, and the larger CHOICE online community about the topics covered in this course or other topics you are interested in. From the Course screen you can also access available resources for a more continuous learning experience.

2 | Working with Lists

Lesson Time: 1 hour, 30 minutes

Lesson Objectives

In this lesson, you will work with lists. You will:

- Sort data.

- Filter data.

- Query data with database functions.

- Outline and subtotal data.

Lesson Introduction

Organizing and presenting your data in a logical and coherent manner is just as important as working with functions to analyze that data. In this lesson, you will use Microsoft® Office Excel® 2016 to sort, filter, and subtotal data. These functions help you organize your data for better analysis and presentation, in addition to the functions you learned in the previous lesson.

TOPIC A

Sort Data

Raw data is often entered into Excel worksheets in random order, or at least not in the order you need for a particular data analysis task. For example, sales data may be entered chronologically, but you may need to examine information related to particular products or store locations. Or, you may need to review employee data based on hire date, but the entries are listed alphabetically by employee last name.

In this topic, you will learn to sort data. By reordering your data, you can more easily locate and interact with specific entries, even in massive worksheets with tens of thousands of entries. Your raw data can be in many formats, such as text, dates, and values that Excel can sort alphabetically or numerically.

Sorting

Sorting is, quite simply, reordering the data in your worksheets based on some defined criteria, such as alphabetically or from highest value to lowest value. Sorting enables you to put data entries in a sequence that makes sense for a particular task. In Excel, you can sort by row or by column, but an overwhelming majority of sorting is done by column because of the way most people enter worksheet data. You can sort on a single row or column, or apply multiple sorts to the same set of data. Additionally, you can sort either range or table data. Excel can sort data based on a number of different values, such as numeric, alphabetical, date and time, and even by cell color or conditional formatting criteria. If you add data to a sorted range or table, you can re-sort it to accommodate the new entries.

It is important to keep in mind that when you sort data, you are not changing the raw data in your worksheets; you are merely changing the display of the data. So, while you may sort on one particular column in a worksheet, say by numeric value, after the sort, each entry (individual row) will have the same data across the entire row. The rows will just appear in a different order based on the sort criteria. This preserving of data integrity is what makes sorting a powerful, useful feature.

 Note: It's a best practice to select only a single cell within a column or row when sorting. When you do this, Excel will automatically preserve the integrity of your data as described. However, if you select an entire column or row and then sort, Excel prompts you to include the surrounding data in the sort. If you do not expand the selection to include the surrounding data, Excel will not maintain your data integrity.

There are a couple of things about sorting that you should keep in mind. First, you cannot clear sorting, but you can use the **Undo** command to revert sorted data to its previous state. Second, when you save and close workbook files, you save sorts along with it. So, if you want to undo a sort, you must do it before saving and closing the file or before performing more actions than your undo settings allow you to undo. You can access the sort commands in the **Sort & Filter** group on the **Data** tab.

	A	B	C	D	E	F
1	**Last Name**	**First Name**	**Hire Date**	**Department**	**Office Location**	**Extention**
2	Burke	Steven	10/30/2011	IT	TS3	4005
3	Howell	Stanley	8/12/1994	Engineering	PB2	4168
4	Mcguire	Pamela	3/25/2003	Development	CC1	4302
5	Quinn	Sophie	2/4/2003	Facilities	TS1	4904
6	Hawkins	Alvin	8/23/1994	Accounting	PB4	4299
7	Redd	Randal	7/12/1998	Human Resources	TS1	4127
8	Dandridge	Ray	8/12/2007	Accounting	PB4	4224
9	Gearheart	Darrell	3/25/2015	Finance	TS3	4165
10	Pellham	Marlon	6/20/2009	Management	TS5	4529
11	Czapla	Cornell	1/29/2004	Development	CC1	4464
12	Rundle	Ruben	6/11/2011	Customer Service	CC1	4503
13	Maines	Mac	3/16/2003	Engineering	PB2	4987
14	Gosselin	Theo	5/3/2001	Marketing	CC3	4939
15	Carnegie	Filiberto	5/17/1994	Training	PB3	4430

Unsorted Data

Sorted by Last Name

	A	B	C	D	E	F
1	**Last Name**	**First Name**	**Hire Date**	**Department**	**Office Location**	**Extention**
2	Bierman	Tommie	9/28/2007	Finance	TS3	4660
3	Burke	Steven	10/30/2011	IT	TS3	4005
4	Cargo	Reva	11/3/1995	Accounting	PB4	4447
5	Carnegie	Filiberto	5/17/1994	Training	PB3	4430
6	Carreiro	Harlan	12/27/2014	Engineering	PB2	4325
7	Charlesworth	Rena	9/1/2007	Human Resources	TS1	4716
8	Charon	Jacques	1/14/2003	IT	TS3	4459
9	Coutu	Crystle	8/28/2013	Management	TS5	4628
10	Czapla	Cornell	1/29/2004	Development	CC1	4464
11	Dahl	Julius	1/27/1997	Marketing	CC3	4132
12	Dandridge	Ray	8/12/2007	Accounting	PB4	4224
13	Dorazio	Jackeline	11/5/1997	Engineering	PB2	4550
14	Gearheart	Darrell	3/25/2015	Finance	TS3	4165
15	Gosselin	Theo	5/3/2001	Marketing	CC3	4939

Figure 2-1: The same Excel worksheet both unsorted and sorted.

Clean Data

When performing sorting or any other list-related function, it is best to have clean data. You will sometimes need to clean your data before you can sort it. To do this, make sure your list has a heading row and no blanks. The list should have a header row and the header row should be formatted differently than the rest of the data. Adding bold formatting to the headings is sufficient to prevent Excel from accidentally treating your heading row as a row of data to sort. The list should have no blank rows or columns separating sections of the data. Excel will stop sorting a list at the point where it finds a blank row or column. Keeping your list contiguous is a good example of clean data.

Multiple Column/Row Sorting

When you sort on multiple columns or rows, it's important to consider that all of the columns or rows on which you're sorting, except for the last one you sort on, should contain some duplicate entries. Otherwise, the sort is of no value. Consider the simple example in the following figure.

◢	A	B	C	D	E	F
1	**Last Name**	**First Name**	**Hire Date**	**Department**	**Office Location**	**Extention**
2	Dandridge	Ray	8/12/2007	Accounting	PB4	4224
3	Hawkins	Alvin	8/23/1994	Accounting	PB4	4299
4	Cargo	Reva	11/3/1995	Accounting	PB4	4447
5	Sandifer	Catheryn	12/23/2006	Accounting	PB4	4931
6	Lipscomb	Phebe	3/28/1999	Customer Service	CC1	4124
7	Rundle	Ruben	6/11/2011	Customer Service	CC1	4503
8	Seibel	Lianne	5/5/2013	Development	CC1	4243
9	Mcguire	Pamela	3/25/2003	Development	CC1	4302
10	Czapla	Cornell	1/29/2004	Development	CC1	4464
11	Ridgley	Jodee	11/6/2010	Development	CC1	4747
12	Howell	Stanley	8/12/1994	Engineering	PB2	4168
13	Mcelligott	Conrad	2/21/2015	Engineering	PB2	4307
14	Carreiro	Harlan	12/27/2015	Engineering	PB2	4325
15	Dorazio	Jackeline	11/5/1997	Engineering	PB2	4550

Data sorted first on column D, then on column E, and then on column F

Figure 2-2: Sorting on multiple columns or rows enables you to organize your data in increasingly meaningful ways.

In this example, the dataset is sorted in ascending order on three different columns. First, it is sorted by Department, then by Office Location, and then by Extension. This sort can provide some analytical value because there are multiple entries with duplicate values in the first two columns the data is sorted on. For example, you can quickly find an employee's extension by locating their Department and Office Location quickly.

Quick Sorts

There are two general categories of sorting in Excel: quick sorts and custom sorts. *Quick sorts* enable you to easily sort the data in a range according to a set of predefined criteria. By using quick sorts, you can sort data one column at a time, in ascending or descending order, according to the type of content stored in the column. For example, if the column contains text, you can sort by alphabetical order. If the cells contain numeric values, you can sort lowest to highest, or highest to lowest. If the cells contain dates, you can sort based on chronological order. With quick sorts, you can sort only by column, not by row. To perform this operation, you will need to turn on **AutoFilter** by selecting **Data→Sort & Filter→Filter** or **Home→Editing→Sort & Filter**.

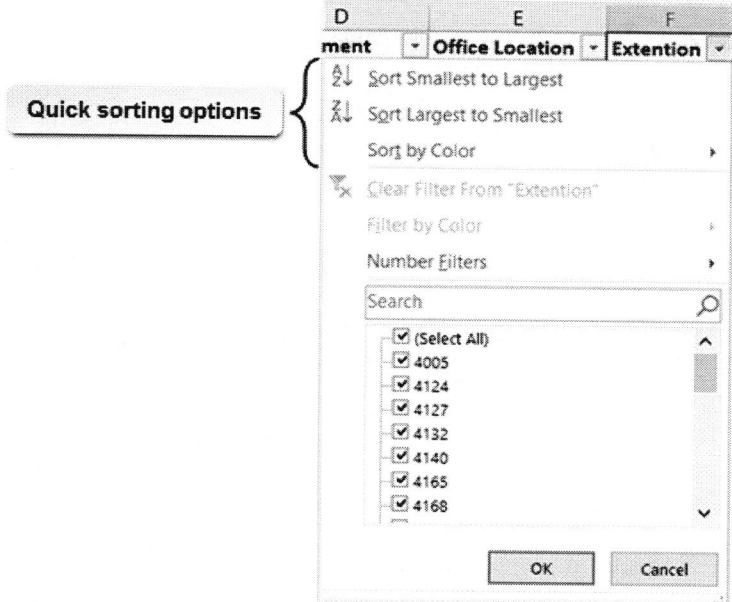

Figure 2-3: Use quick sorts to easily reorder your range data.

 Note: Ranges or lists of data that need to be sorted should have a distinct heading row so that Excel does not inadvertently sort the heading row along with the rest of the data. Formatting the heading row bold is all that is needed to avoid problems.

Custom Sorts

To sort your range data by using more highly defined criteria than is possible by using quick sorts, you can define a *custom sort*. Custom sorting enables you to sort by row or column, to sort on multiple rows or columns simultaneously, and to define specific sort criteria. In addition to the sort criteria that are available by using quick sorts, custom sorts enable you to sort based on cell and font color, and based on conditional formatting icons.

Each specific criterion you assign to a custom sort is called a *level*. Excel evaluates and sorts your data based on the order in which you assign sort levels to the data. You can add, delete, edit, and reorder sort levels. Custom sorting is only possible by using ribbon commands.

 Note: You cannot apply both column and row sorting to the same data range.

The Sort Dialog Box

You use the **Sort** dialog box to define and manage your custom sorts. You can access the **Sort** dialog box by selecting **Data→Sort & Filer→Sort**.

Figure 2-4: The Sort dialog box displaying multiple sort levels for a data range.

Note: Because sorting is such a useful function, you can also access the **Sort** dialog box by selecting **Home→Editing→Sort & Filter→Sort**.

The following table describes the functions of the various **Sort** dialog box elements.

Sort Dialog Box Element	Description
Add Level button	Adds new blank sort levels to a custom sort.
Delete Level button	Removes the currently selected sort level from a custom sort.
Copy Level button	Creates a copy of the currently selected sort level and places it immediately after the selected level.
Move Up/Move Down buttons	Enables you to reorder the sort levels in a custom sort.
Options button	Opens the **Sort Options** dialog box.
Column/Row drop-down menu	Use this to select the column or the row upon which to sort your data. Setting your sort options determines whether you sort by row or column.
Sort On drop-down menu	Use this to select the criteria by which you want to sort your data.
Order drop-down menu	Use this to determine the order in which Excel will display sorted data; for example, alphabetical or oldest to newest. The options that the **Order** drop-down menu displays depend on the selections you make in the **Column/Row** drop-down menus and the **Sort On** drop-down menus.
Defined sort levels	The sort levels appear in the order in which Excel will evaluate and apply data sorting.

The Sort Options Dialog Box

Use the **Sort Options** dialog box to determine whether Excel will sort by column or row, and to define the precedence Excel applies to capitalization while sorting. When the **Case sensitive** check box is unchecked, Excel gives precedence to capital letters. When the **Case sensitive** check box is checked, it gives precedence to lowercase letters. The **Orientation** section has two options. The default, **Sort top to bottom**, sorts by column and the **Sort left to right** option sorts by row. You can access the **Sort Options** dialog box by selecting the **Options** button in the **Sort** dialog box.

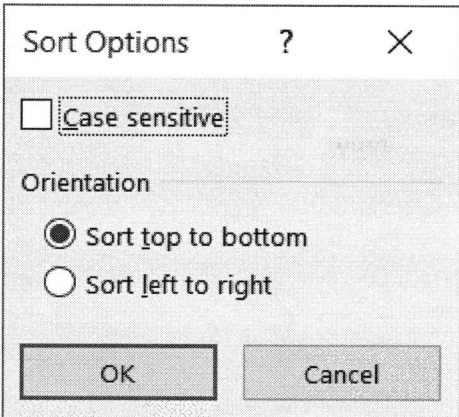

Figure 2-5: Use the Sort Options dialog box to assign sorts to rows or columns and to define the precedence Excel applies to capitalization.

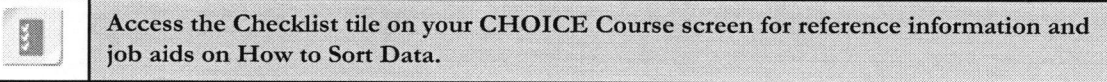
Access the Checklist tile on your CHOICE Course screen for reference information and job aids on How to Sort Data.

ACTIVITY 2–1
Sorting Data

Data File
C:\091056Data\Working with Lists\Develetech Lists.xlsx

Before You Begin
Excel 2016 is open.

Scenario
You are an HR Generalist with Develetech Industries and your manager has asked you to organize the employees list. You want to quickly look up employees in various ways by sorting data. The employees list contains data that will allow you to sort by name, date, department and office location.

1. Sort the employees list by Last Name.
   a) In Excel, open the workbook **Develetech Lists.xlsx**.
   b) Verify that the **Employees** worksheet is selected.
   c) Verify that cell **A1** is selected, and on the **Data** tab, in the **Sort & Filter** group, select **Sort A to Z**. ⬇
   d) Confirm that the employees list is sorted by Last Name.

	A
1	**Last Name**
2	Bierman
3	Burke
4	Cargo
5	Carnegie
6	Carreiro
7	Charlesworth
8	Charon
9	Coutu
10	Czapla

   e) Select cell **D1** and select **Data→Sort & Filter→Sort**.
   f) Select the **Sort by** drop-down arrow and select **Department**.
   g) Select **OK**.

h) Verify that the employees list is sorted by Department.

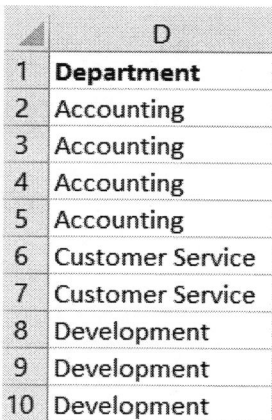

	D
1	**Department**
2	Accounting
3	Accounting
4	Accounting
5	Accounting
6	Customer Service
7	Customer Service
8	Development
9	Development
10	Development

2. Sort the employees list by Last Name, then by Department, and then by Extension.

   a) Select **Data→Sort & Filter→Sort**.
   b) Observe that Excel maintained the previous sort on Department.
   c) Select the **Sort by** drop-down arrow and select **Last Name**.
   d) Select **Add Level**.
   e) Select the **Then by** drop-down arrow and select **Department**.
   f) Select **Add Level** again.
   g) Select the last **Then by** drop-down arrow and select **Extension**.
   h) Verify that Excel is sorting by Last Name and Department alphabetically and that Extension is sorted smallest to largest and then select **OK**.

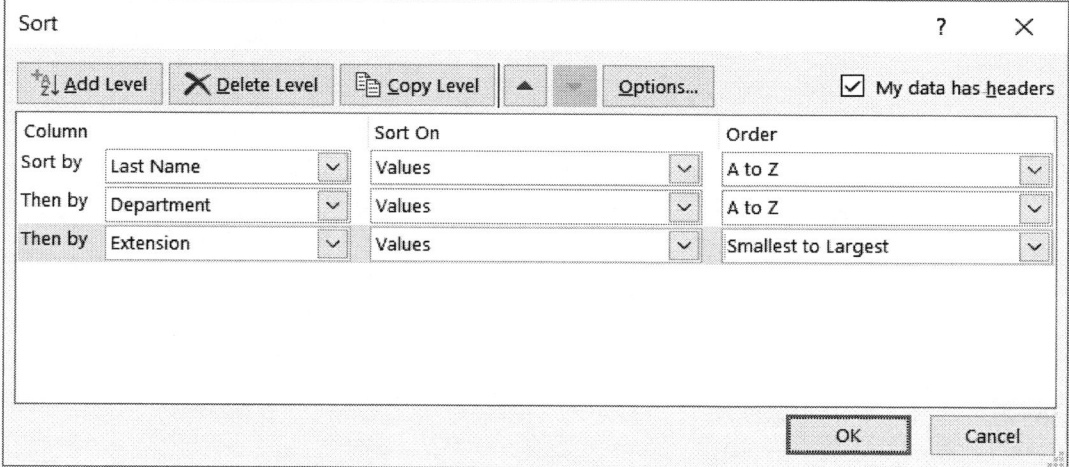

 i) Confirm that the employees list has been sorted by Last Name, then by Department, and then by Extension.

⁄	A	B	C	D	E	F
1	**Last Name**	**First Name**	**Hire Date**	**Department**	**Office Location**	**Extension**
2	Bierman	Tommie	9/28/2007	Finance	TS3	4660
3	Burke	Steven	10/30/2011	IT	TS3	4005
4	Cargo	Reva	11/3/1995	Accounting	PB4	4447
5	Carnegie	Filiberto	5/17/1994	Training	PB3	4430
6	Carreiro	Harlan	12/27/2015	Engineering	PB2	4325
7	Charlesworth	Rena	9/1/2007	Human Resources	TS1	4716
8	Charon	Jacques	1/14/2003	IT	TS3	4459
9	Coutu	Crystle	8/28/2013	Management	TS5	4628
10	Czapla	Cornell	1/29/2004	Development	CC1	4464

3. Save the workbook as *My Develetech Lists.xlsx* and keep the file open.

TOPIC B

Filter Data

Though sorting can help you locate and review data in large worksheets, it does nothing to cut down on the number of displayed entries. Even with ordered data, you may often still need to sift through large volumes of data to find what you're looking for, which can be challenging and time consuming. In this topic, you will learn to filter data, which limits the rows of data you have to review in order to find what you are looking for.

Filtering

As with the sorting feature, you can use the *filtering* feature to make data far easier to work with. While sorting rearranges your data based on particular defined criteria, filtering removes from view any data entries that do not match the specified criteria. When you filter data in Excel, you do not affect the actual data entries; you alter only how Excel displays your data. It is important to note that filtering affects entire worksheet rows. If you have data in a range or a table next to data that you filter, rows that are suppressed from view in the data you're filtering are also suppressed from view in the adjacent tables or ranges.

You can filter data ranges in Excel, and you can filter on more than one column. However, you can filter only by column, and not by row. You can combine sorting and filtering to fine tune the display of your data. Typically, when you combine sorting and filtering, it's a best practice to filter first and then sort just the data you wish to work with. You can toggle filtering on and off for ranges by selecting any cell within the desired range and select **Data→Sort & Filter→Filter**.

> **Note:** When you turn on filtering for a data range, you also activate quick sorting functionality for the range. Be sure that you select either only a single cell within the range or the entire data range when turning on filtering for a range. If you select only certain columns within a range when turning on filtering, when you use quick sorts to sort the range, columns not included in the selection when you turned on filtering will not sort with the rest of the data. Remember that the **Filter** command is also located on the **Home** tab by selecting **Home→Editing→Sort & Filter→Filter**.

Unlike sorting, filtering can be cleared at any time to re-display all rows that the filtering temporarily suppressed. When you apply functions to or search through filtered data, Excel applies the function to or searches through only the data that is displayed. When you clear filters, Excel applies the function to or searches through the entire dataset.

Unfiltered data

	A	B	C	D	E	F
1	Last Name	First Name	Hire Date	Department	Office Location	Extention
2	Burke	Steven	10/30/2011	IT	TS3	4005
3	Howell	Stanley	8/12/1994	Engineering	PB2	4168
4	Mcguire	Pamela	3/25/2003	Development	CC1	4302
5	Quinn	Sophie	2/4/2003	Facilities	TS1	4904
6	Hawkins	Alvin	8/23/1994	Accounting	PB4	4299
7	Redd	Randal	7/12/1998	Human Resources	TS1	4127
8	Dandridge	Ray	8/12/2007	Accounting	PB4	4224
9	Gearheart	Darrell	3/25/2015	Finance	TS3	4165
10	Pellham	Marlon	6/20/2009	Management	TS5	4529
11	Czapla	Cornell	1/29/2004	Development	CC1	4464
12	Rundle	Ruben	6/11/2011	Customer Service	CC1	4503
13	Maines	Mac	3/16/2003	Engineering	PB2	4987
14	Gosselin	Theo	5/3/2001	Marketing	CC3	4939
15	Carnegie	Filiberto	5/17/1994	Training	PB3	4430

	A	B	C	D	E	F
1	Last Name	First Name	Hire Date	Department	Office Location	Extention
3	Howell	Stanley	8/12/1994	Engineering	PB2	4168
13	Maines	Mac	3/16/2003	Engineering	PB2	4987
17	Dorazio	Jackeline	11/5/1997	Engineering	PB2	4550
27	Carreiro	Harlan	12/27/2015	Engineering	PB2	4325
31	Mcelligott	Conrad	2/21/2015	Engineering	PB2	4307

Filtered data with suppressed rows

Figure 2-6: Filtering data removes all non-pertinent entries from view, making it easier to review and work with your data.

> **Caution:** Filtering data and hiding rows or columns can have a wide range of effects on the **Cut** and **Copy** commands. When cutting or copying and then pasting data from filtered datasets or datasets with hidden columns or rows, always ensure that your pasted values appear as expected.

AutoFilters

AutoFilters enable you to quickly filter range data or datasets based on unique cell entries or applied cell formatting in a column. AutoFilter options appear in two ways: as check boxes or as pop-up menu options in the header row drop-down menu of ranges that have filtering turned on. You use the list of check boxes to filter based on cell values. Checked items will appear in the filtered dataset; unchecked items will not. You can check or uncheck any number of entries for each column, and you can search for specific entry values to pare down the list of AutoFilter options. The search functionality for AutoFilter values is dynamic, so Excel filters the AutoFilter options as you type each character of your search term.

You use the pop-up menu options to filter cells based on font or fill color, or based on icon sets. Again, for whichever formatting criteria you select in the pop-up menu, Excel will display rows containing that particular formatting; all other rows are hidden. You can use AutoFilters to filter blended criteria. In other words, you can filter by cell value and by formatting in the same column, but you can filter based on only one formatting criterion at a time.

The AutoFilter feature is most useful in columns that contain multiple duplicate entries or formatting options. Excel will display only one check box for each unique data entry (up to 10,000 unique values) in the column and one formatting option for each unique formatting element. Columns that you have applied filtering to will display a slightly different header row down-arrow.

For unfiltered columns, the header row down-arrow looks like this: ▼; in filtered columns, it looks like this: ⏷.

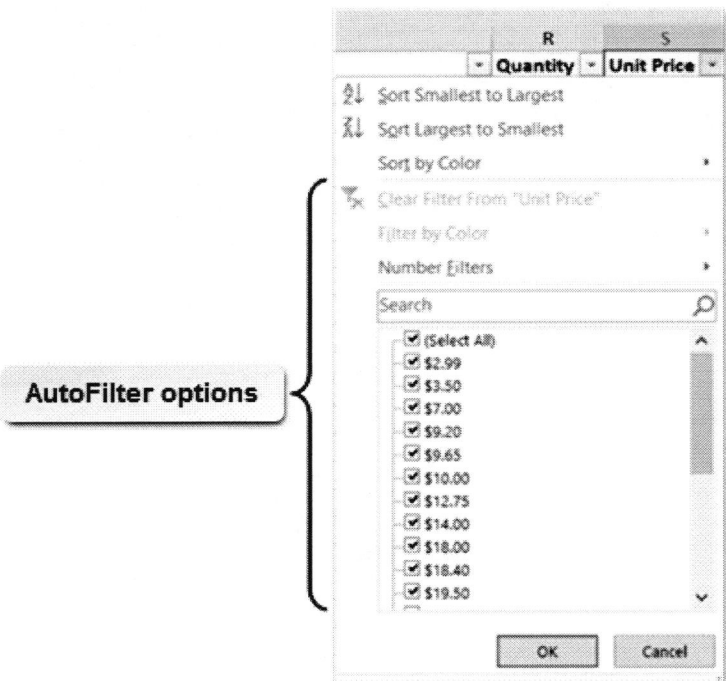

Figure 2–7: AutoFilters enable you to quickly filter datasets based on unique column entries or cell formatting.

Note: Two visual changes appear in Excel to let you know that filtering has been applied. The row labels change color to blue, as well as the status bar indicates the number of records found after applying a filter.

Custom AutoFilters

In addition to using the default AutoFilters available in Excel, you can customize AutoFilters to filter datasets according to specific criteria. You can use *custom AutoFilters* to filter by such criteria as a particular range of numeric values, text entries that begin with a particular character, or all entries made before or after a particular date. The custom AutoFilter options available to you depend on the type of data stored in the column. You can access these options by selecting either **Text Filters**, **Number Filters**, or **Date Filters** from the header row drop-down menu of ranges that have filtering turned on. Selecting any of these options from the drop-down menu opens a secondary menu. In the secondary menu, some of the filter options have no configurable parameters, such as filtering for the top or bottom 10 percent of numerical values, so selecting them will simply apply the filter. Others do need to be configured, so, when you select them, Excel opens the **Custom AutoFilter** dialog box.

The Custom AutoFilter Dialog Box

Use the **Custom AutoFilter** dialog box to configure the parameters for some of Excel's custom AutoFilters. The options available in the **Custom AutoFilter** dialog box vary depending on the type of data in the column. You can set one or two parameters in the **Custom AutoFilter** dialog box. For example, if you'd like to filter for a certain range of numeric values, you would enter the top and bottom values of the desired range. You can also select whether Excel should filter data based on entries that meet both defined criteria or based on meeting only one of the two criteria. If you don't enter a value in the lower fields, Excel ignores them.

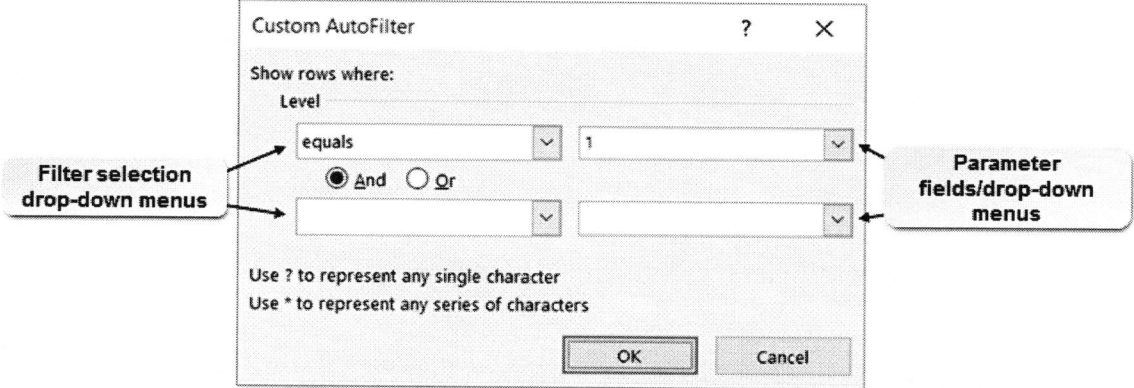

Figure 2–8: Use the Custom AutoFilter dialog box to set the parameters for custom AutoFilters.

The following table describes the function of the various elements of the **Custom AutoFilter** dialog box.

Custom AutoFilter Dialog Box Element	Allow You To
Filter selection drop-down menus	Select the specific custom AutoFilters you wish to apply to your dataset. Typically, Excel automatically populates the top menu with the filter you selected to open the **Custom AutoFilter** dialog box.

Custom AutoFilter Dialog Box Element	Allow You To
And/Or radio buttons	Choose between requiring both filter parameters or applying the filter to entries matching either one or the other. Choosing **And** will narrow the results and choosing **Or** will expand the results.
Parameter entry text fields/ drop-down menus	Define the specific criteria for the search. You can manually type the entries or select them from the drop-down menu, which is populated with the column's data entries.

Advanced Filtering

Excel's built-in AutoFilter functionality is a fast and easy way to pare down large volumes of data into manageable, easy-to-view chunks. However, there will likely be times when you will need to filter your data based on much more complex criteria than the AutoFilter options can support. In these cases, you can create advanced filters. When you filter data by using Excel's **Advanced** filtering command, you enter filter criteria directly on the worksheet containing the dataset you want to filter. Advanced filtering uses a set of filter operators that are similar to Excel's comparison operators. Although you can filter the original dataset in its original location, you can also ask Excel to return the filtered dataset in a different location within the workbook. This provides you with both an unfiltered and a filtered view of your data simultaneously. You can access the **Advanced** filter command by selecting **Data→Sort & Filter→Advanced**.

Figure 2-9: The Advanced filtering command enables you to filter your data using highly complex, user-defined criteria.

 Note: Applying advanced filtering to a range with filtering (AutoFilter) turned on automatically turns off filtering.

The Criteria Range

As previously mentioned, to use advanced filtering, you enter the desired filter criteria directly on the worksheet containing the dataset you wish to filter. The area on the worksheet in which you do this is called the *criteria range*. To properly enter filter criteria in the criteria range, you must follow the correct protocol. Here are the requirements for creating a valid criteria range:

- It is a best practice to have the criteria range be located directly above the dataset you wish to filter.
- The criteria range must contain the same column headings as the columns in the dataset.
- Criteria entered into cells on the same row in the criteria range use the AND operator. In other words, rows displayed in the filtered dataset must meet all of the specified criteria in the criteria range row.
- Criteria entered in different rows use the OR operator.
- Each criterion that you wish to include by using the OR operator must be in its own row in the criteria range.

- You can enter more than one filter operator in the same column. Not all columns have to include a filter operator.
- There must be at least one blank row between the criteria range and the dataset you wish to filter.

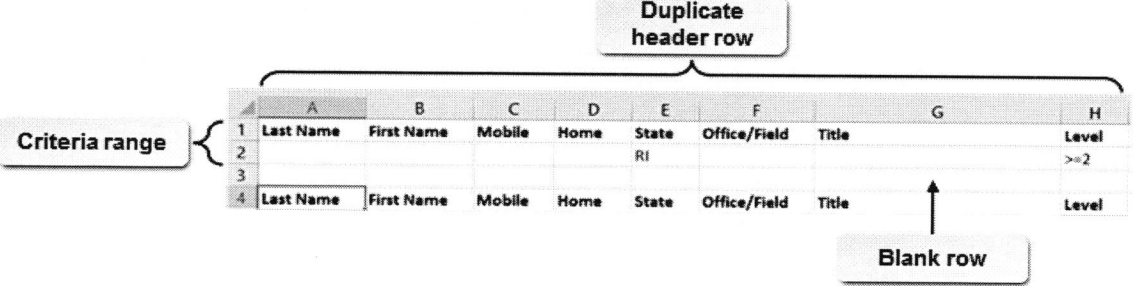

Figure 2-10: Use the criteria range to specify advanced filtering criteria.

Filter Operators

To define the criteria for advanced filtering, you use filter operators. These function very much like the comparison operators you use to create logical functions. Filter operators help you narrow your search for specific data, and you can use these in nearly any combination.

Filter Operator	What It Does
=	Filters data based on an exact content match. As Excel interprets the equal sign as the beginning of a formula or function, you must enclose the = operator in a set of double quotation marks (" "). So, if you want to filter for all entries that include the text "NY," you must enter the filter criteria as *"=NY"* To filter for an exact numerical match, you can simply enter the numerical value.
<	Filters for numerical or date and time values that are less than the defined criteria.
>	Filters for numerical or date and time values that are greater than the defined criteria.
<=	Filters for numerical or date and time values that are less than or equal to the defined criteria.
>=	Filters for numerical or date and time values that are greater than or equal to the defined criteria.
<>	Filters for numerical, textual, or date and time values that are not equal to the defined criteria.
?	Serves as a wildcard character for a single character in the same position as the question mark. So, if you want to filter a list of employee numbers that begin with "100," but can have any number as the last digit, you could type *100?* as the filter criterion.
*	Serves as a wildcard character for multiple characters in the same position as the asterisk. So, if you want to filter a list of product names for entries that begin with the letter S and end with the letter L, you could enter *"=S*L"* as the criterion. In this case, both "sail" and "stool" would appear in the filtered dataset.

 Note: You cannot use cell or range references to define advanced filter criteria. You must manually enter values in the criteria range.

Note: Be aware that there may be some occasions where you do not need to enter an equal sign (=) operator. Simply entering your criteria may constitute that criteria equals what you are looking to find.

 Access the Checklist tile on your **CHOICE** Course screen for reference information and job aids on **How to Filter Data.**

ACTIVITY 2-2
Filtering Data

Before You Begin
The My Develetech Lists.xlsx file is open.

Scenario
As an HR Generalist at Develetech Industries, you were asked to sort the employees list. Now you are being asked which employees are in specific offices and departments. In order to find this information, you will filter the employees list.

1. Filter the data for all employees in the PB4 Office Location.
   a) Select cell **A1** and select **Data→Sort & Filter→Filter**.
   b) Select the Office Location **AutoFilter** drop-down arrow and uncheck **Select All**.
   c) Select **PB4** and select **OK**.
   d) Verify that only the Office Location PB4 is shown.

	A	B	C	D	E	F
1	Last Name	First Name	Hire Date	Department	Office Location	Extension
4	Cargo	Reva	11/3/1995	Accounting	PB4	4447
12	Dandridge	Ray	8/12/2007	Accounting	PB4	4224
16	Hawkins	Alvin	8/23/1994	Accounting	PB4	4299
29	Sandifer	Catheryn	12/23/2006	Accounting	PB4	4931

2. Filter for management and marketing employees.
   a) Select the **AutoFilter** drop-down arrow for Office Location and select **Clear Filter from "Office Location"**.
   b) Select the Department **AutoFilter** drop-down arrow and uncheck **Select All**.
   c) Select **Management** and **Marketing** and then select **OK**.
   d) Verify that the Management and Marketing departments are shown.

	A	B	C	D	E	F
1	Last Name	First Name	Hire Date	Department	Office Location	Extension
9	Coutu	Crystle	8/28/2013	Management	TS5	4628
11	Dahl	Julius	1/27/1997	Marketing	CC3	4132
15	Gosselin	Theo	5/3/2001	Marketing	CC3	4939
24	Pellham	Marlon	6/20/2009	Management	TS5	4529

3. Create an advanced filter for employees in either engineering or facilities.
   a) Select the Department **AutoFilter** drop-down arrow and select **Clear Filter from "Department"**.

b) Select the Department **AutoFilter** drop-down arrow again and select **Text Filters→Custom Filter**.

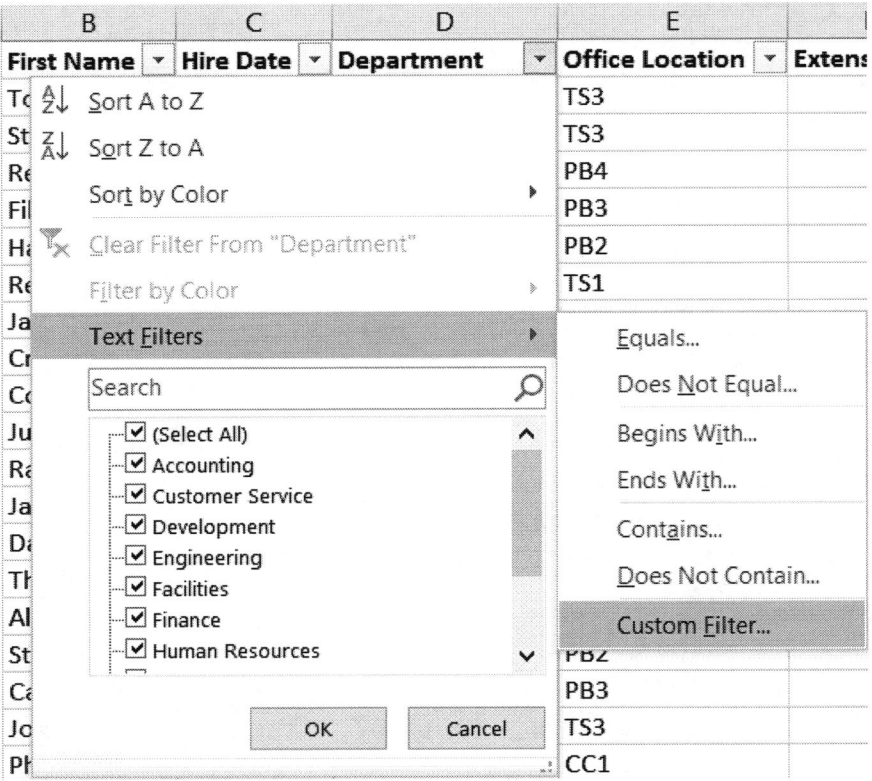

c) Select the **Parameter fields** drop-down arrow on the first row and select **Engineering**.
d) Select the **Or** option.
e) Select the **Filter selection** drop-down arrow on the second row and select **equals**.
f) Select the **Parameter fields** drop-down arrow on the second row and select **Facilities**.

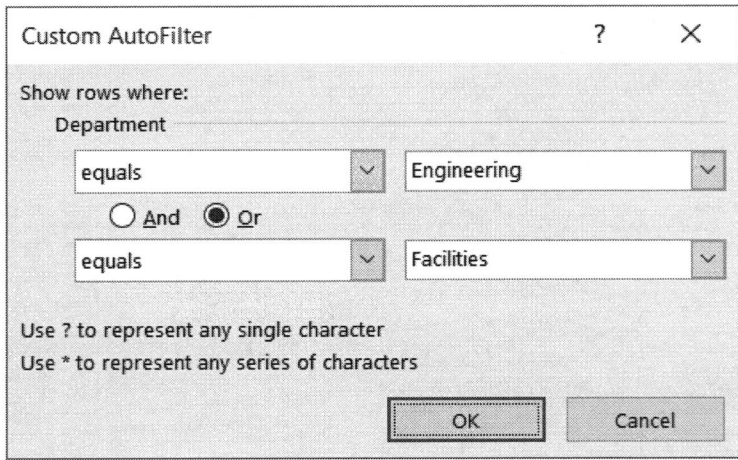

g) Select **OK**.

h) Verify that the Employees list has been filtered for the Engineering and Facilities departments.

	A	B	C	D	E	F
1	Last Name ▾	First Name ▾	Hire Date ▾	Department ⏷	Office Location ▾	Extension ▾
6	Carreiro	Harlan	12/27/2015	Engineering	PB2	4325
13	Dorazio	Jackeline	11/5/1997	Engineering	PB2	4550
17	Howell	Stanley	8/12/1994	Engineering	PB2	4168
21	Maines	Mac	3/16/2003	Engineering	PB2	4987
22	Mcelligott	Conrad	2/21/2015	Engineering	PB2	4307
25	Quinn	Sophie	2/4/2003	Facilities	TS1	4904
31	Stickland	Kasie	12/28/2002	Facilities	TS1	4420

4. Save the workbook and keep the file open.

TOPIC C

Query Data with Database Functions

After sorting and filtering your data, you may want to perform calculations on the data. Similar to advanced filters, you can use database functions. These functions allow you to find the data you are looking for and perform calculations all in one step. If your company has thousands of products, customers, or data entries of any kind, database functions can help you find specific items in the dataset and perform calculations to sum or average subsets of that data. In this topic, you will query data with database functions.

Database Functions

Excel 2016 provides you with a powerful set of functions that can help you drill down into your data to ask highly focused questions: *database functions*. Database functions enable you to perform calculations on ranges of data based on specific criteria. Essentially, these allow you to perform calculations on particular data by incorporating a database-query-like level of functionality. Basically, you query the dataset to find a particular value or set of values, and then perform some calculation on only the specific data.

Mathematically speaking, the calculations that database functions perform are similar to their standard counterparts. Database functions, essentially, combine the functionality of Excel functions with the functionality of advanced filters. Database functions use the same operators that advanced filters use to identify the specific data you wish to perform a calculation on. To enter criteria for database functions, you must follow the same rules as you do for creating advanced filters.

A flat file list in Excel can also be considered a database. A column of data in a database is known as a field and a row of data is either an entry or a record.

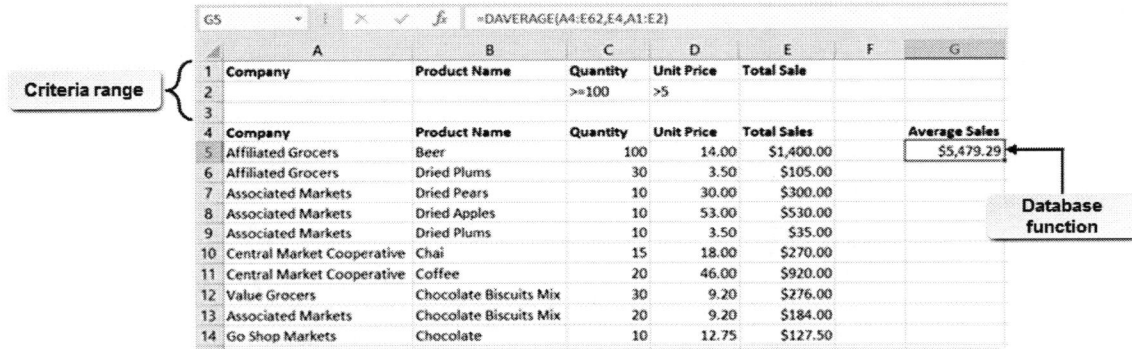

Figure 2–11: The database function in cell G5 returns the average sales for sales greater than or equal to a quantity of 100 and a unit price greater than $5.00.

The following table lists all of the database functions in Excel 2016.

Function Name	Function Definition
DAVERAGE	Averages the values in a column in a list or database that match your criteria.
DCOUNT	Counts the cells containing numbers in the field (column) in the database that match your criteria.
DCOUNTA	Counts nonblank cells in the field (column) in the database that match your criteria.

Function Name	Function Definition
DGET	Extracts from a database a single record that matches your criteria.
DMAX	Returns the largest number in the field (column) in the database that match your criteria.
DMIN	Returns the smallest number in the field (column) in the database that match your criteria.
DPRODUCT	Multiplies the values in the field (column) in the database that match your criteria.
DSTDEV	Estimates the standard deviation based on a sample from selected database entries.
DSTDEVP	Calculates the standard deviation based on the entire population of selected database entries.
DSUM	Adds the numbers in the field (column) in the database that match your criteria.
DVAR	Estimates the variance based on a sample from the selected database entries.
DVARP	Calculates variance based on the entire population of selected database entries.

Database Function Syntax

You can distinguish database functions from their counterparts because the function names all begin with the letter "D." The database function equivalent of the SUM function is the DSUM function, and the database function equivalent of the AVERAGE function is the DAVERAGE function. All database functions have the same three arguments, which are all required. Let's look at the DSUM function as an example.

Syntax: =DSUM(**database,field,criteria**)

The DSUM function calculates the sum of values within a range that all meet the specified criteria. In the function's arguments, **database** is the reference to the range of cells that make up the entire dataset. This range should include column labels (headers). In addition, you can use range names in place of the database argument.

The **field** argument specifies the column that the function will perform a calculation on. You can include this argument in one of three ways. The first is by enclosing the column label in double quotation marks (example: "Total Sales"). The second is by entering the cell reference of the cell containing the column label. Or, in the third and final way, you can simply refer to the column by its numerical place in the dataset. So, if you want the function to perform the calculation on the third column in a table or dataset, you could enter *3* as the **field** argument.

The **criteria** argument specifies the criteria range. You enter this argument as a range of cells; the range must include the duplicate header row and all criteria you wish to include. It does not have to include the empty row between the criteria range and the dataset.

 Note: All the database functions in Excel contain the same arguments.

Let's take another look at the previous example, which uses the DAVERAGE function.

G5		:	×	✓	f_x	=DAVERAGE(A4:E62,E4,A1:E2)		

▲	A	B	C	D	E	F	G
1	Company	Product Name	Quantity	Unit Price	Total Sale		
2			>=100	>5			
3							
4	Company	Product Name	Quantity	Unit Price	Total Sales		Average Sales
5	Affiliated Grocers	Beer	100	14.00	$1,400.00		$5,479.29
6	Affiliated Grocers	Dried Plums	30	3.50	$105.00		
7	Associated Markets	Dried Pears	10	30.00	$300.00		
8	Associated Markets	Dried Apples	10	53.00	$530.00		
9	Associated Markets	Dried Plums	10	3.50	$35.00		
10	Central Market Cooperative	Chai	15	18.00	$270.00		
11	Central Market Cooperative	Coffee	20	46.00	$920.00		
12	Value Grocers	Chocolate Biscuits Mix	30	9.20	$276.00		
13	Associated Markets	Chocolate Biscuits Mix	20	9.20	$184.00		
14	Go Shop Markets	Chocolate	10	12.75	$127.50		

Figure 2-12: The DAVERAGE function.

As you can enter the field argument in three different ways, this function could be entered in any of the following ways:

=DAVERAGE(A4:E62,E4,A1:E2)

=DAVERAGE(A4:E62,"Total Sales",A1:E2)

=DAVERAGE(A4:E62,5,A1:E2)

In the first example, the **field** argument is specified by the cell name. The second example uses the columns label's. The third example specifies the argument by the column's position in the dataset. As the **Total Sales** column is the fifth column in the dataset, you can simply enter *5* to define the **field** argument.

 Access the Checklist tile on your CHOICE Course screen for reference information and job aids on How to Use Database Functions.

ACTIVITY 2-3
Using Database Functions

Before You Begin
The My Develetech Lists.xlsx file is open.

Scenario
As a sales manager at Develetech Industries, you want to analyze the second quarter sales figures in order to identify the impact of sales in various regions across the nation. You want to know the total sales and average sales in the quarter where sales in the Northeast and Southeast were less than $1,000. In addition, calculating the total and average sales for the month of May will aid in your national sales analysis. You decide to use database functions to calculate the totals and averages utilizing the range name Q2Sales to simplify the formula.

---

1. Calculate the total and average sales in the northeast and southeast where sales were less than $1,000.

   a) Select the **Quarter 2 Sales** worksheet.

   b) Verify that cell **J2** is selected and type *=DSUM(*

   c) From the **Formula Bar**, select **Insert Function**.

   d) In the **Function Arguments** dialog box, in the **Database** text box, select **Formulas→Defined Names→Use in Formula→Q2Sales**.

   e) Press **Tab** and in the **Field** text box, select or type *H4*, and press **Tab**.

    Note: Remember that the field is the column of data you wish to summarize. In the data file, you can also total any region.

   f) In the **Criteria** text box, select or type *A1:H2* and select **OK**.

    **Note:** Advanced queries and database functions set up the criteria area in the same manner. The criteria area comprises at least three rows above the list with the headings from the list copied into row one. The following rows are used for the comparison criteria. Be sure to leave a blank row between the criteria area and the list.

   g) Verify that total sales for the Northeast and Southeast region, where sales were less than $1,000, is $32,839.

	A	B	C	D	E	F	G	H	I	J
1	Date	Month	Northeast	Southeast	Midwest	Southwest	West	Total		Sum
2			<1000	<1000						$32,839

Formula bar: J2 — =DSUM(Q2Sales,H4,A1:H2)

   h) Select cell **K2** and enter *=DAVERAGE(Q2Sales,H4,A1:H2)*

i) Verify the average total sales for the Northeast and Southeast region, where sales were less than $1,000, is $6,568.

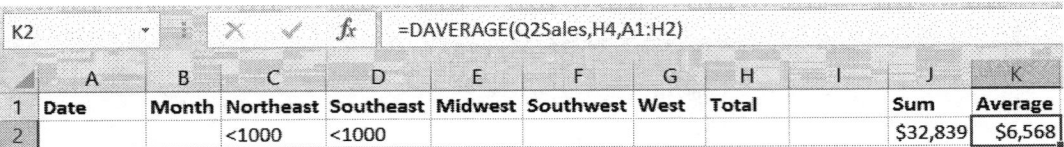

	A	B	C	D	E	F	G	H	I	J	K
1	Date	Month	Northeast	Southeast	Midwest	Southwest	West	Total		Sum	Average
2			<1000	<1000						$32,839	$6,568

2. Edit the criteria to calculate the total and average sales for May.
   a) Select cells **C2:D2** and press **Delete**.
   b) Select cell **B2** and enter *May*
   c) If necessary, adjust the width of column J and verify the total and average sales for May.

	A	B	C	D	E	F	G	H	I	J	K
1	Date	Month	Northeast	Southeast	Midwest	Southwest	West	Total		Sum	Average
2		May								$169,566	$7,708

3. Save the workbook and keep the file open.

TOPIC D

Outline and Subtotal Data

As you have worked with Excel, you have learned how to hide rows and columns of data to present a summary view of the data for reporting purposes. In addition, as you enter data, you may want to periodically summarize the data, by region or quarter for example, rather than creating a grand total for all regions or quarters. In this topic, you will learn how to outline and subtotal your data which may be especially useful when you are working on a spreadsheet with a large amount of data.

Outlines

Outlining is the process of grouping rows and columns to create a hierarchy called an *outline*. In an outline, subtotaled datasets are arranged into groups of varying levels of detail that you can expand or collapse depending on how much detail you want to see. For example, if you want to carefully analyze individual data entries for the worksheet, you would want to expand all levels in the hierarchy so that all populated cells appear in the worksheet. But if you want to present summary data to your supervisor on a per-region basis, you may want to display only the subtotal rows that contain the summary information.

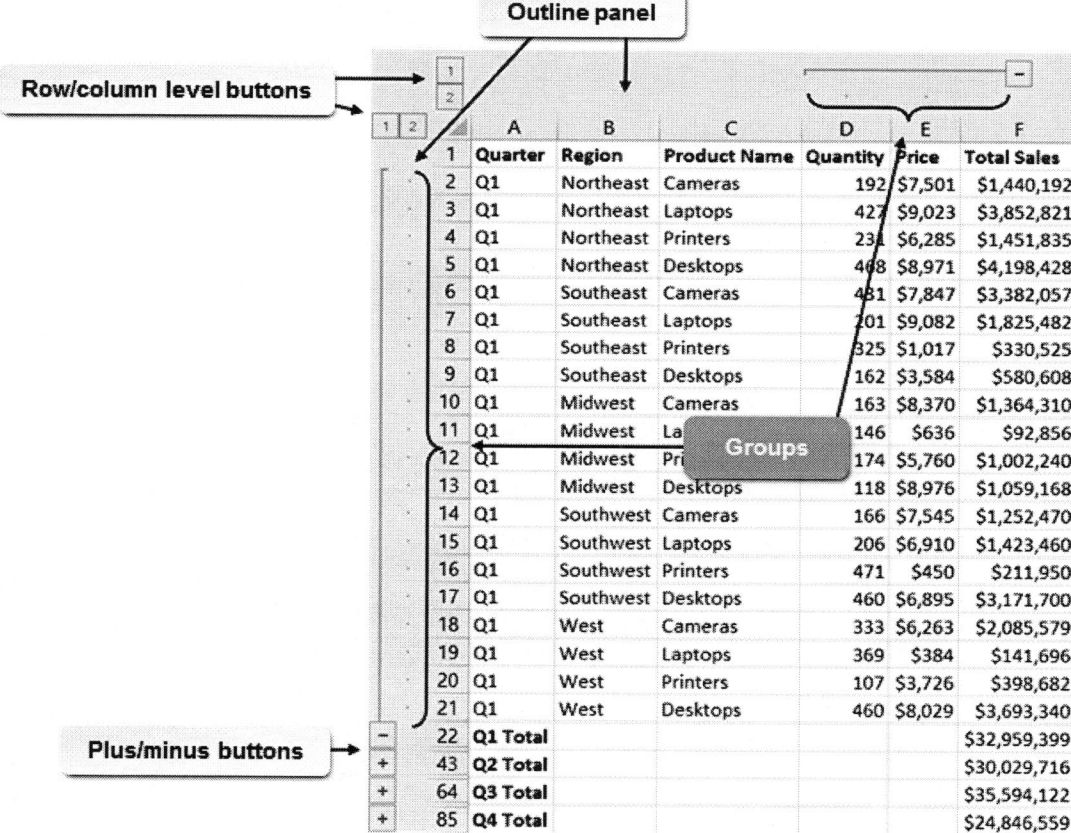

Figure 2–13: Outlines enable you to control how much detail is displayed in worksheets containing subtotals.

Outlines can contain up to eight levels of detail. Each level is nested within the previous level. The level buttons along the top of the **Outline** panel enable you to instantly change the view of your worksheet to display only the summary information of that level. The higher the number of the level button, the more detailed a view of your data you will see. Data subsets are represented in the outline by square brackets. These brackets display plus and minus buttons that enable you to collapse and expand individual data subsets as desired.

The commands to manually create outlines are found on the **Data** tab, in the **Outline** group.

The SUBTOTAL Function

Before you look at two key elements of Excel functionality that will help you analyze your data on a more granular level, it will be helpful to look at a different type of Excel function, one that lies at the core of this functionality: the SUBTOTAL function. *SUBTOTAL functions* are a specific set of Excel functions that perform calculations on subsets of data.

 Note: Although it is important to have an understanding of how SUBTOTAL functions work in terms of syntax, most users take advantage of them through ribbon commands and other UI-based functionality, as opposed to manually typing them into cells.

The most common calculation you will likely make using SUBTOTAL functions is not, surprisingly, finding subtotals. Take a look at this example to get a sense of how useful these functions can be.

F22 | | × ✓ *fx* | =SUBTOTAL(9,F2:F21)

	A	B	C	D	E	F
1	**Quarter**	**Region**	**Product Name**	**Quantity**	**Price**	**Total Sales**
2	Q1	Northeast	Cameras	192	$7,501	$1,440,192
3	Q1	Northeast	Laptops	427	$9,023	$3,852,821
4	Q1	Northeast	Printers	231	$6,285	$1,451,835
5	Q1	Northeast	Desktops	468	$8,971	$4,198,428
6	Q1	Southeast	Cameras	431	$7,847	$3,382,057
7	Q1	Southeast	Laptops	201	$9,082	$1,825,482
8	Q1	Southeast	Printers	325	$1,017	$330,525
9	Q1	Southeast	Desktops	162	$3,584	$580,608
10	Q1	Midwest	Cameras	163	$8,370	$1,364,310
11	Q1	Midwest	Laptops	146	$636	$92,856
12	Q1	Midwest	Printers	174	$5,760	$1,002,240
13	Q1	Midwest	Desktops	118	$8,976	$1,059,168
14	Q1	Southwest	Cameras	166	$7,545	$1,252,470
15	Q1	Southwest	Laptops	206	$6,910	$1,423,460
16	Q1	Southwest	Printers	471	$450	$211,950
17	Q1	Southwest	Desktops	460	$6,895	$3,171,700
18	Q1	West	Cameras	333	$6,263	$2,085,579
19	Q1	West	Laptops	369	$384	$141,696
20	Q1	West	Printers	107	$3,726	$398,682
21	Q1	West	Desktops	460	$8,029	$3,693,340
22	**Q1 Total**					$32,959,399

Figure 2–14: The SUBTOTAL Function.

In this example, a range of sales data has been sorted by quarter. To find the sales totals by quarter, extra rows have been added in the worksheet. Normally you would simply use the SUM function to calculate each quarter's total sales, which are subtotals of the company's overall sales. This is simple enough to do if you're dealing with a relatively small worksheet, but this could quickly become quite a chore in larger ones. So, having a function that can perform the subtotal calculation on a very large dataset can be quite advantageous. The example shown here shows the SUBTOTAL function used in place of the SUM function.

Technically speaking, the SUBTOTAL function is a single function that calls one other function out of a set of available functions, such as SUM, AVERAGE, MAX, and MIN, depending on the specific calculation you want Excel to perform. It then performs the selected function on the range or ranges you stipulate in the arguments. Here is the function's syntax:

=SUBTOTAL(**function_num,ref1**,[ref2],...,[ref254])

In the function's syntax, the reference arguments, **ref1**, **ref2**, and so on, simply tell the function which ranges to perform the calculations on. The **function_num** argument calls the specific function you want to use to calculate your subtotals. You express this argument as a single numeric value of 1 to 11, or 101 to 111. Of the available functions the SUBTOTAL function can call, there are two different groups, hence the two sets of possible values for the **function_num** argument. These are two identical sets of functions: if you enter a value from 1 to 11 as the argument, the selected function will include hidden values (because of hidden rows or columns in your worksheet); if you enter a value from 101 to 111 as the argument, the selected function will ignore hidden values.

The following table outlines the functions each value in the **function_num** argument calls.

function_num Argument (Includes Hidden Values)	function_num Argument (Ignores Hidden Values)	Called Function
1	101	AVERAGE
2	102	COUNT
3	103	COUNTA
4	104	MAX
5	105	MIN
6	106	PRODUCT
7	107	STDEV
8	108	STDEVP
9	109	SUM
10	110	VAR
11	111	VARP

So, if you have a large set of data in column A of a worksheet, and you want the subtotal for the first 20 values, you would enter the following function: **=SUBTOTAL(9, A1:A20)**. If you wanted to find the average value of that same range, you would enter **=SUBTOTAL(1,A1:A20)**. If that range contained hidden rows that you wanted to ignore while performing the same calculations, you would use **109** and **101** for the **function_num** arguments, respectively.

The Subtotals Feature

As previously mentioned, although it's good to have a grasp of the SUBTOTAL function's syntax, it isn't necessary to manually enter these functions. This is because Excel 2016 includes several features that enter the appropriate function for you automatically. One of these is the *Subtotals feature*. Selecting the **Subtotals** command enables you to automatically perform SUBTOTAL function calculations on subsets of data within a particular dataset. The Subtotals feature does not work on tables which you will learn about in the next lesson.

Two of the most important things to remember about the Subtotals feature are that it is most effective when you have included column headers in the dataset and when you have already sorted your data by some specific criteria, such as a region or financial period for which you wish to calculate subtotals. This is because the Subtotals feature looks for changes in the column entries of one column, and then performs the desired calculation on the corresponding values in another column.

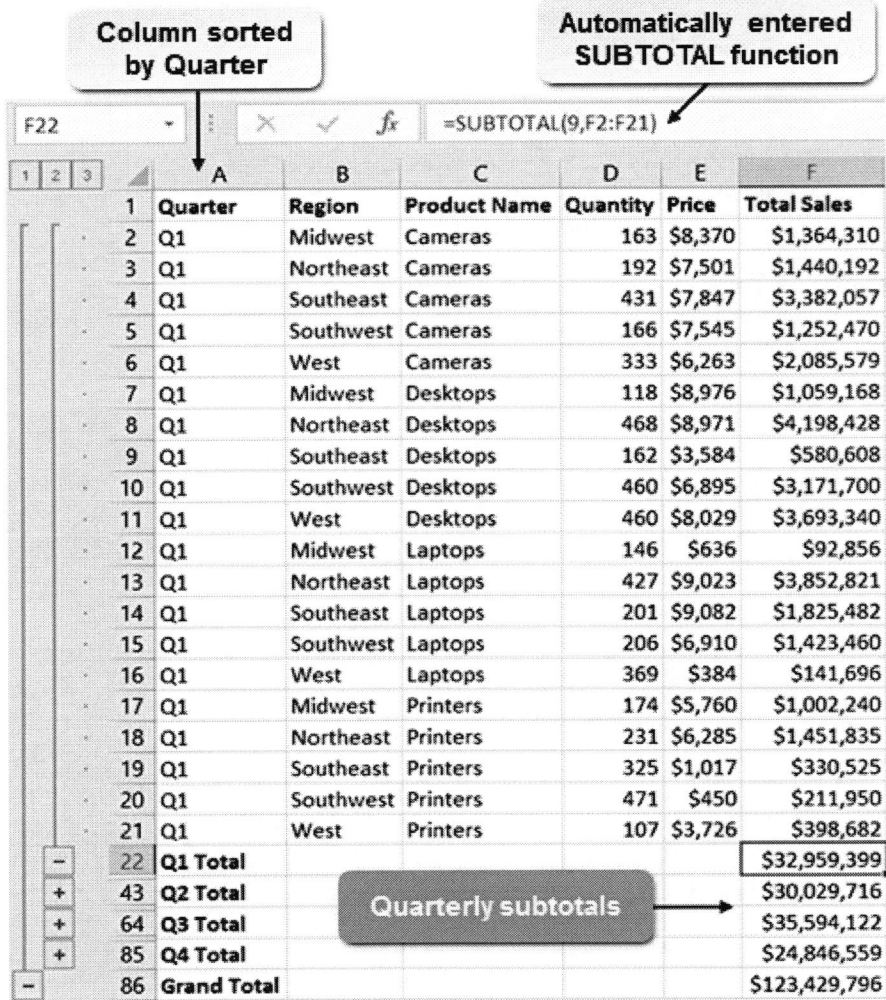

Figure 2-15: The Subtotals feature applied to a dataset. Here, the data is sorted by quarter and the Subtotals feature has applied the SUM function to the values in the Total Sales column.

The Subtotal Dialog Box

You can use the **Subtotal** dialog box to perform SUBTOTAL function calculations on data ranges without having to manually enter the desired SUBTOTAL function. From here, you specify the criteria by which Excel will organize subsets of data, select the desired function, and select the column on which the calculation will be performed. The **Subtotal** dialog box also includes several options for configuring the display of subtotals. You can access the **Subtotal** dialog box by selecting **Data→Outline→Subtotal**.

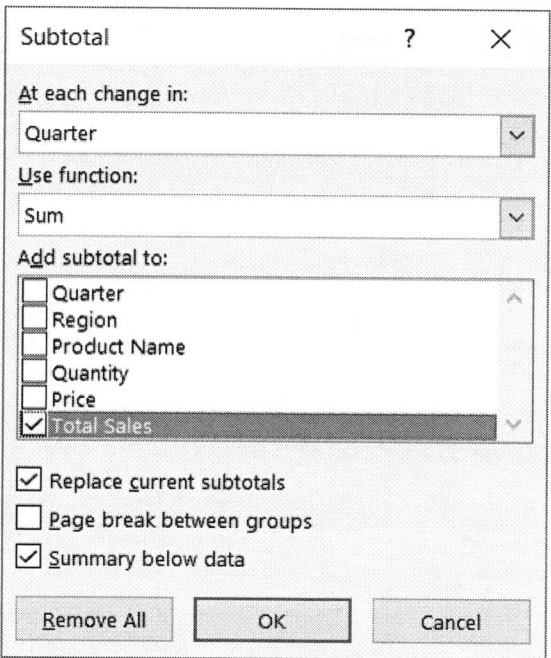

Figure 2–16: Use the Subtotal dialog box to configure your subtotal calculations.

The following table describes the function of the various elements of the **Subtotal** dialog box.

Subtotal Dialog Box Element	Enables You To
At each change in drop-down menu	Select the criteria by which to organize subsets of data. You do this by selecting the column that contains the desired entries. For example, you can tell Excel to perform subtotal calculations on data entries based on a particular region, department, or product. Remember to first sort your data on the column you will select in the **At each change in** drop-down menu, and then apply the subtotal calculation.
Use function drop-down menu	Select the desired SUBTOTAL function.
Add subtotal to menu	Select the column on which you wish to perform the calculation. Like the **At each change in** drop-down menu, this drop-down menu is populated with the column headers in the selected dataset.
Replace current subtotals check box	Decide between replacing existing subtotals with new subtotal calculations or including multiple subtotals in your dataset.
Page break between groups check box	Place a page break after each subtotal so you can print each subset of data separately.
Summary below data check box	Include a summary row at the bottom of the dataset. This will include the grand total from all of the individual subtotals.
Remove All button	Clear all subtotals and subsets from the original dataset.

 Access the Checklist tile on your CHOICE Course screen for reference information and job aids on How to Summarize Data with the Subtotal Feature.

ACTIVITY 2–4
Using Subtotals to Summarize Data

Before You Begin

The My Develetech Lists.xlsx file is open.

Scenario

As a data analyst for Develetech Industries, it is your responsibility to analyze the 2016 sales data. You have been asked to provide subtotals for the total sales of each region. You decide to use the subtotal feature to group each region and sum total sales.

1. Use the Subtotal feature to sum total sales for each region.
   a) Select the **2016 Sales** worksheet.
   b) Select cell **B1** and **Sort A to Z**.
   c) Select **Data→Outline→Subtotal**.
   d) From the **At each change in** drop-down menu, select **Region**.
   e) In the **Use function** field, verify that **Sum** is selected.
   f) In the **Add subtotal to** field, verify that **Total Sales** is selected.

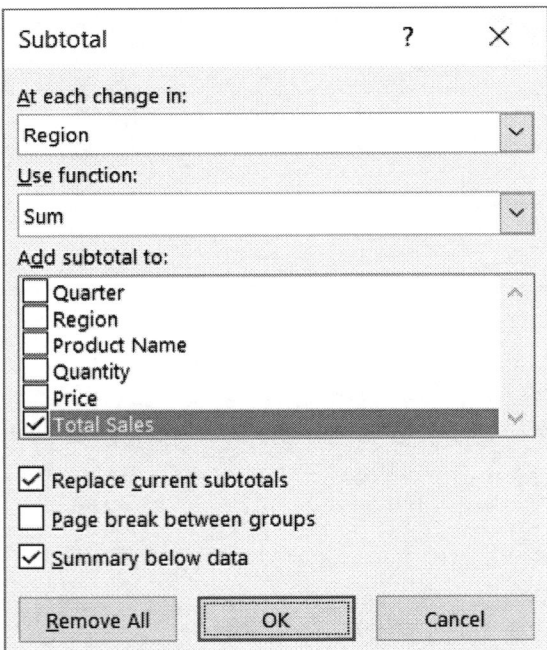

   g) Select **OK**.

2. Manipulate the subtotal outline to show only the regional totals.
   a) Next to row 18, select the minus button.
   b) Select the outline level 2 in the rows outline area.

c) AutoFit column **F**, if necessary, and verify the subtotals for each region and grand total of sales.

			Quarter	Region	Product Name	Quantity	Price	Total Sales
	+	18		Midwest Total				$20,757,540
	+	35		Northeast Total				$32,793,687
	+	52		Southeast Total				$21,702,944
	+	69		Southwest Total				$26,240,811
	+	86		West Total				$21,934,814
−		87		Grand Total				$123,429,796

3. Save the workbook and then close the file.

Summary

In this lesson, you learned to sort, filter, and subtotal data. Learning to extract subsets of your raw data can be an invaluable analysis tool. When data is organized in smaller groups, it is often easier and faster to analyze.

How do you think sorting and filtering will benefit you with current or future workbooks?

How do you plan to incorporate the Subtotal feature in future workbooks?

 Note: Check your CHOICE Course screen for opportunities to interact with your classmates, peers, and the larger CHOICE online community about the topics covered in this course or other topics you are interested in. From the Course screen you can also access available resources for a more continuous learning experience.

3 | Analyzing Data

Lesson Time: 1 hour

Lesson Objectives

In this lesson, you will analyze data. You will:

- Create and modify tables.

- Apply intermediate conditional formatting.

- Apply advanced conditional formatting.

Lesson Introduction

As you progress with the features of Microsoft® Office Excel® 2016, you see that many of its features build on the concepts and topics introduced in the previous lessons. You have already learned that data analysis is an integral part of what you can do with Excel.

As you have learned, manipulating raw data for analysis can be done in many ways, and each method has its merits. In this lesson, you will learn how to create tables to make reviewing data easier. In addition, you will learn how to format data in order to show highs, lows, or trends.

TOPIC A

Create and Modify Tables

While most work in Excel does not require much formatting to present a well-organized, good-looking worksheet, one feature known as tables can have a huge visual impact on how your data is presented. In the previous lesson, you learned how to work with lists by sorting and filtering and this topic on creating and modifying tables builds on that knowledge. By converting your raw data into tables, you will be able to take advantage of additional reporting features without affecting any of the data you have entered into your worksheets.

Tables

In Excel, a *table* is simply a dataset composed of contiguous rows and columns that Excel treats as a single, independent object. Excel tables contain robust functionality that enables you to organize, change the display of, and perform calculations on worksheet data quickly and easily. Regardless of how many ways you manipulate your table data, the raw data you initially entered remains intact. You can create tables from existing ranges, or create empty tables and then populate them. You can also revert tables to simple ranges.

As with cells and ranges, you can apply defined names to tables for ease of reference. When you create a table, Excel automatically assigns it a generic name, such as Table1 or Table2, but you can change this to suit your needs. You can also expand existing tables to accommodate additional data, and you can insert or delete columns and rows within tables, just as you can in a range.

	A	B	C	D	E	F
1	Quarter	Region	Product Name	Quantity	Price	Total Sales
2	Q3	Northeast	Cameras	406	$8,985	$3,647,910
3	Q3	Northeast	Laptops	127	$3,704	$470,408
4	Q3	Northeast	Printers	468	$4,211	$1,970,748
5	Q3	Northeast	Desktops	475	$5,507	$2,615,825
6	Q3	Southeast	Cameras	413	$4,574	$1,889,062
7	Q3	Southeast	Laptops	311	$5,455	$1,696,505
8	Q3	Southeast	Printers	328	$3,834	$1,257,552
9	Q3	Southeast	Desktops	144	$1,308	$188,352
10	Q3	Midwest	Cameras	431	$3,585	$1,545,135
11	Q3	Midwest	Laptops	409	$9,745	$3,985,705
12	Q3	Midwest	Printers	277	$2,863	$793,051
13	Q3	Midwest	Desktops	104	$897	$93,288
14	Q3	Southwest	Cameras	246	$8,449	$2,078,454
15	Q3	Southwest	Laptops	494	$6,172	$3,048,968
16	Q3	Southwest	Printers	463	$3,271	$1,514,473
17	Q3	Southwest	Desktops	317	$1,245	$394,665
18	Q3	West	Cameras	180	$6,434	$1,158,120
19	Q3	West	Laptops	487	$4,111	$2,002,057
20	Q3	West	Printers	339	$8,072	$2,736,408
21	Q3	West	Desktops	327	$7,668	$2,507,436
22	Total					$35,594,122

Figure 3-1: Data in an Excel table.

Note: Named tables must adhere to the same naming conventions as other named elements.

Table Components

There is a basic set of table components that Excel tables can, but don't necessarily have to, contain. By default, Excel tables contain a header row and appear with banded rows. You can toggle the display of these and other components on or off to suit your needs and to provide access to or suppress various functionality.

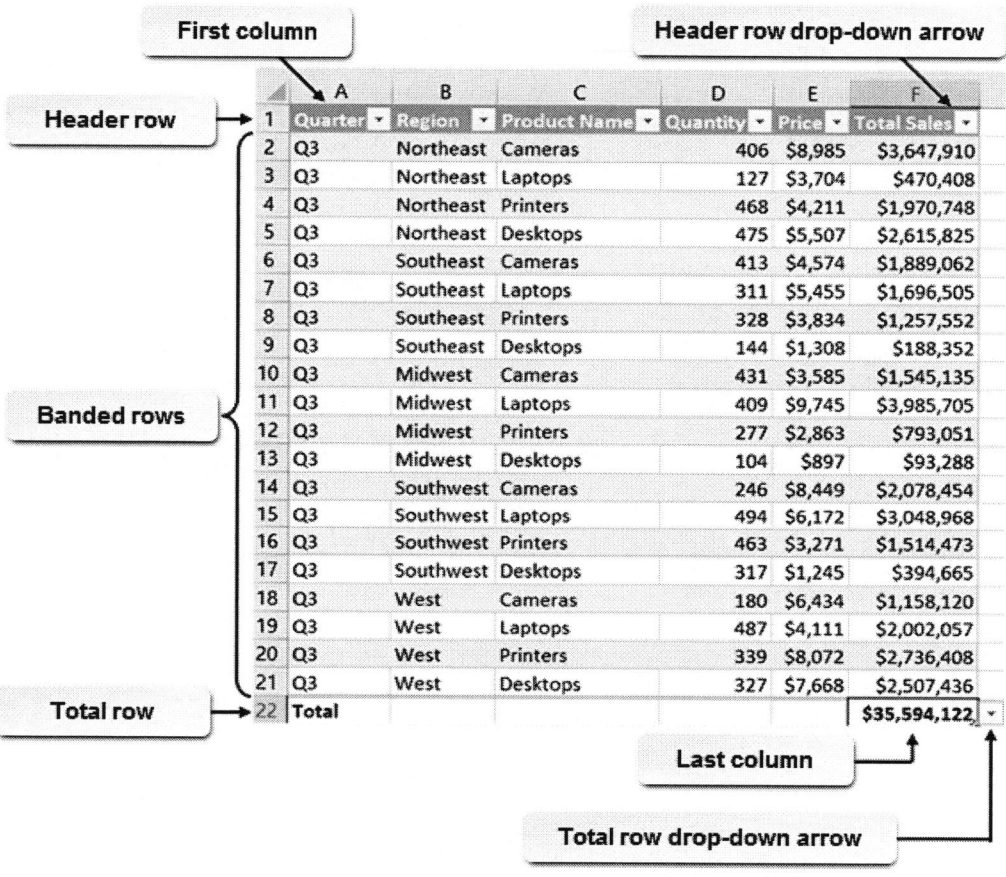

Figure 3-2: An Excel table with most of its components displayed.

The following table describes the various components of Excel tables, along with their functions.

Excel Table Component	Description
Header row	Displays column labels for the table and provides you with access to some of Excel's table-organization functionality.
Header row drop-down arrow	Displays a drop-down menu that provides you with access to commands you can use to organize and change the display of your table data.
Total row	Displays the results of column-specific calculations and provides you with access to some of Excel's built-in table *summary function* capabilities.
Total row drop-down arrow	Displays a drop-down menu that provides you with quick and easy access to functions for performing calculations on table-column data.

Excel Table Component	Description
Banded rows	These make it easier to view individual rows of data by applying different formatting to alternating table rows.
Banded columns	These make it easier to view individual columns of data by applying different formatting to alternating table columns.
First column	Sets off the display of the first column of data by applying specific formatting (typically bolding) to it.
Last column	Sets off the display of the last column of data by applying specific formatting (typically bolding) to it.
Sizing handle	Enables you to manually increase or decrease the size of a table. Generally speaking, changing the size of an Excel table does not affect the entries in any of the cells you either add to or remove from the table. But, cell formatting is affected. For example, if you add cells to a table by using the sizing handle to increase the size of a table, the new cells inherit the table's formatting. If you remove those same cells from the table using the sizing handle, the formatting reverts. This only applies, however, to the table's formatting; formatting you manually added to the cells may not change.

The Create Table Dialog Box

You can use the **Create Table** dialog box to convert simple ranges of data into tables. From here, you can confirm the range selection you wish to convert into a table or modify that range to ensure that the correct data becomes part of the table. The **Create Table** dialog box also enables you to decide whether or not you wish to include the top row of the selected range in the new table as a header row. Typically, you would do this if the selected range contains column labels in the top row. You can access the **Create Table** dialog box by selecting **Insert→Tables→Table**.

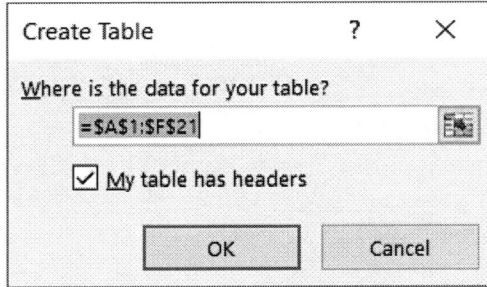

Figure 3-3: Use the Create Table dialog box to convert raw data into a table.

 Note: Another way to create a table is to use the **Format as Table** command located on the **Home** tab in the **Styles** group. This command lets you format a list as a table by choosing the style first and then confirming where the data is for your table. The only difference between the two commands is that **Format as Table** lets you choose a table style before the table is created.

The Table Tools Design Contextual Tab

The **Design** contextual tab contains various commands and options that are specific to working with tables. It appears when you select a worksheet table, or any part of a table, and disappears when you select outside the table. The **Table Tools** contextual tab group contains only one tab, the **Design** tab, which is divided into five command groups.

The following table identifies the types of commands and options contained in the various groups on the **Table Tools Design** contextual tab.

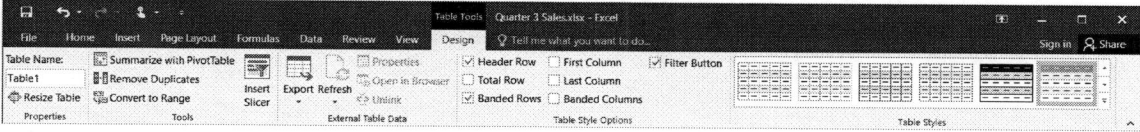

Figure 3–4: The Table Tools Design contextual tab.

Table Tools Design Contextual Tab Group	Contains Commands or Options For
Properties	Resizing and naming worksheet tables. This group also displays the name of the currently selected table.
Tools	Removing duplicate values from tables; converting tables back into ranges; creating PivotTables out of tables; and adding filtering objects, known as slicers, to tables.
External Table Data	Exporting table data to external applications and managing data links with external sources.
Table Style Options	Toggling the display of table components on or off.
Table Styles	Applying styles to Excel tables.

Table Styles and Quick Styles

Like cell styles, *table styles* are particular configurations of formatting options you can apply to your worksheet tables. Table styles help make your tables more visually appealing and easier to read. Table styles can consist of font, border, and fill formatting, and you can create your own customized table styles or select from among a variety of preconfigured table styles, which are known as *quick styles*.

	A	B	C	D	E	F
1	Quarter	Region	Product Name	Quantity	Price	Total Sales
2	Q3	Northeast	Cameras	406	$8,985	$3,647,910
3	Q3	Northeast	Laptops	127	$3,704	$470,408
4	Q3	Northeast	Printers	468	$4,211	$1,970,748
5	Q3	Northeast	Desktops	475	$5,507	$2,615,825
6	Q3	Southeast	Cameras	413	$4,574	$1,889,062
7	Q3	Southeast	Laptops	311	$5,455	$1,696,505
8	Q3	Southeast	Printers	328	$3,834	$1,257,552
9	Q3	Southeast	Desktops	144	$1,308	$188,352
10	Q3	Midwest	Cameras	431	$3,585	$1,545,135
11	Q3	Midwest	Laptops	409	$9,745	$3,985,705
12	Q3	Midwest	Printers	277	$2,863	$793,051
13	Q3	Midwest	Desktops	104	$897	$93,288
14	Q3	Southwest	Cameras	246	$8,449	$2,078,454
15	Q3	Southwest	Laptops	494	$6,172	$3,048,968
16	Q3	Southwest	Printers	463	$3,271	$1,514,473
17	Q3	Southwest	Desktops	317	$1,245	$394,665
18	Q3	West	Cameras	180	$6,434	$1,158,120
19	Q3	West	Laptops	487	$4,111	$2,002,057
20	Q3	West	Printers	339	$8,072	$2,736,408
21	Q3	West	Desktops	327	$7,668	$2,507,436
22	Total					$35,594,122

Figure 3–5: A highly stylized Excel table.

The New Table Style Dialog Box

You can use the **New Table Style** dialog box to create and save custom table styles. From here, you can select which table component you wish to apply formatting to; access the **Format Cells** dialog box to configure the desired font, border, and fill formatting; and name and save your custom styles. To access the **New Table Style** dialog box, on the **Design** tab of the **Table Tools** contextual tab, in the **Table Styles** group, select the **Table Styles** gallery's **More** button, and then select **New Table Style**.

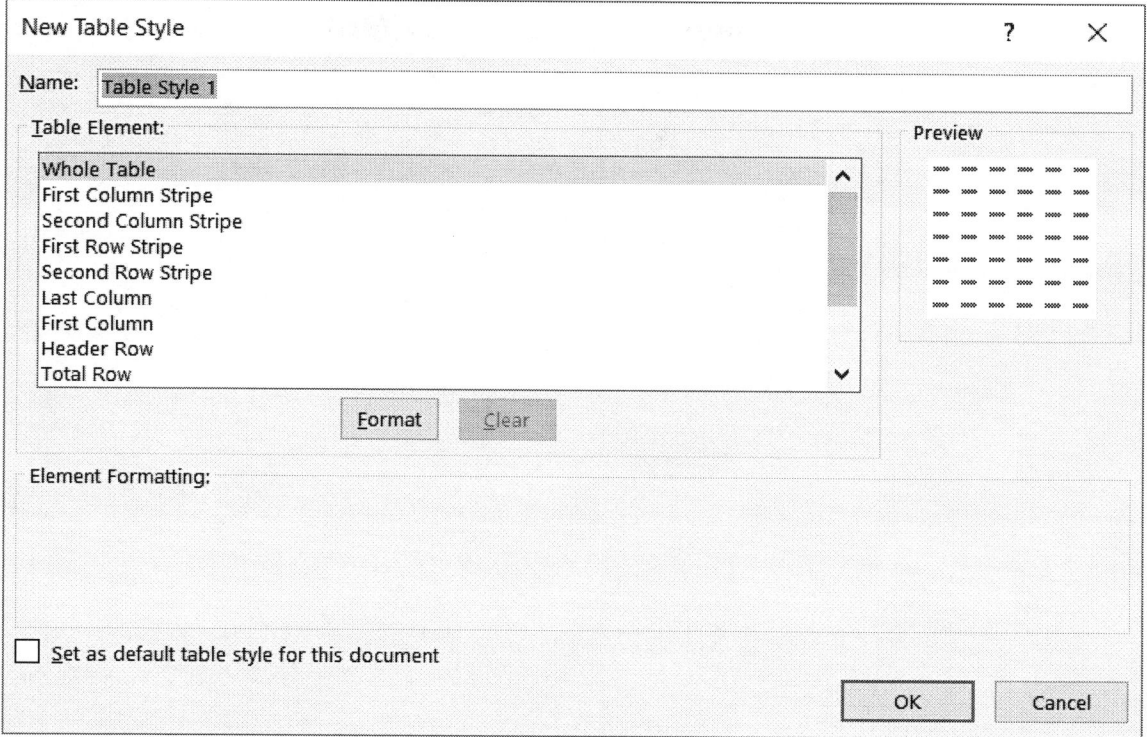

Figure 3–6: The New Table Style dialog box.

Quick Analysis

You've likely already noticed the little icon that appears whenever you select multiple populated cells, or a combination of populated and empty cells, on your worksheets. This icon is the **Quick Analysis** button, which provides you with access to a set of commands for quickly performing a variety of common data-analysis tasks. Among these is the ability to quickly convert a range to a table. Excel 2016's **Quick Analysis** tools appear in a pop-up gallery when you select the **Quick Analysis** button. This gallery is divided into a series of five tabs that each display a set of Quick Analysis commands related to a particular type of analysis. These commands are, to a degree, context specific, and so can change depending on the current selection. Pointing the cursor at the various commands in the **Quick Analysis** gallery displays a live preview of what applying that option would look like.

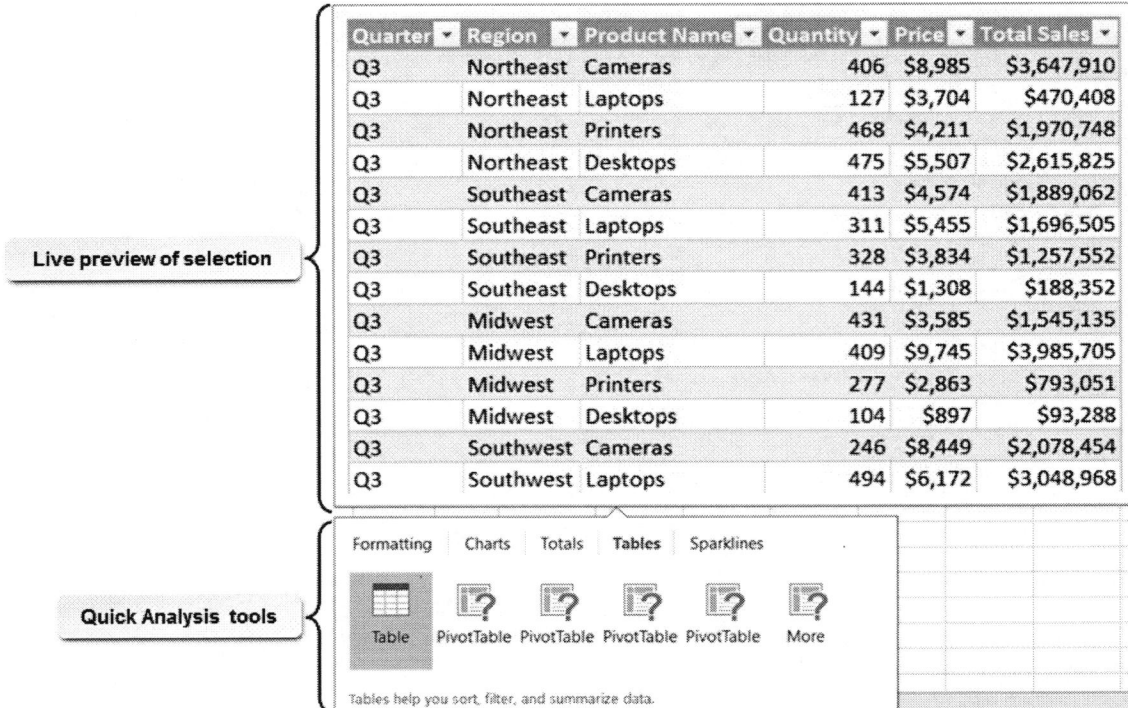

Quarter ▾	Region ▾	Product Name ▾	Quantity ▾	Price ▾	Total Sales ▾
Q3	Northeast	Cameras	406	$8,985	$3,647,910
Q3	Northeast	Laptops	127	$3,704	$470,408
Q3	Northeast	Printers	468	$4,211	$1,970,748
Q3	Northeast	Desktops	475	$5,507	$2,615,825
Q3	Southeast	Cameras	413	$4,574	$1,889,062
Q3	Southeast	Laptops	311	$5,455	$1,696,505
Q3	Southeast	Printers	328	$3,834	$1,257,552
Q3	Southeast	Desktops	144	$1,308	$188,352
Q3	Midwest	Cameras	431	$3,585	$1,545,135
Q3	Midwest	Laptops	409	$9,745	$3,985,705
Q3	Midwest	Printers	277	$2,863	$793,051
Q3	Midwest	Desktops	104	$897	$93,288
Q3	Southwest	Cameras	246	$8,449	$2,078,454
Q3	Southwest	Laptops	494	$6,172	$3,048,968

Live preview of selection

Quick Analysis tools

Formatting Charts Totals **Tables** Sparklines

Table PivotTable PivotTable PivotTable PivotTable More

Tables help you sort, filter, and summarize data.

Figure 3-7: Quick Analysis tools display live previews when you point the mouse pointer at them.

 Note: When you create a table using the **Quick Analysis** tools, Excel does not display the **Create Table** dialog box, which enables you to verify or change the cells that will be included in the table. Using the Quick Analysis method automatically coverts the entire selected range into a table.

The following table describes the types of **Quick Analysis** tools you will find on the various **Quick Analysis** gallery tabs.

Quick Analysis Gallery Tab	Contains Commands For
Formatting	Applying conditional formatting to the current selection.
Charts	Creating charts out of the current selection.
Totals	Automatically inserting various functions to perform calculations on the current selection.
Tables	Converting the current selection to a table or inserting a PivotTable.
Sparklines	Inserting graphical data-analysis objects into the selected cells based on their values.

 Access the Checklist tile on your CHOICE Course screen for reference information and job aids on How to Use Quick Analysis Tools.

 Access the Checklist tile on your CHOICE Course screen for reference information and job aids on How to Create and Modify Tables.

ACTIVITY 3-1
Creating and Modifying Tables

Data File

C:\091056Data\Analyzing Data\Develetech Sales.xlsx

Before You Begin

Excel 2016 is open.

Scenario

As an administrative assistant to the vice president of sales at Develetech Industries you have been asked to create a report of the third quarter sales. The third quarter sales report should delineate each of the quarter's records. You decide the best way to present this data is to create a table from the data.

1. In Excel, open the workbook **Develetech Sales.xlsx**.

2. Convert the data for the third quarter sales in to a table.
   a) On the **Quarter 3 Sales** worksheet, verify that there are no blank rows or columns within the dataset.
   b) With cell **A1** selected, select **Insert→Tables→Table**.
   c) In the **Create Table** dialog box, ensure that the range listed is =$A$1:$F$21.
   d) Verify that the **My table has headers** check box is selected and select **OK**.

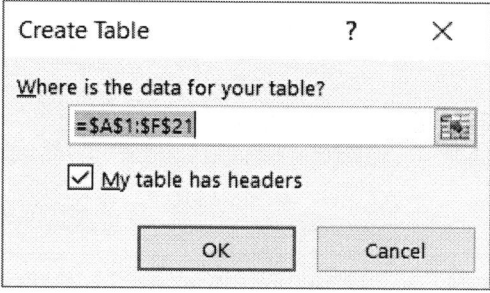

3. Apply a quick style to the table.
   a) If necessary, select any cell within the table to display the **Table Tools Design** contextual tab.
   b) Select the **Table Tools Design** contextual tab, then in the **Table Styles** group, select the **More** button.

c) Select **Table Style Medium 12** from the **Medium** section, in the **Table Styles** gallery.

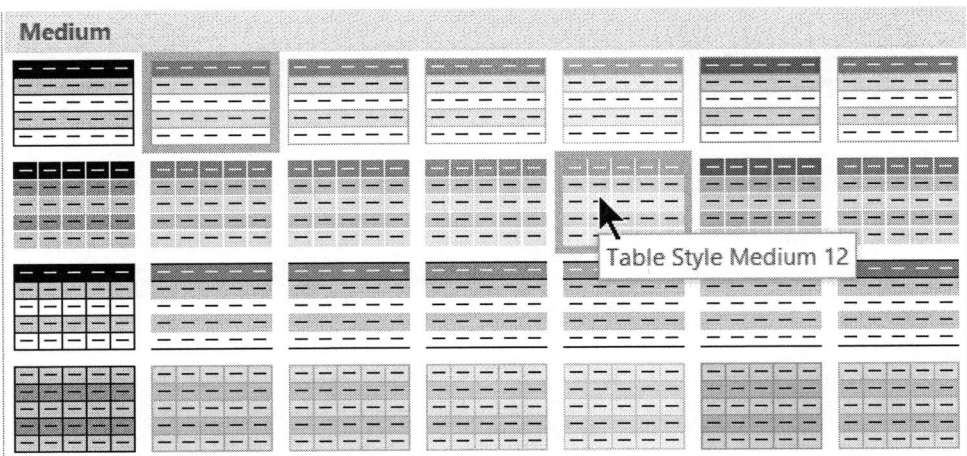

4. Add a new sales entry to the table and a new column.

   a) Select cell **A22** and type *Q3* and press **Tab**.

 Note: As you enter the new record Excel automatically formats the row according to the table style.

   b) Enter the remaining values for the entry in row 22.

- B22: *West*
- C22: *Desktops*
- D22: *327*
- E22: *7,668*

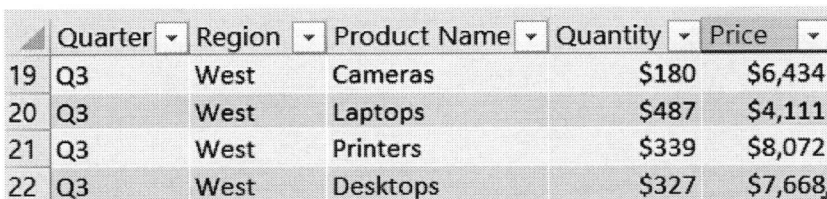

	Quarter ▾	Region ▾	Product Name ▾	Quantity ▾	Price ▾
19	Q3	West	Cameras	$180	$6,434
20	Q3	West	Laptops	$487	$4,111
21	Q3	West	Printers	$339	$8,072
22	Q3	West	Desktops	$327	$7,668

 Note: While a cell in the table is selected, when you scroll down the worksheet Excel will change the column headings from A-F into the column headings of your table.

   c) Select cell **F1** and enter *Total Sales*

5. Remove the duplicate Northeast region data for cameras from the table.

   a) Verify that the table is selected and select **Table Tools Design→Tools→Remove Duplicates**.

b) In the **Remove Duplicates** dialog box, verify that **My data has headers** is selected and that all columns are selected.

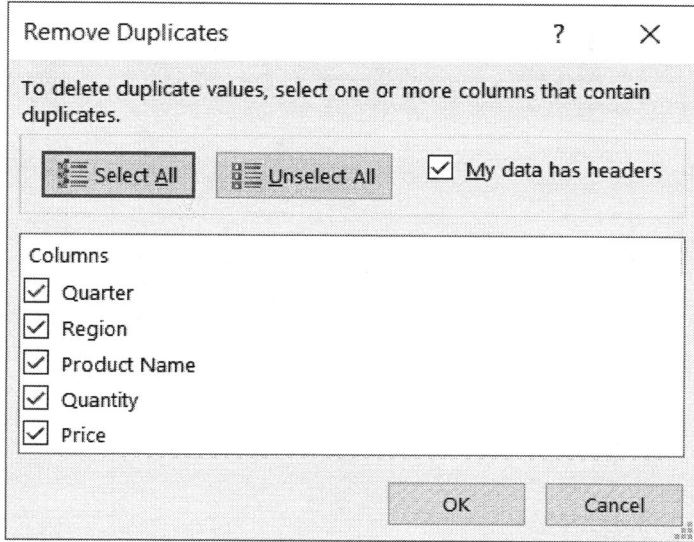

c) Select **OK**.
d) Verify that one duplicate value was found and removed from the table and select **OK**.

6. Create a defined name for the table.

a) Select the **Table Tools Design** contextual tab, if necessary, then in the **Properties** group, select the **Table Name** text box and type *Q3Sales_tbl*

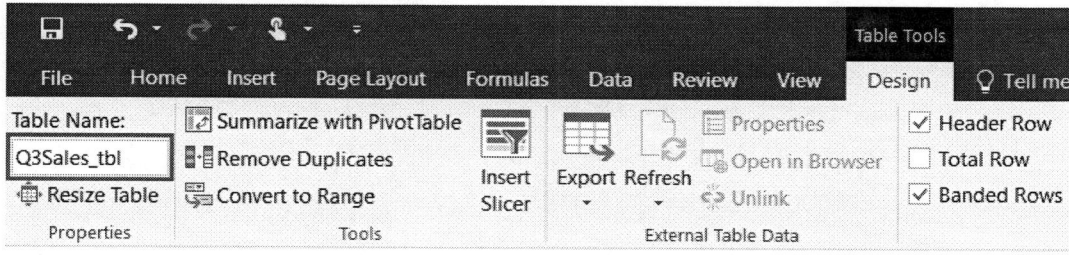

b) Press **Enter**.

7. Save the workbook as *My Develetech Sales.xlsx* and keep the file open.

ACTIVITY 3-2
Using Summary Functions in Tables

Before You Begin
The workbook My Develetech Sales.xlsx is open.

Scenario
The vice president is pleased with your work on the third quarter sales. Now the vice president wants to know the total sales for each row of the table and for the Southwest region, and by each product in the Southwest region. You decide the best way to accomplish this is to enable the total row for the table and to filter for the Southwest region.

---

1. Calculate the Total Sales for each table row, multiplying quantity times price.
   a) Select cell **F2** and type **=** and select cell **D2**.
   b) Type ***** and then select cell **E2** and press **Enter**.
   c) Verify that Excel automatically calculated the formula for the remaining table rows.

    Note: When you create an Excel table, Excel assigns a name to the table and to each column in the table. When you add formulas to an Excel table, those names can appear automatically as you enter the formula and select the cell references in the table instead of manually entering them. These are called structured references.

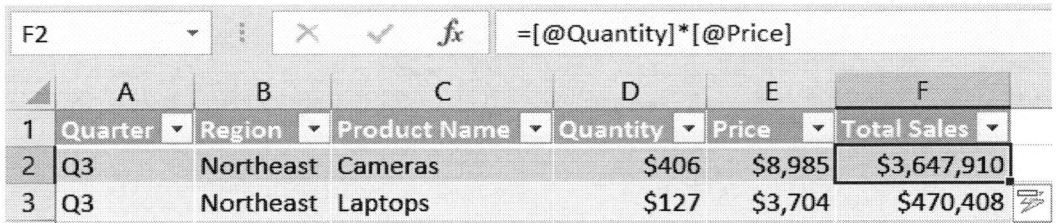

2. Enable the Total Row for the table.
   a) With any cell of the table selected, select **Table Tools Design** and in the **Table Style Options** group, select the **Total Row** check box.
   b) Select cell **F22** and select the **Total Row** drop-down arrow.
   c) Verify that the function **Sum** is selected.
   d) Select any cell within the table to close the drop-down menu.

e) Verify the total for the quarter is $35,594,122.

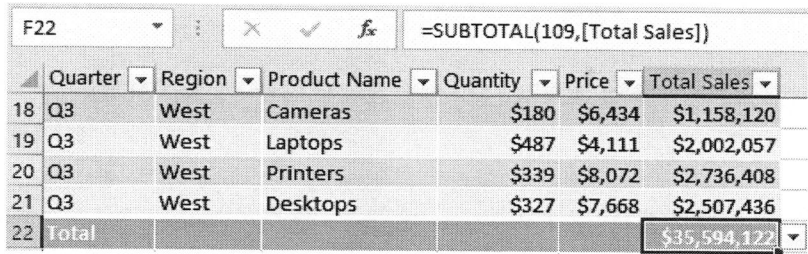

3. Filter the third quarter sales for the Southwest region.
   a) Select the **Region AutoFilter** drop-down arrow in cell **B1** and uncheck the **Select All** check box.
   b) Select the **Southwest** check box and select **OK**.
   c) Verify the third quarter totals for the Southwest region.

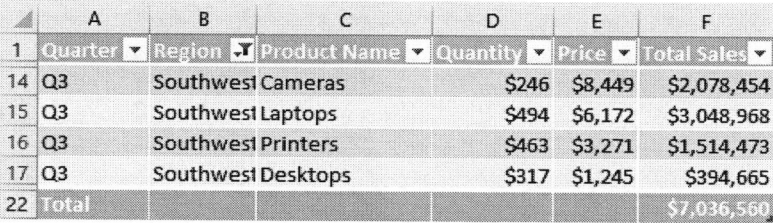

4. Save the workbook and keep the file open.

TOPIC B

Apply Intermediate Conditional Formatting

In *Microsoft® Office Excel® 2016: Part 1*, you learned basic conditional formatting can be applied to ranges of data to highlight data outliers and compare data as a set. Learning additional conditional formatting options beyond the basics is the next step to help you analyze data trends. In this topic, you will learn to apply intermediate conditional formatting.

Custom Conditional Formats

In addition to the preconfigured conditional formatting options available in Excel 2016, you have the option of creating completely custom conditional formats to suit your needs. The tools available in Excel enable you to create specific rules you can use to apply conditional formatting and to tailor the display of conditionally formatted cells using an incredible array of options. You can start with one of Excel's pre-formatted options and then adjust it to better suit your needs. Or, you can create sets of rules and formatting options completely from scratch. In addition to the built-in cell formatting options and the data bars, color scales, and icon sets, you can use nearly any of Excel's cell formatting options, such as number, font, and border formatting, to format cells that meet the conditions you set. The cell formatting options not available for use as conditional formats are those on the **Alignment** and **Protection** tabs in the **Format Cells** dialog box.

The New Formatting Rule Dialog Box

The **New Formatting Rule** dialog box enables you to create fully customized conditional formatting rules and to customize the display of cells that meet the given criteria. The **New Formatting Rule** dialog box is divided into two sections: the **Select a Rule Type** list and the **Edit the Rule Description** section. The **New Formatting Rule** dialog box is accessible by selecting **Home→Styles→Conditional Formatting→New Rule**.

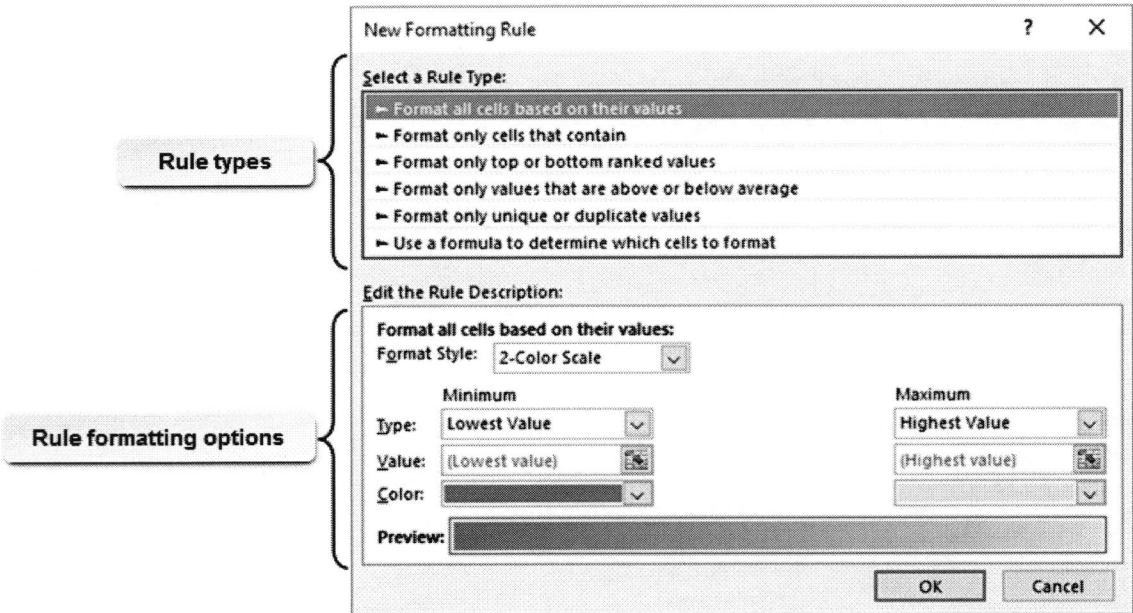

Figure 3–8: Add new conditional formatting rules by using the New Formatting Rule dialog box.

The **Select a Rule Type** list displays six categories of rule types from which you can select the general kind of rule you wish to use to apply conditional formatting. The following table provides some detail on what these categories represent.

Rule Type	Will Apply Formatting to Cells
Format all cells based on their values	Based on the relative values of the data in a range. This is the same rule type used by data bar, color scale, and icon set conditional formatting.
Format only cells that contain	Based on both the type of data contained in a specified range and the specific values. You can use this rule type to format cells based on criteria such as numerical values, specific text entries, particular dates, or cell errors.
Format only top or bottom ranked values	Containing values that fall within a specified percentage of the top or bottom range of values. For example, you can apply formatting to the top 5 percent of values or the bottom 22 percent of values.
Format only values that are above or below average	Containing values that are either above or below the average value of all data in the selected range. You can also use this rule type to apply formatting to values that fall either above or below the first, second, or third standard deviation.
Format only unique or duplicate values	Containing data that is either unique in the specified range or that duplicates values in other cells in the specified range.
Use a formula to determine which cells to format	That pass a logical test specified by a formula or function.

The **Edit the Rule Description** section displays the commands and options you will use to configure the parameters of whichever rule you select and to customize the display of cell formatting. The commands and options that appear in the **Edit the Rule Description** section vary dramatically depending on the rule type you select in the **Select a Rule Type** list. Typically, you will be presented with options for setting the particular values or content types Excel will use as thresholds/identifiers to apply the selected formatting. The specific formatting options also vary greatly, but selecting several of the rule types will prompt Excel to display the **Format** button in the **Edit the Rule Description** section. Selecting the **Format** button opens the **Format Cells** dialog box, providing you with access to a wide array of formatting options. You can access the **New Formatting Rule** dialog box by selecting **Home→Styles→Conditional Formatting→New Rule**.

The Conditional Formatting Rules Manager Dialog Box

You can use the **Conditional Formatting Rules Manager** dialog box to add, delete, edit, and manage conditional formatting rules in your workbooks. The **Conditional Formatting Rules Manager** dialog box contains a number of commands, components, and options that provide you with a high level of control over your conditional formatting rules. From here, you can simultaneously manage all conditional formatting rules present in an entire workbook. You can access the **Conditional Formatting Rules Manager** dialog box by selecting **Home→Styles→Conditional Formatting→Manage Rules.**

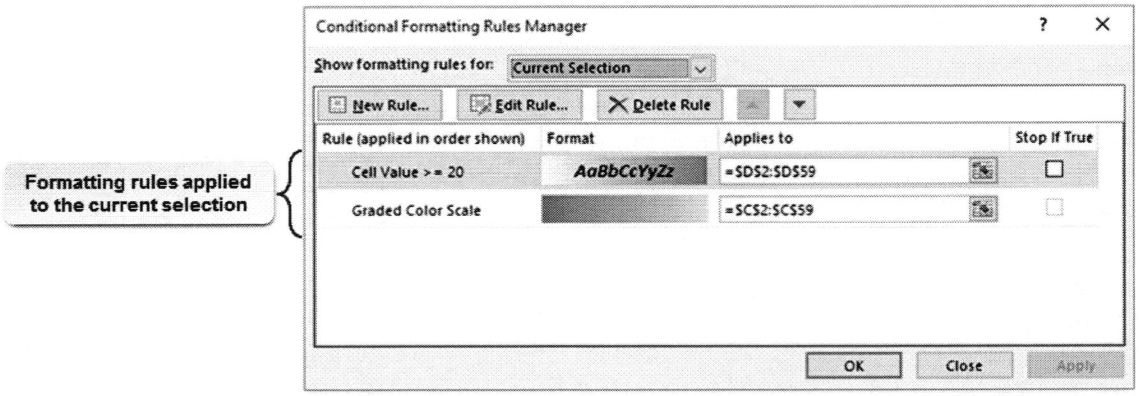

Figure 3-9: Use the Conditional Formatting Rules Manager dialog box to manage all conditional formatting within a particular workbook.

The following table describes the various elements of the **Conditional Formatting Rules Manager** dialog box.

Conditional Formatting Rules Manager Dialog Box Element	Description
Show formatting rules for drop-down menu	Enables you to select which workbook element to display applied formatting rules for. This can be for the currently selected range of cells, for any of the worksheets in the workbook, and for particular objects like tables.
New Rule button	Opens the **New Formatting Rule** dialog box, which you can use to create a new conditional formatting rule.
Edit Rule button	Opens the **Edit Formatting Rule** dialog box, which enables you to edit the currently selected rule. This is essentially the same as the **New Formatting Rule** dialog box, only you use it to edit existing conditional formatting rules.
Delete Rule button	Deletes the currently selected rule.
Move Up and **Move Down** buttons	Use these to change the order of rule precedence.
Rule (applied in order shown) column	Displays all of the specific rules applied to the selection in the **Show formatting rules for** drop-down menu.
Format column	Displays a preview of the specific formatting associated with each rule.
Applies to column	Displays the cell or range to which each rule applies.
Stop If True check boxes	Enables you to select how far down the list of displayed rules to stop applying formatting. You use this feature if you need to open a workbook in an earlier version of Excel that does not support the same type or the same number of conditional formatting rules. For example, if you have five conditional formatting rules applied to a particular worksheet, but you have the workbook containing that worksheet open in an older version of Excel that supports only three rules, you could check the **Stop If True** check box for the third rule to tell Excel to apply only the top three rules.

Rule Precedence

The **Conditional Formatting Rules Manager** dialog box displays all rules applied to the selection in the **Show formatting rules for** drop-down menu in order of *rule precedence*. This is the order in which Excel evaluates and applies conditional formatting to the cells. Rules that appear above other rules have a higher precedence.

Where there are no conflicts, all conditional formatting applied to the same range of cells will appear simultaneously. Where there are conflicts, Excel will default to displaying the formatting with a higher precedence. For example, let's say you apply two conditional formatting rules to the same cell, and both of the formats indicate applying a background fill, one blue and one red, to the cells. In cells containing data that matches the criteria of both rules, Excel will display the formatting that has a higher precedence in the **Conditional Formatting Rules Manager** dialog box. This is because a cell cannot have two different background fills applied to it at the same time. However, you can, for example, display a data bar on top of a cell background. If those are the two formats applied to a cell, both will appear in the cell and the precedence is moot.

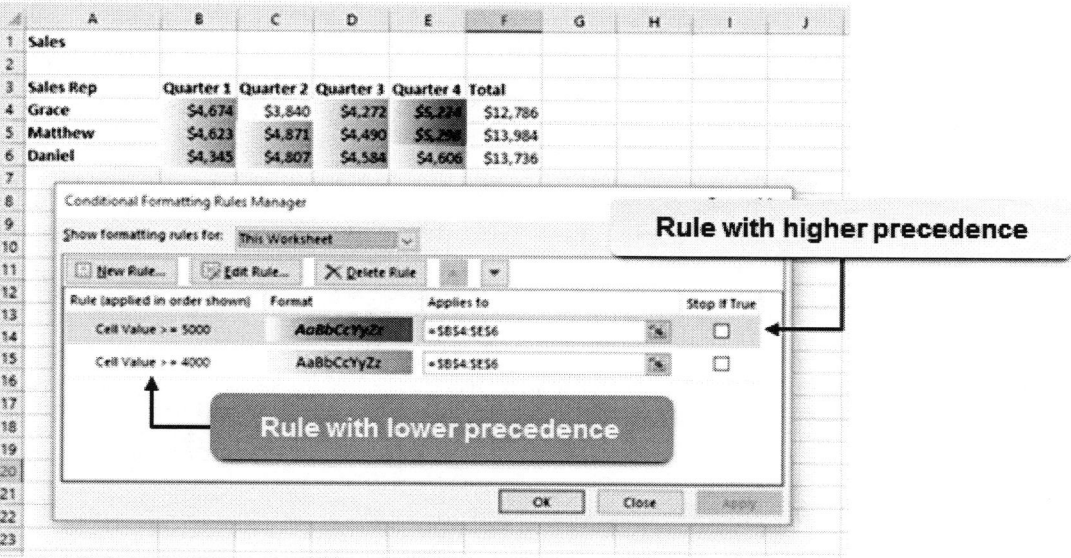

Figure 3-10: Here, most cells meet the criteria for the rule applying blue fill formatting, but only two cells meet the criteria for the red fill formatting. As the red fill formatting rule has precedence, the red fill appears in cells that meet its rule's condition.

 Access the Checklist tile on your CHOICE Course screen for reference information and job aids on How to Apply Intermediate Conditional Formatting.

ACTIVITY 3-3
Applying Intermediate Conditional Formatting

Before You Begin
The workbook My Develetech Sales.xlsx is open.

Scenario
As the vice president of sales for Develetech Industries you have collected the 2016 sales data and organized it for each of the quarters, regions, and products. You want to find out which regions and products are above the average. In order to accomplish this task, you decide to apply conditional formatting.

1. Apply conditional formatting in order to see total sales that are above the average.
   a) Select the **Total Sales** worksheet.
   b) Select the range **C2:C21**.
   c) Select **Home→Styles→Conditional Formatting→New Rule**.
   d) In the **New Formatting Rule** dialog box, from the **Select a Rule Type** list, select **Format only values that are above or below average**.
   e) In the **Edit the Rule Description** section, in the **Format values that are** drop-down list, verify that **above** is selected.
   f) Select the **Format** button.
   g) In the **Format Cells** dialog box, select the **Fill** tab.
   h) Select the **Fill Effects** button and in the **Shading styles** section, select the option **Vertical**.
   i) In the **Fill Effects** dialog box, on the **Gradient** tab, in the **Variants** section, select the **upper right variant** and select **OK**.
   j) In the **Format Cells** dialog box, select **OK**.

k) In the **New Formatting Rule** dialog box, select **OK**.

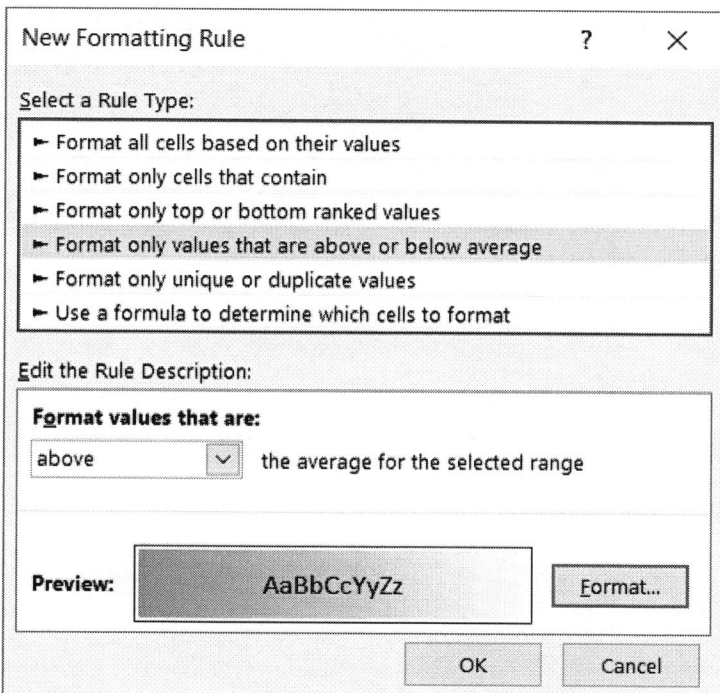

l) Verify that the conditional formatting has been applied to the sales data that are above the average of $6,171,490.

 Note: Note that the average of the selected range will appear on the status bar if Average is enabled. Right-click the status bar to customize its settings.

	A	B	C
1	Region	Product Name	Total Sales
2	Northeast	Cameras	$7,222,322
3	Northeast	Laptops	$6,321,037
4	Northeast	Printers	$6,284,587
5	Northeast	Desktops	$12,965,741
6	Southeast	Cameras	$6,459,779
7	Southeast	Laptops	$4,193,765
8	Southeast	Printers	$6,097,807
9	Southeast	Desktops	$4,951,593
10	Midwest	Cameras	$5,147,974
11	Midwest	Laptops	$5,956,485
12	Midwest	Printers	$6,524,010
13	Midwest	Desktops	$3,129,071
14	Southwest	Cameras	$7,081,467
15	Southwest	Laptops	$10,389,948
16	Southwest	Printers	$3,832,051
17	Southwest	Desktops	$4,937,345
18	West	Cameras	$4,217,353
19	West	Laptops	$3,567,725
20	West	Printers	$5,223,515
21	West	Desktops	$8,926,221

2. Save the workbook and keep the file open.

TOPIC C

Apply Advanced Conditional Formatting

Applying conditional formatting to worksheets is a convenient way to help users quickly make sense of the data in a particular column. But applying conditional formatting using some of the more common methods can be limiting. Many users simply apply conditional formatting to the same range of cells they ask Excel to evaluate. But, what if you want Excel to examine and evaluate the data in one column, but then apply the specified conditional formatting to another column? Or, suppose you wish to format the cells in numerous columns based on criteria in a different column.

In Excel, you can create a formula to evaluate a condition and when that condition is met, you can apply formatting. In this topic, you will learn to apply conditional formatting based on formulas.

The Use a Formula to Determine Which Cells to Format Rule

Typically, when you apply conditional formatting to a range of cells, say a particular column of data, you're asking Excel to evaluate the entries in that range and then apply the specified formatting to any cell that meets the specified criteria. Any of the basic, preconfigured conditional formatting rules, and most of the rules available in the **New Formatting Rule** dialog box, are well-suited to performing this task. But applying formatting to cells based on the data entered in other cells will require the use of formulas or functions. This means you'll need to select the **Use a formula to determine which cells to format** option in the **New Formatting Rule** dialog box when you go to define the conditional formatting rule.

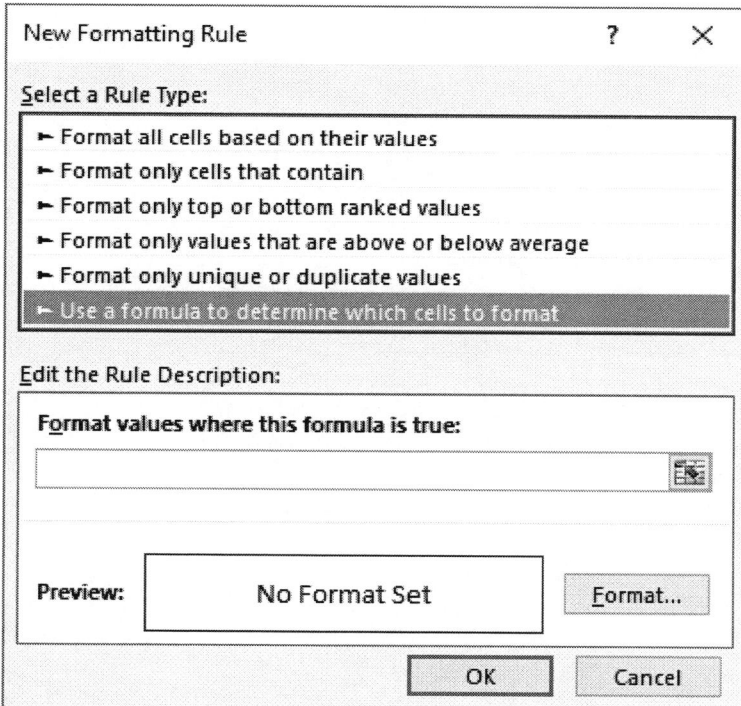

Figure 3–11: Excel enables you to define your own custom rules for the application of conditional formatting.

This option is, essentially, an IF function that Excel uses to determine which cells to apply formatting to. Excel treats any formula or function you enter in the **Format values where this formula is true** field like the **logical_test** argument in a standard IF function. The difference here is that the **value_if_true** argument is the application of the specified conditional formatting, whereas the **value_if_false** argument is not applying the specified formatting. To get a better idea of how this works, let's take a look at an extremely simple example, one in which we ask Excel to highlight the number of years an employee, in this case a sales rep, has been with the company if more than 10 years.

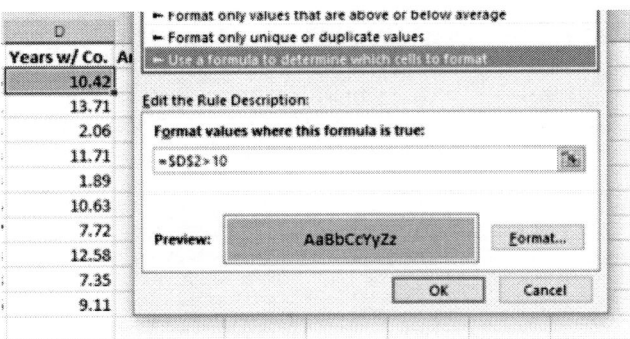

Figure 3-12: An example of highlighting the number of years an employee has been with the company if greater than 10 years.

 Note: As with entering formulas or functions in worksheet cells, you must add the equal sign (=) before the formula or function in the **Format values where this formula is true** field.

Here, we are using a formula to apply formatting to the same cell Excel is evaluating. In this example, if you were to read aloud the "IF" function Excel is applying, it would sound something like "If the value in cell **D2** is greater than 10, then apply the formatting. Otherwise, don't apply the formatting." Obviously, this is a task Excel could easily perform using one of the preconfigured **Highlight Cells Rules** from the **Conditional Formatting** drop-down menu. But, let's say we want to use the value in cell **D2** to apply the formatting to the sales rep's name instead of the value itself. That would look something like the following image.

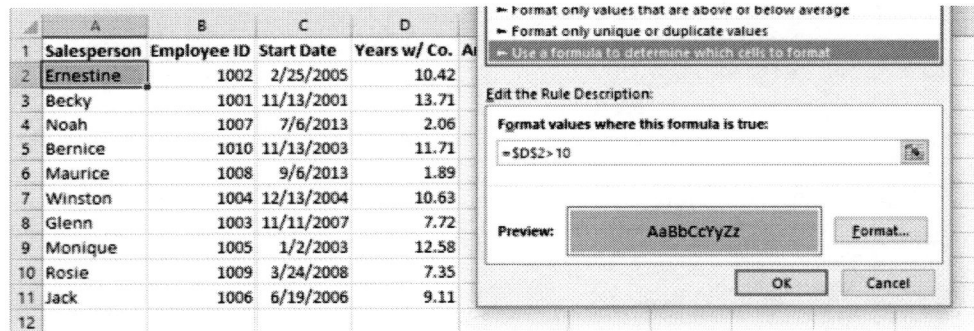

Figure 3-13: An example of highlighting the sales rep's name if the number of years the employee has been with the company is greater than 10 years.

The only difference between the first example and this example is that we highlighted cell **A2**, not cell **D2**, before creating the conditional formatting rule. So, although the formula is still looking to cell **D2** to perform the logical test, Excel is applying the conditional formatting to cell **A2**. This forms the basis for using formulas to apply conditional formatting to cells other than those Excel evaluates. In order to apply the same formatting across a much wider range of cells, you'll first need to consider how absolute and relative references come into play.

 Note: Although the main focus of this topic is on using formulas and functions to apply conditional formatting to multiple columns simultaneously and to cells other than the ones Excel evaluates, it is important to understand that you can also use formulas and functions to create custom formatting rules when the existing conditional formatting options don't suit your needs.

Cell References and Conditional Formatting

Excel provides you with several options for applying a conditional formatting rule to more than one cell, row, or column at a time. You can select the entire range to which you wish to apply the formatting before defining the rule, or you can use the **Format Painter** or the **Paste Special** options to copy and paste the formatting to other cells once you've already defined the rule. But there is an extremely important consideration to keep in mind when doing this: whether you select the entire range first or you copy the formatting later, Excel treats the operation as if you were dragging (or copying and pasting) the formatting to the new cells. This means that, as with reusing formulas and functions themselves, absolute and relative cell references become extremely important once you begin to reuse conditional formatting rules. When you define your conditional formatting rule, you must think in these terms or you won't get the results you desire. Let's take a look at a few examples to see how this works.

In this first example, we are trying to apply the same conditional formatting we did for the salesperson that has been with the company greater than 10 years. We used the **Format Painter** to apply the conditional formatting rule to the remaining cells in the first column.

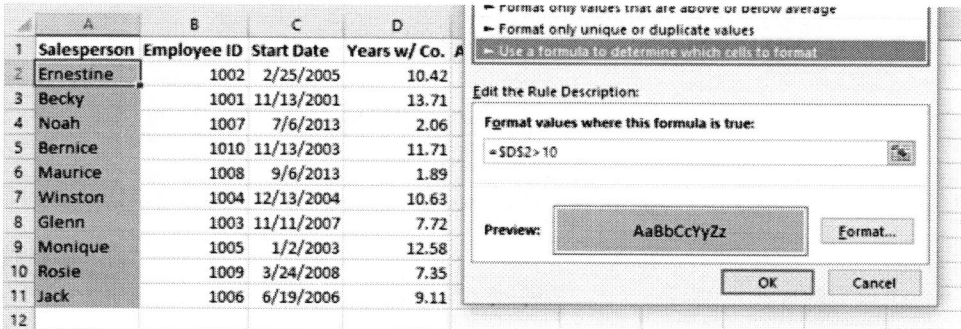

Figure 3-14: An example of using Format Painter to apply conditional formatting.

Clearly, there is an issue as salespersons who have been with the company less than 10 years are still highlighted. This is because the reference to cell **D2** in the formula is an absolute reference. Excel is looking to that cell for all of the cells in column **A** when applying the rule. To resolve this, simply change the reference to cell **D2** from an absolute reference to a relative reference.

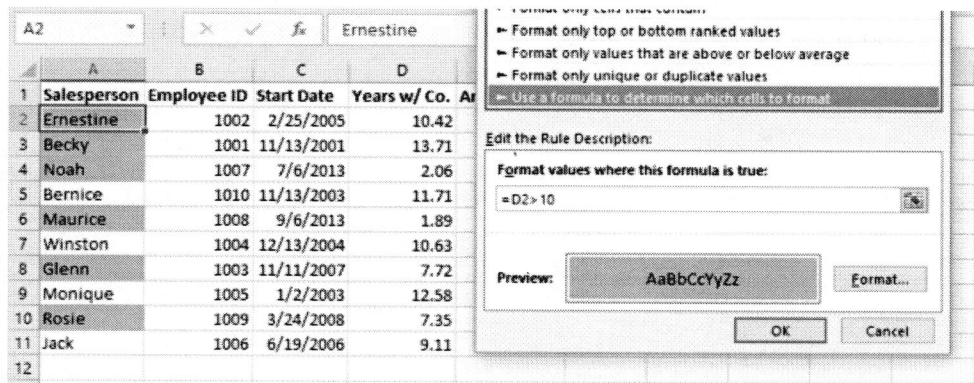

Figure 3-15: An example of changing an absolute reference to a relative reference.

Now the rule is behaving as you'd expect it to. However, things get a bit more complex when you try to apply the same conditional formatting rule to more than one column at a time. Continuing with this example, let's say we now want to use the same rule to apply formatting to both the Salesperson name and Employee ID based on the values in column **D**. If we simply copy the formatting to the second column without changing the formula, this would be the result.

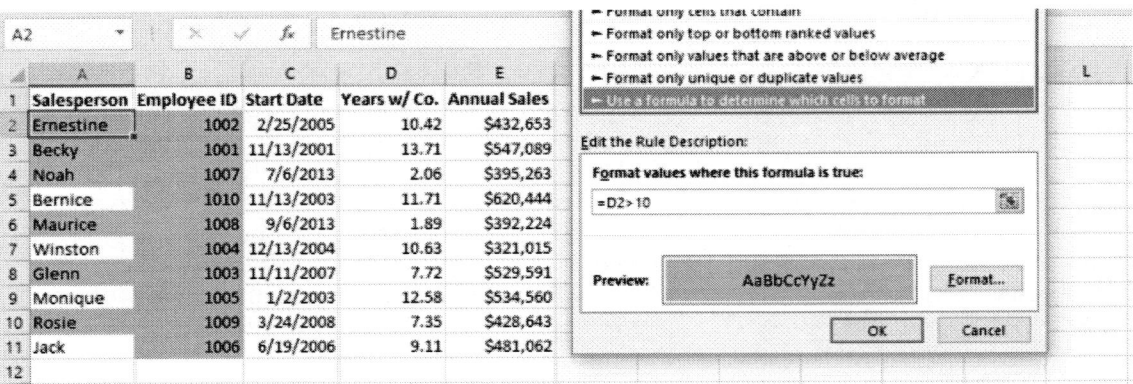

Figure 3-16: An example of applying conditional formatting to more than one column at a time.

Although Excel applied the correct formatting in column **A**, it did not do so in column **B**. This is because both the column and the row are relative references for cell **D2** in the formula. Keep in mind that regardless of how you apply the conditional formatting rule to the range, Excel treats it as if you entered it in cell **A2** and then dragged it down column **A** and then across to column **B**. For all of the cells in column **B**, Excel is looking to the values in column **E**, not column **D**. As all of those values are well above 10, Excel applied the formatting to all of the cells in column **B**. In this example, we want Excel to always look in column **D** to find the value to evaluate. We also want it to look for the values per salesperson, so the row will need to change. Because of this we need to use a mixed reference that locks the column reference but allows the row reference to change. To get this example working the way we want it to, the formula would look like the following.

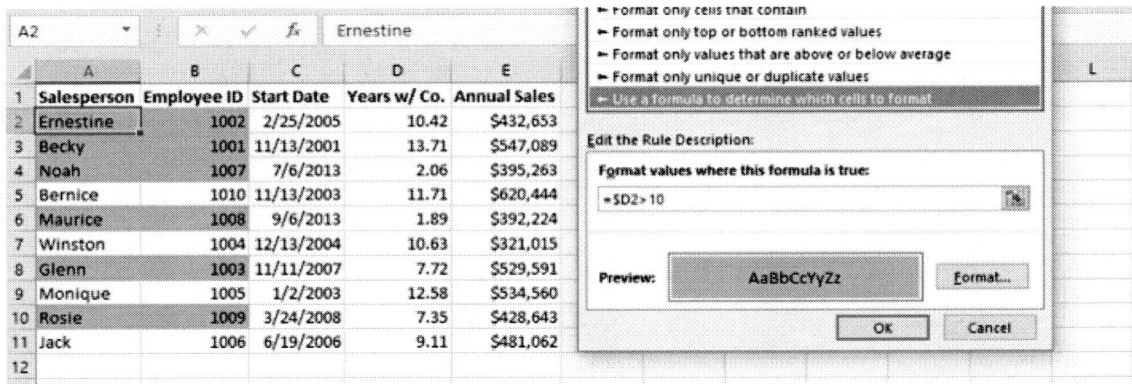

Figure 3-17: An example of using a mixed reference to apply conditional formatting.

When using formulas or functions to apply conditional formatting across ranges of cells, always think in terms of dragging the formula or function from the first cell to all others, and then write your cell and range references accordingly.

 Access the Checklist tile on your CHOICE Course screen for reference information and job aids on How to Use Formulas and Functions to Apply Conditional Formatting.

Guidelines for Applying Conditional Formatting to Cells Based on Values in Other Cells

 Note: All of the Guidelines for this lesson are available as checklists from the **Checklist** tile on the CHOICE Course screen.

Although you can use formulas and functions to apply conditional formatting to wide ranges of data, when doing so based on data in other cells, you must keep absolute and relative references in mind. Excel treats all conditional formatting rules applied in this manner as if they were entered into a single cell and then dragged across the rest of the range. When applying conditional formatting to cells based on data stored in other cells:

- You must use a formula or a function to define the conditional formatting rule.
- You must enter the formula or function in the **Format values where this formula is true** field in the **New Formatting Rule** dialog box.
- The formula or function must begin with an equal sign (=).
- If you are applying the rule to a single cell, you can use either a relative or an absolute reference to the evaluated cell in the formula or function.
- If you are applying the rule to multiple cells in a single column and the rule will be evaluating the data in only a single cell, you must use an absolute reference to the evaluated cell in the formula or function.
- If you are applying the rule to multiple cells in a single column and the rule will be evaluating the associated data stored in multiple rows in another column, you must use a mixed reference that locks the column for the evaluated cells, but that is relative for rows, in the formula or function.
- If you are applying the rule to a range that includes multiple rows and columns and the rule will be evaluating the associated data stored in a single cell, you must use an absolute reference for the evaluated cell in the formula or function.
- If you are applying the rule to a range that includes multiple rows and columns and the rule will be evaluating the associated data stored in multiple rows in another column, you must use a mixed reference that locks the column for the evaluated cells, but that is relative for rows, in the formula or function.

ACTIVITY 3–4
Using Logical Functions to Apply Conditional Formatting

Before You Begin

The workbook My Develetech Sales.xlsx is open.

Scenario

As the sales manager for Develetech Industries you want to recognize sales personnel that have been with the company for ten or more years. You have created a workbook with each of the sales persons and their tenure calculated. You decide to use a formula to apply conditional formatting to the salesperson name and Employee ID.

---

1. Apply conditional formatting to the salesperson names based on their tenure with the company.
   a) Select the **Sales Tenure** worksheet.
   b) Select cells **A2:A11**.
   c) Select **Home→Styles→Conditional Formatting→New Rule**.
   d) From the **Select a Rule Type** list box, select the **Use a formula to determine which cells to format** rule.
   e) Select the **Format values where this formula is true** text box and type *=$D2>10*

    Note: Using the mixed reference in this formula prevents the column from changing when this rule is copied to the Employee IDs later in this activity.

   f) Select the **Format** button.
   g) In the **Format Cells** dialog box, select the **Fill** tab, if necessary, and in the last row of the **Background Color** section, select **Light Green** which is the fifth color from the left, and select **OK**.

h) In the **New Formatting Rule** dialog box, select **OK**.

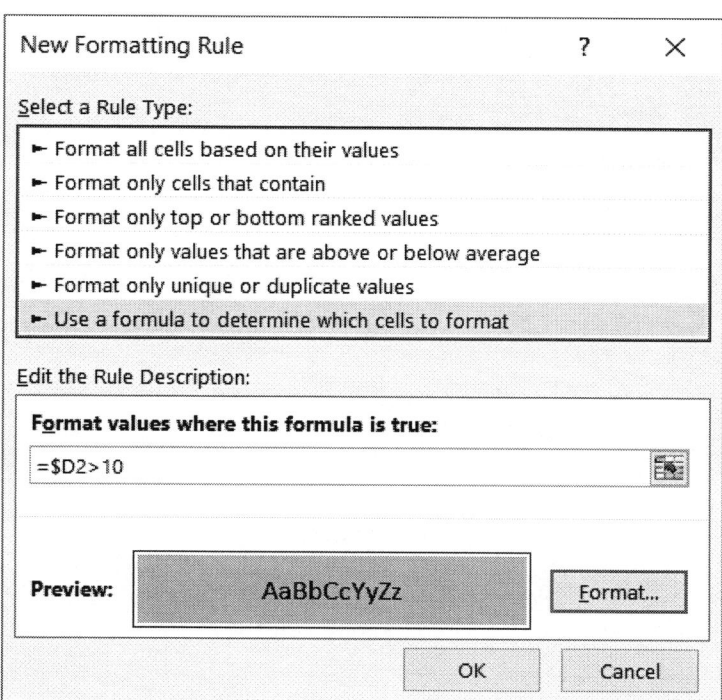

i) Verify that correct fill formatting has been applied to the salesperson names who have been with the company greater than 10 years.

	A	B	C	D	E
1	**Salesperson**	**Employee ID**	**Start Date**	**Years w/ Co.**	**Annual Sales**
2	Ernestine	1002	2/25/2005	10.52	$432,653
3	Becky	1001	11/13/2001	13.81	$547,089
4	Noah	1007	7/6/2013	2.15	$395,263
5	Bernice	1010	11/13/2005	9.80	$620,444
6	Maurice	1008	9/6/2013	1.98	$392,224
7	Winston	1004	12/13/2004	10.72	$321,015
8	Glenn	1003	11/11/2007	7.81	$529,591
9	Monique	1005	1/2/2003	12.67	$534,560
10	Rosie	1009	3/24/2008	7.44	$428,643
11	Jack	1006	6/19/2006	9.21	$481,062

2. Apply the same formatting to the employee IDs.

a) If necessary, reselect **A2:A11**, **AutoFill** right to **B2:B11**.

 Note: Remember that the AutoFill handle is in cell A11 after the range A2:A11 is selected.

a) Select the **AutoFill** icon and select **Fill Formatting Only**.

b) Verify the correct fill formatting has been applied to the employee IDs.

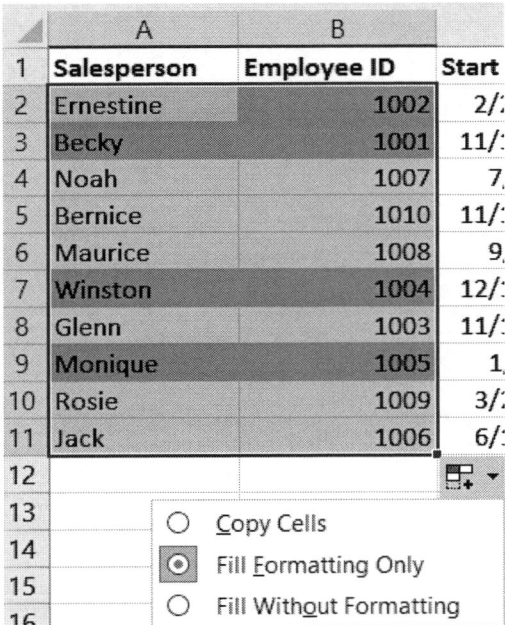

3. Verify the **Conditional Formatting Rules Manager** updated the rule to include the range B2:B11.
   a) If necessary, select **A2:B11**, and select **Home→Styles→Conditional Formatting→Manage Rules**.
   b) In the **Conditional Formatting Rules Manager** dialog box, in the **Show formatting rules for** drop-down list **Current Selection** is selected and in the **Applies to** section the range **=$A$2:$B$11** is displayed.

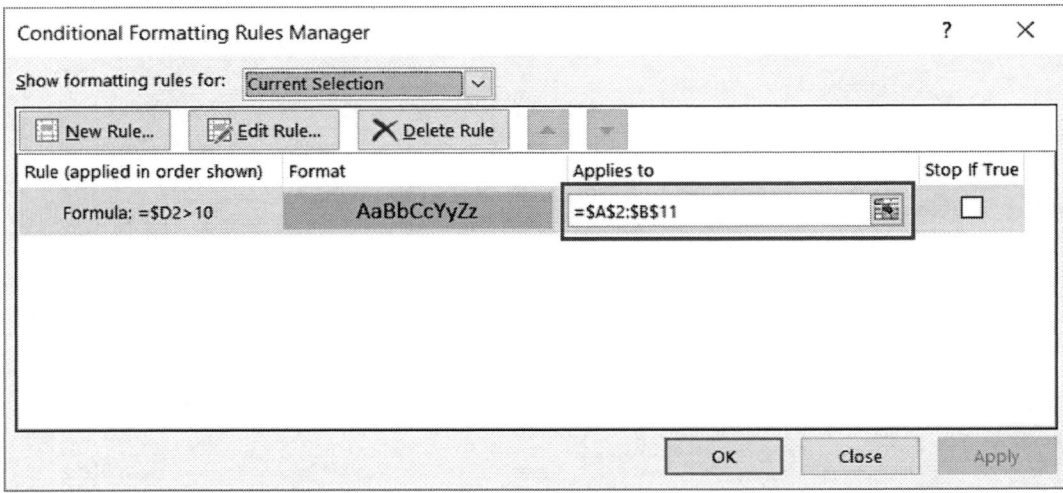

   c) Select **Close**.

4. Save the workbook and then close the file.

Summary

In this lesson, you learned to create and modify tables, and you learned multiple ways to apply conditional formatting. The ability to create and summarize data quickly using tables to present that data in a professional manner is an important skill. Another important skill is the ability to highlight key values in your data through the use of conditional formatting. Excel provides many different methods of analyzing your data because every business need is different.

What advantages do you see tables providing in addition to data ranges?

What tasks will Excel's advanced conditional formatting options make easier for you in your current role?

 Note: Check your CHOICE Course screen for opportunities to interact with your classmates, peers, and the larger CHOICE online community about the topics covered in this course or other topics you are interested in. From the Course screen you can also access available resources for a more continuous learning experience.

4 | Visualizing Data with Charts

Lesson Time: 1 hour

Lesson Objectives

In this lesson, you will visualize data with charts. You will:

- Create charts.

- Modify and format charts.

- Use advanced chart features.

Lesson Introduction

Microsoft® Office Excel® 2016 provides you with powerful features to help you organize and analyze your data. As you become more familiar with these features, you'll find you can ask Excel a vast array of questions and get the answers you need. However, not everyone who you report to or present data to will have the same comfort level or expertise when it comes to viewing worksheets. Viewing information in the form of ranges of data entries is simply not natural for many people. You may find yourself presenting information to large audiences on a regular basis. In these cases, you don't want people scanning lines of data on a worksheet when you're trying to present. You want to give them a simple, easy-to-digest view of important data so they can quickly understand what's really important.

In short, you need a way to generate visual representations of your data. Excel 2016 includes some handy functionality that can convert your raw or analyzed data into visually clear, easy-to-interpret diagrams with just a few steps. Taking the time to understand how this functionality works will give you the ability to generate high-impact visuals to present to nearly any audience, nearly any time, almost instantly.

TOPIC A

Create Charts

Charts are a great way to interpret data, as many people need to see data visually to comprehend it better. Plotting data in charts can make spreadsheets less confusing when incorporated in your workbooks. In this topic, you will learn to create charts.

Charts

Charts are graphical representations of the numeric values and relationships in a dataset. Charts help worksheet viewers to quickly and easily interpret the data in a worksheet. Excel charts update automatically when you update the data feeding them. And, some chart types contain animation functionality that helps worksheet viewers more easily discern overall patterns in the changing data as you update it.

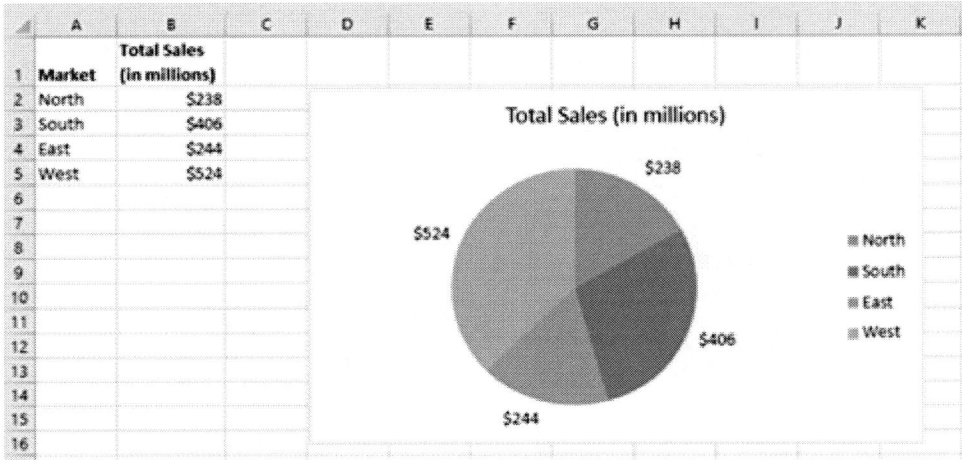

Figure 4-1: A pie chart on an Excel worksheet.

In this figure, while you can tell from the values in the **Total Sales (in millions)** column what the sales are for each market, the pie chart to the right of the data is much easier to interpret. With just a glance, you can tell that Western sales are greater than the other three regions, and that they account for more than a third of all sales. Getting this information from the raw data would require a bit of analysis and some calculating.

Chart Basics

Although there is a wide variety of charts available to display a number of different types of data in Excel 2016, most of the chart types follow the same basic conventions. Most of the commonly used chart types in Excel plot data along two axes: the X axis and the Y axis. The X axis is the one that runs horizontally along the chart. It is typically used to represent a category of information, such as fiscal quarter or department. The Y, or vertical, axis is typically used to represent values within your dataset, such as sales totals or number of products shipped. The objects displayed in the chart, such as bars, columns, or lines, typically represent the individual items, or series, for which you wish to represent the data, such as particular regions or individual sales reps.

Because Excel pulls data from your worksheets to create charts, it's important to understand how Excel reads your data in order to create them. Excel pulls the elements plotted along the X axis, or the categories, from your column labels. It identifies a data series based on the row labels from the selected dataset. Excel reads the values in the remaining cells as the values to plot against the Y axis.

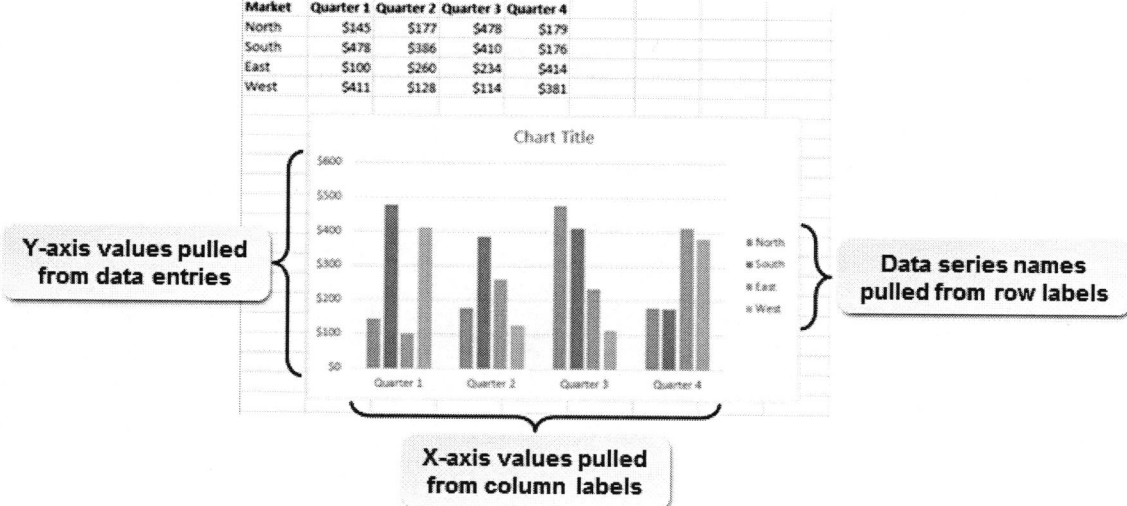

Figure 4-2: Using simple sales data to chart relative sales by region.

Note that, in the figure, the categories along the X axis correspond to the worksheet column labels, which in this case are fiscal quarters. The data series, represented by the columns on the chart, represent different regions, which Excel pulled from the row labels. The data entered into the remaining cells are the values against which the series are plotted.

Of course, not all charts work exactly like this, but most of the commonly used charts do. The most notable exceptions are the pie chart, which you will typically use only to chart a single column of data, and the bar chart, which essentially turns a column chart on its side.

Chart Types

Excel 2016 includes 15 different chart types, each of which is ideal for displaying a particular type of data or set of relationships. Each type of chart contains a variety of specific subtypes that you can use to tailor the presentation of your data. You can access the chart types and subtypes in the **Insert Chart** dialog box, which you can use to insert charts into your worksheets. You can access the **Insert Chart** dialog box by selecting the **Insert→Charts→dialog box launcher**, or by selecting the **More** option from any of the chart type drop-down menus in the **Charts** group on the **Insert** tab.

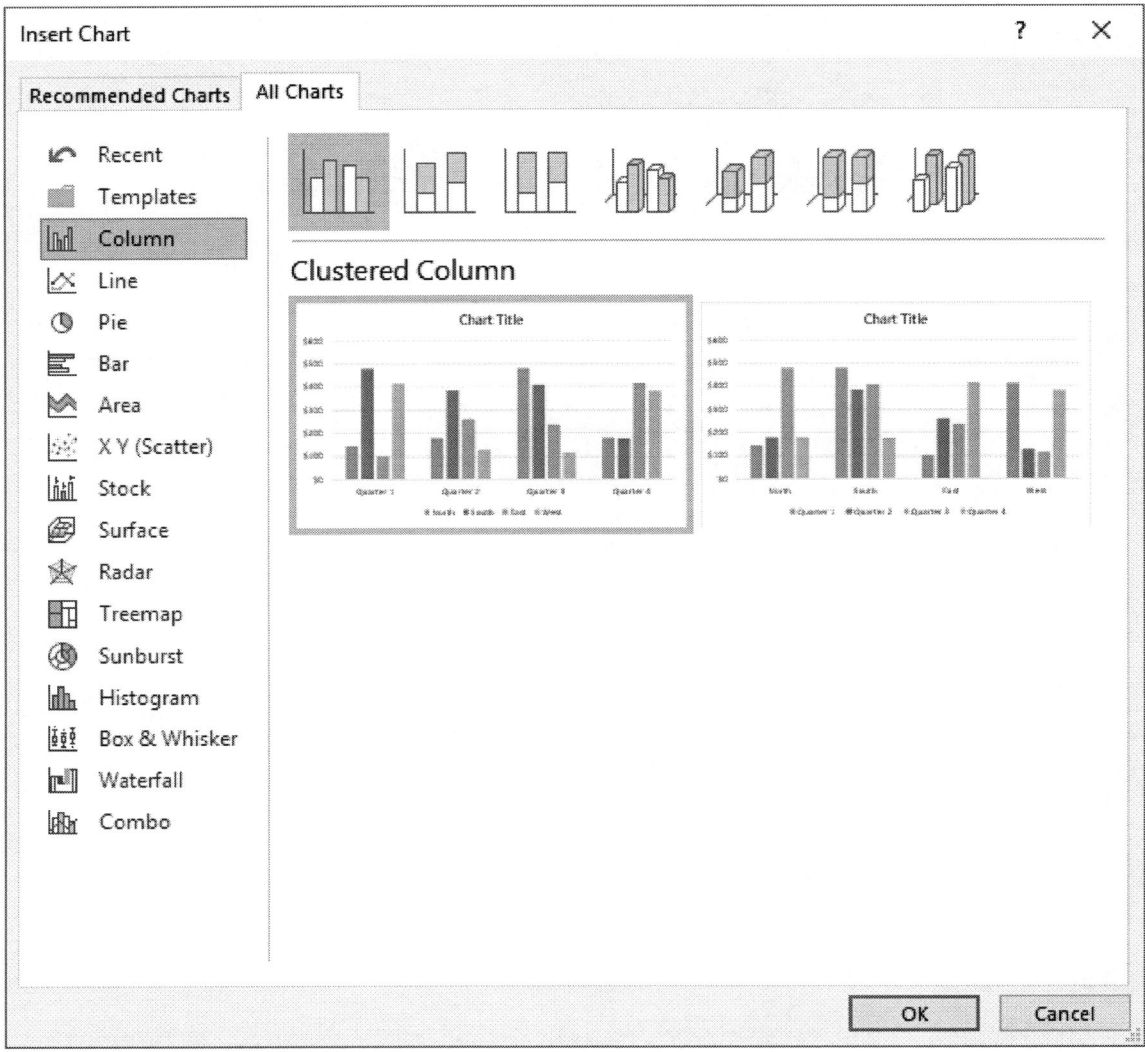

Figure 4–3: Use the All Charts tab on the Insert Chart dialog box to select the desired chart type and subtype to suit your needs.

The following table describes the ideal uses for the various Excel chart types.

Chart Type	Is Best Used to Display
Column	Relationships among values in a number of categories or changes in values over time.
Line	Trends in data over a period of time at consistent intervals; for example, quarterly or annually.
Pie	The relative size of values compared to the whole and to other parts of the whole. This is the best chart to use when you are charting only a single column or row of data.
Bar	Relationships among values in a number of categories.
Area	Relationships among values in a number of categories over time with visual emphasis on the magnitude of each data category.

Chart Type	Is Best Used to Display
X Y (Scatter)	The relationship between two categories of measured data, as opposed to one category of measured data across evenly spaced periods of time. Use this chart type to determine if there is a trend in the relationship between two sets of variables.
Stock	The change in stock prices over time or other similar fluctuating sets of values, such as daily or annual temperatures.
Surface	Three-dimensional representations of data. Typically, you would use a surface chart when working with three sets of data. An example of this would be charting the relative change in density of several materials, at a variety of temperatures, over a period of time.
Radar	The aggregate relational sizes of multiple data categories in terms of multiple criteria. For example, you could use a radar chart to track the popularity of a particular item in multiple countries for each year in a decade.
Treemap	A hierarchical chart; it shows a hierarchical view of your data and how the parts of hierarchy compare in size to each other.
Sunburst	Visual comparisons of relative sizes, similar to Treemap. The difference with Sunburst is showing the links between groups and sub-groups.
Histogram	A column chart that shows frequency data. The difference is that each column represents a range of values (called a bin) instead of a single value.
Box & Whisker	Statistical information about a set of data; the distribution of data into quartiles, highlighting the mean and outliers.
Waterfall	A running total as values are added or subtracted. It's useful for understanding how an initial value (for example, net income) is affected by a series of positive and negative values.
Combo	Relationships among values of widely differing ranges of data. For example, if you want to chart both unit sales measured in thousands of units on the same chart as sales in billions of dollars, you could use a combo chart so that both sets of values, which are on vastly different scales, can be displayed simultaneously. Combo charts are also referred to as dual-axis charts.

Chart Insertion Methods

Before inserting a chart into a worksheet, you should select the dataset the chart will be based on. If you select a single cell within the desired dataset, Excel will try to guess at the proper range. This does not always generate the desired outcome, however, so it's a best practice to manually select the desired dataset.

It's important to remember to include row and column labels in your selection and to have your data entered correctly. For example, the categories you want plotted along the X axis should be your column labels, and the desired data series should be the row labels. Once you have ensured that your data is properly entered on the worksheet, and you have selected the desired range, you have four general options for inserting a chart: the **Quick Analysis** tools, ribbon commands, the **Insert Chart** dialog box, or inserting the default chart type. For either of the middle two methods, simply select the desired chart type and subtype from the **Insert Chart** dialog box or from the chart type drop-down menus in the **Charts** group on the **Insert** tab.

If you know you will be inserting the same type of chart a number of times in your workbook, you can set that chart type as the default chart type. Then you can use one of two keyboard shortcuts to instantly create the default chart type out of any selected dataset.

Keyboard Shortcut	Inserts
Alt+F1	The default chart type on the same worksheet the dataset is on.
F11	The default chart type on a new worksheet.

 Note: You set the default chart type for Excel by right-clicking the desired chart subtype from the **Insert Chart** dialog box, and then selecting **Set as Default Chart**. This is an application-level setting, so what you set here will be the default chart type for any workbook file until you change the default chart type.

Recommended Charts

Excel 2016 includes a handy feature to assist you with selecting the most appropriate chart subtype when inserting charts: Recommended Charts. Based on the dataset you select, Excel 2016 uses an algorithm to determine which of the chart subtypes would best suit your needs. You have access to Recommended Charts in two places: the **Quick Analysis** tools and from the **Recommended Charts** tab in the **Insert Chart** dialog box.

Figure 4–4: You can access Recommended Charts from the Quick Analysis tools or from the Insert Chart dialog box.

The Insert Chart Dialog Box

As previously mentioned, the **Insert Chart** dialog box is one of the methods you can use to insert charts into a worksheet. The **Insert Chart** dialog box is divided into two tabs: the **Recommended Charts** tab and the **All Charts** tab. From the **Recommended Charts** tab, you can view a list of the chart subtypes Excel recommends for you based on the dataset you select. You can also view a live preview of what each of the recommendations would look like if you inserted them. The **All Charts** tab enables you to browse through all of the available chart types and subtypes so you can select the appropriate chart subtype yourself. The **All Charts** tab also displays a live preview of each of the choices. On the **All Charts** tab, these live previews also include variations on the chart subtypes with various formatting options applied to them.

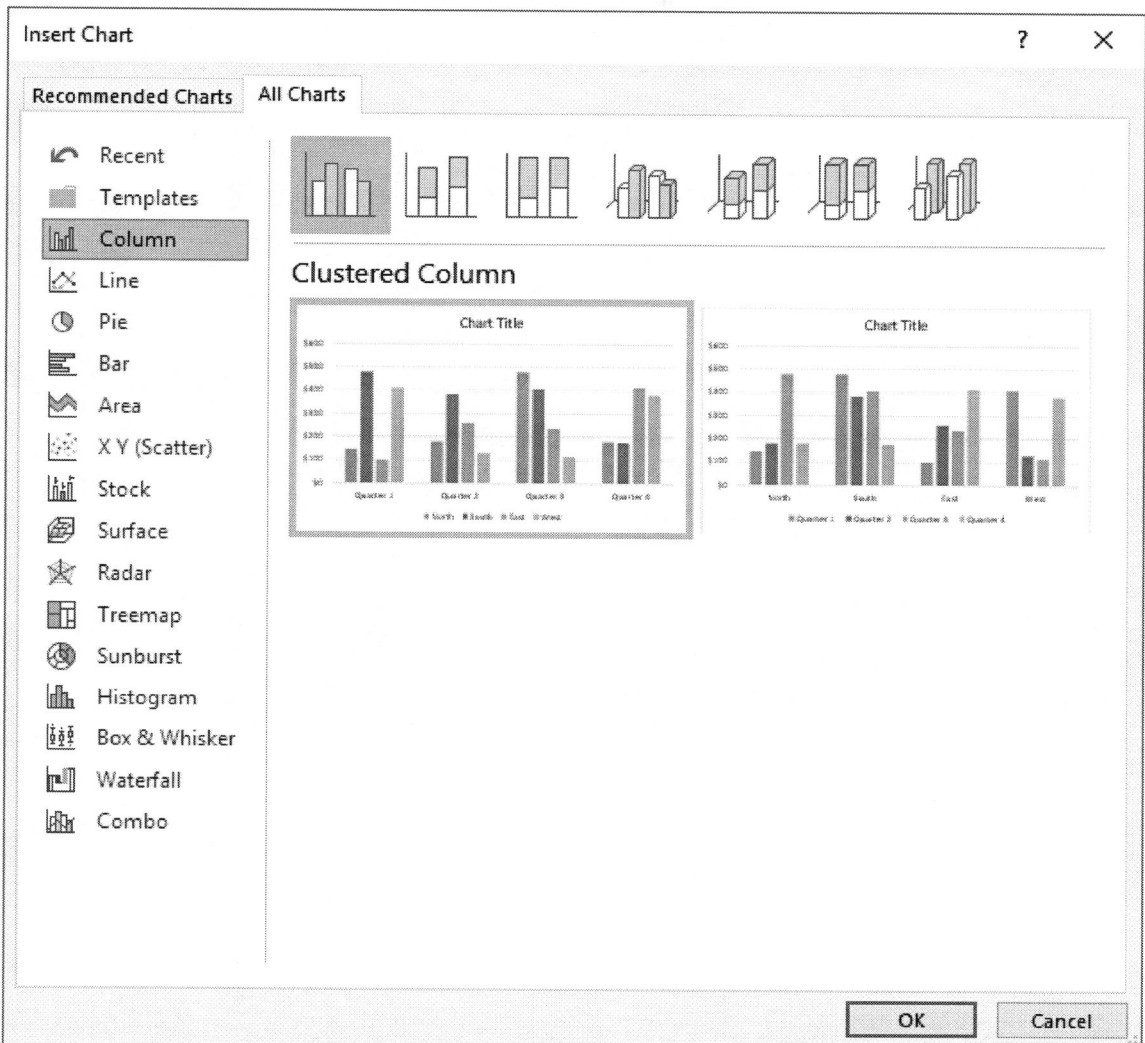

Figure 4-5: The All Charts tab on the Insert Chart dialog box.

Access the Checklist tile on your CHOICE Course screen for reference information and job aids on **How to Create Charts.**

ACTIVITY 4–1
Creating Charts

Data File

C:\091056Data\Visualizing Data with Charts\Annual Sales.xlsx

Before You Begin

Excel 2016 is open.

Scenario

As a marketing analyst for Develetech Industries, the sales team has given you the Annual Sales workbook. The sales manager has asked you to build charts for the data in the workbook to be used in the annual company meeting.

---

1. In Excel, open the workbook **Annual Sales.xlsx**.

2. Create a clustered column chart from the quarterly sales data.
   a) Verify that the **Quarterly Sales** worksheet is selected and select the range **A1:E5**.
   b) Select **Insert→Charts→dialog box launcher**.
   c) Explore the **Recommended Charts** by selecting the chart thumbnails.

d) Select the first recommended chart, a **Clustered Column** chart and select **OK**.

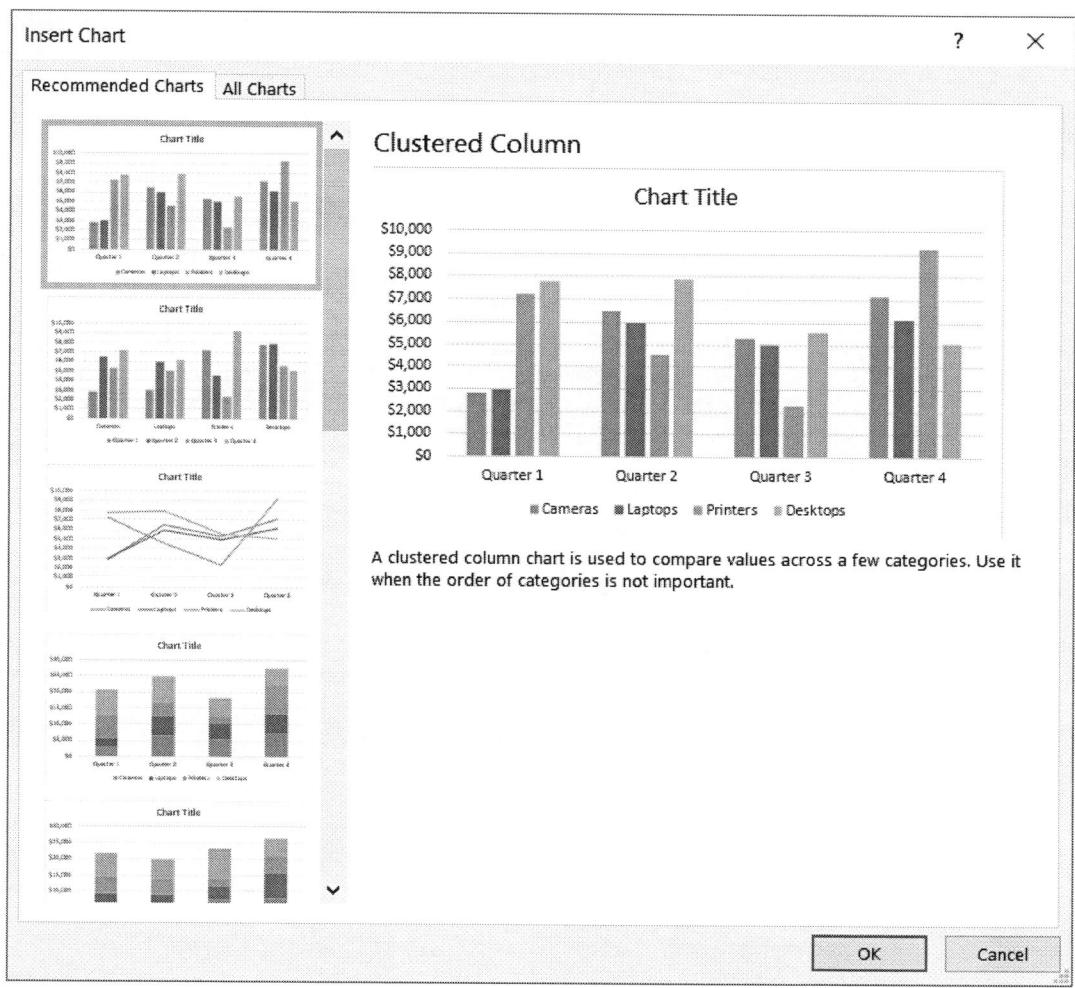

e) Verify that the clustered column chart was created.

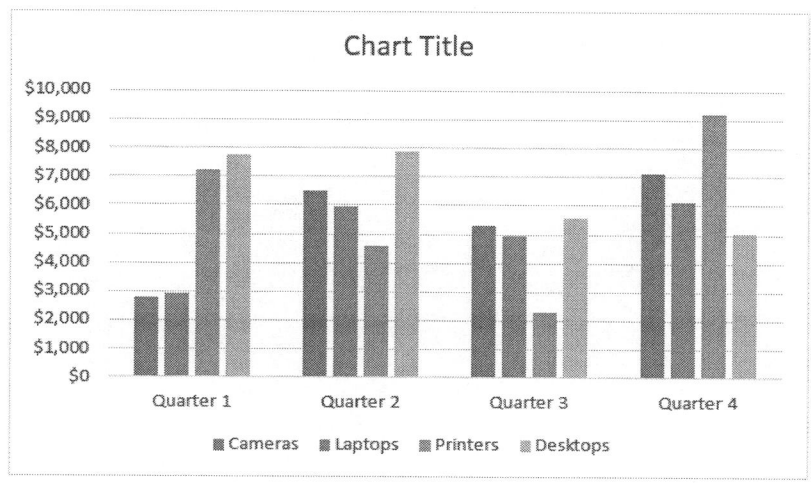

3. Create a line chart from the monthly sales of laptops.
   a) Select the **Sales Trends** worksheet and then select the range **A1:A13**.

    b) Hold **Ctrl** and select **C1:C13**.

    c) Select **Insert→Charts→Insert Line or Area Chart** and select **Line**, the first 2-D line chart variant.

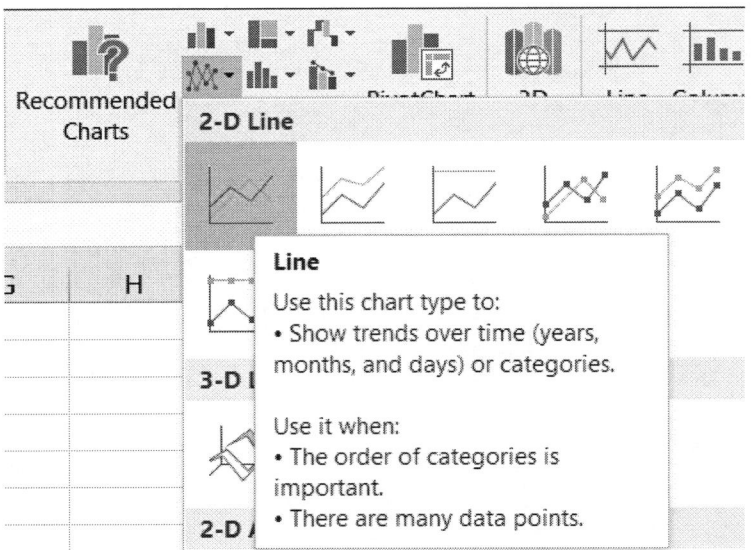

4. Create a pie chart from the sales comparison data.

    a) Select the **Sales Comparison** worksheet and select the range **A1:B5**.

    b) Select the **Quick Analysis** button and then select the **Charts** tab.

    c) Hover over the various chart types and select the **Pie** chart type.

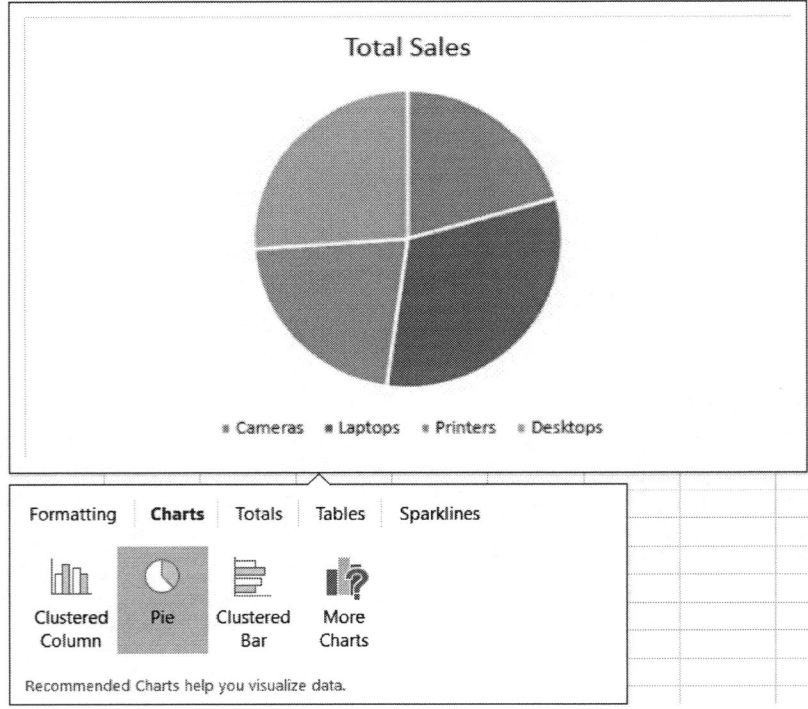

5. Save the workbook as *My Annual Sales.xlsx* and keep the file open.

TOPIC B

Modify and Format Charts

Although you can create charts with just a few mouse clicks, the default chart configurations aren't always exactly what you need to present your data. Depending on your audience and the venue, you may want to include more or less information than the default configurations include, present your data with organizational branding, or simply make your charts larger or easier to read.

Excel 2016 provides you with a vast array of options when it comes to modifying and formatting your charts. By configuring the display of your charts, you take full control over the message your charts convey and their overall visual impact. A well-formatted chart can mean the difference between simply delivering information and making an impact on your audience.

Modification vs. Formatting

Modifying and formatting charts go hand-in-hand. Although many people use these terms synonymously, they are actually two different things. Modifying a chart includes making changes such as moving chart elements, adding or removing chart elements, turning the display of particular data on or off, and changing the chart type. Think of modifying a chart as working with the display of data. You modify a chart to change the audience's understanding of the information you're presenting.

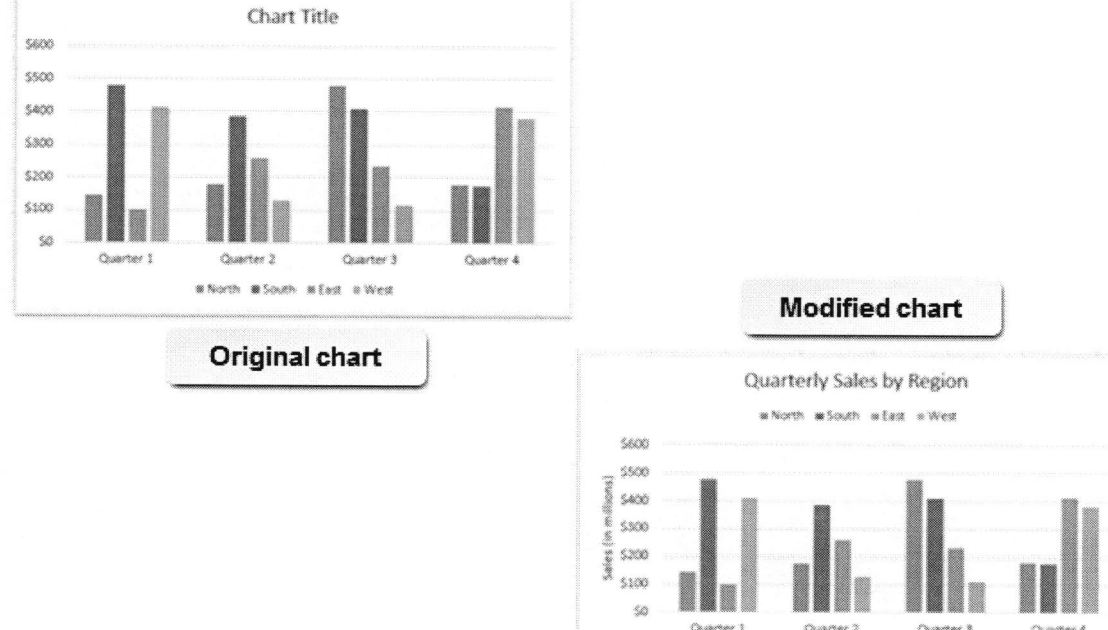

Figure 4–6: This chart has been modified to make the data easier to interpret.

Formatting refers to altering the overall look and feel of a chart. Formatting a chart typically includes tasks such as changing the color scheme or the font, and altering the size of the chart. You format a chart to comply with branding standards or to convey a particular mood or feel.

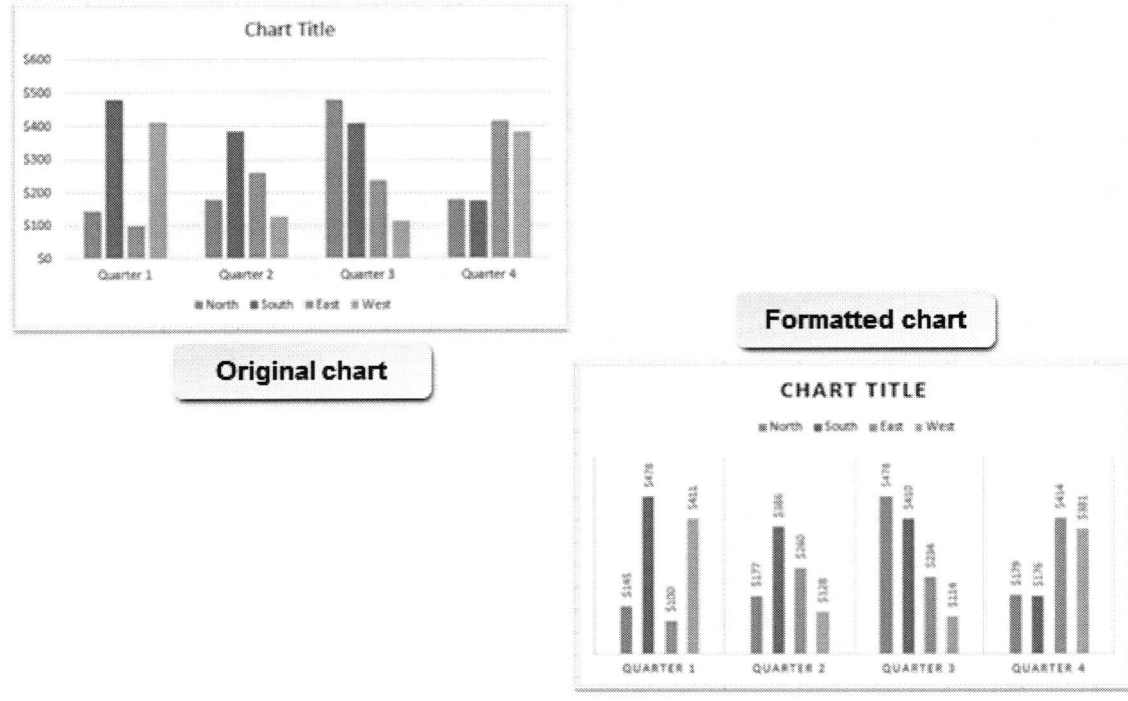

Figure 4-7: This chart has been formatted to comply with branding guidelines.

Chart Elements

Chart elements are the individual objects that can appear on charts and that convey some level of information to a viewer about the chart's data. While all Excel charts contain at least one chart element, by default, the various chart types display different chart elements. For example, while bar and column charts typically display an X axis and a Y axis, surface charts display three axes. Pie charts don't contain axes as they deal with only a single column of data. Each chart element serves a different role in visually communicating information about data and trends.

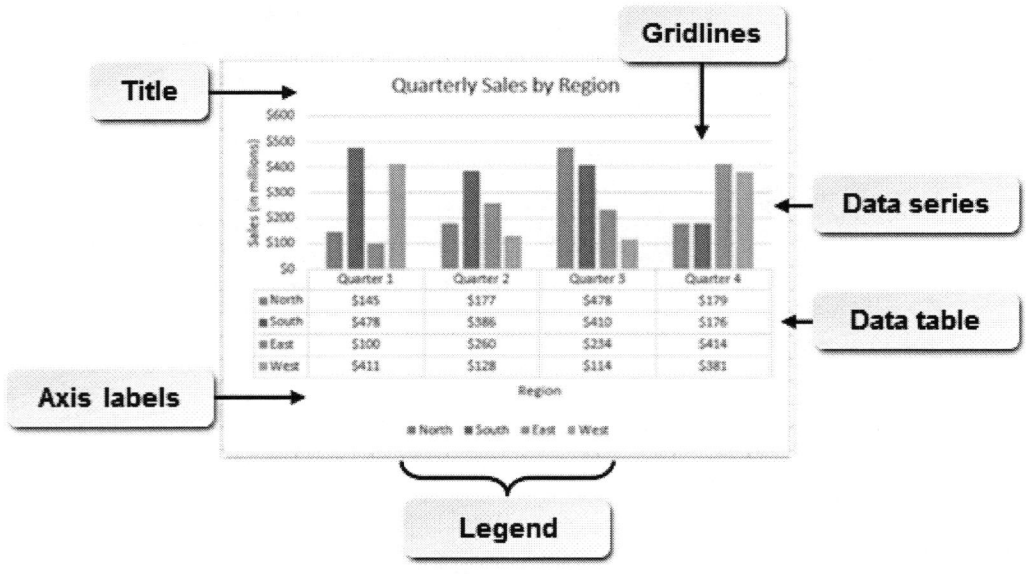

Figure 4-8: Chart elements help the audience interpret chart data.

Chart Elements Guidelines

 Note: All of the Guidelines for this lesson are available as checklists from the **Checklist** tile on the CHOICE Course screen.

Formatting charts has relatively little impact on an audience's ability to interpret your data. Modifying chart elements, on the other hand, can have a significant impact. As a general rule, it's best to include only those chart elements that are absolutely necessary for conveying meaning. Cluttered charts can muddy your main point and make the chart confusing to view, which is exactly what you create charts to avoid. However, some chart elements do actually help add meaning. Until you gain an intuitive sense of what chart elements to include for various purposes, you may want to consider adding chart elements that you feel will help your target audience interpret your data, analyzing your chart, and then removing anything that doesn't directly contribute to the message you intend to deliver. When analyzing your charts, ask yourself questions, such as:

- If I remove the gridlines, will the chart still convey meaning?
- Do I need a legend? Can I remove the legend and use data labels instead?
- How much precision do I need for axis labels?
- Do the axes really need titles?
- Will using a three-dimensional layout enhance visual appeal or distort proportions?
- Does including the data table aid understanding?
- Do I really need major and minor tick marks on the axes?

 Note: Before finalizing your charts, keep the old adage "less is more" in mind. If the audience needs an element to acquire meaning, keep it. Otherwise, remove it.

The Chart Tools Contextual Tab

You can access many of the commands you will use to modify and format your charts on the **Chart Tools** contextual tab. Similar to other contextual tabs, the **Chart Tools** contextual tab appears whenever you select a chart or a chart element, and it disappears when you select a worksheet element outside the chart. The **Chart Tools** contextual tab contains two tabs that each contain task-related groups and commands for working with your charts. Let's take a look at the various command groups on both of these tabs.

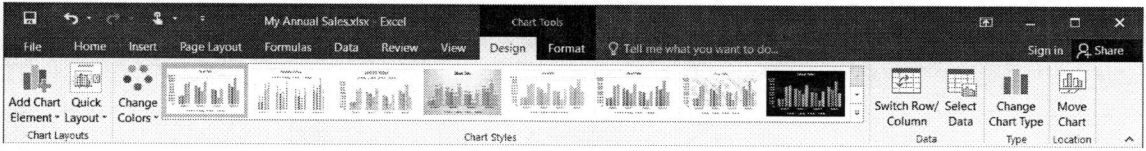

Figure 4-9: The Design tab.

Use the commands on the **Design** tab to quickly change the overall look and feel of your charts.

Design Tab Command Group	Contains Commands For
Chart Layouts	Adding or removing individual chart elements, and quickly configuring the display of all chart elements according to predefined configurations.
Chart Styles	Quickly formatting a chart by using predefined sets of formatting options.
Data	Changing the chart's dataset range and switching the row and column data. Keep in mind that this does not switch the data that is displayed on the X axis with the data that is displayed on the Y axis. This switches the categories with the data series.

Design Tab Command Group	Contains Commands For
Type	Changing the chart type.
Location	Moving charts to different worksheets within a workbook.

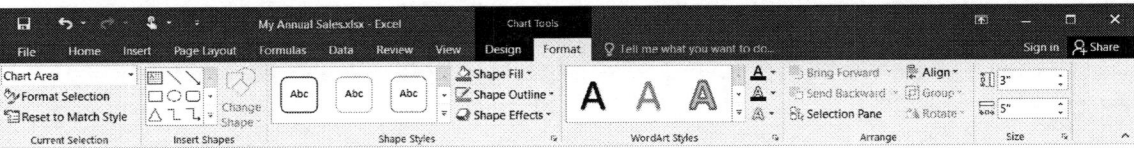

Figure 4-10: The Format tab.

Use the commands on the **Format** tab to configure chart formatting.

Format Tab Command Group	Contains Commands For
Current Selection	Selecting particular chart elements and accessing the **Format** task pane.
Insert Shapes	Inserting or changing shapes on worksheets.
Shape Styles	Configuring formatting options for chart elements.
WordArt Styles	Configuring formatting options for chart text.
Arrange	Changing the front-to-back placement of chart elements and configuring the orientation of chart elements.
Size	Changing the size of charts and chart elements.

The Format Task Pane

You can use the commands available in the **Format** task pane to fine-tune the overall formatting of your charts. Excel 2016 opens the **Format** task pane when you select **Format→Current Selection→Format Selection** from the **Chart Tools** contextual tab. It will display with a slightly different name depending on the chart element you currently have selected. For example, if you have one of the axes selected, it will appear as the **Format Axis** task pane; if you have the chart title selected, it will appear as the **Format Chart Title** task pane.

The **Format** task pane also displays a different configuration of tabs and commands based on the chart element you have selected. At the highest level, depending on your current selection, it may display two tabs that essentially divide the formatting commands between text and other objects. Under each of these tabs is a series of other tabs that further divide the commands into functional groups. Within these lower-level tabs is a series of expandable sections that display the commands and options you will use to apply specific formatting to the selected chart element.

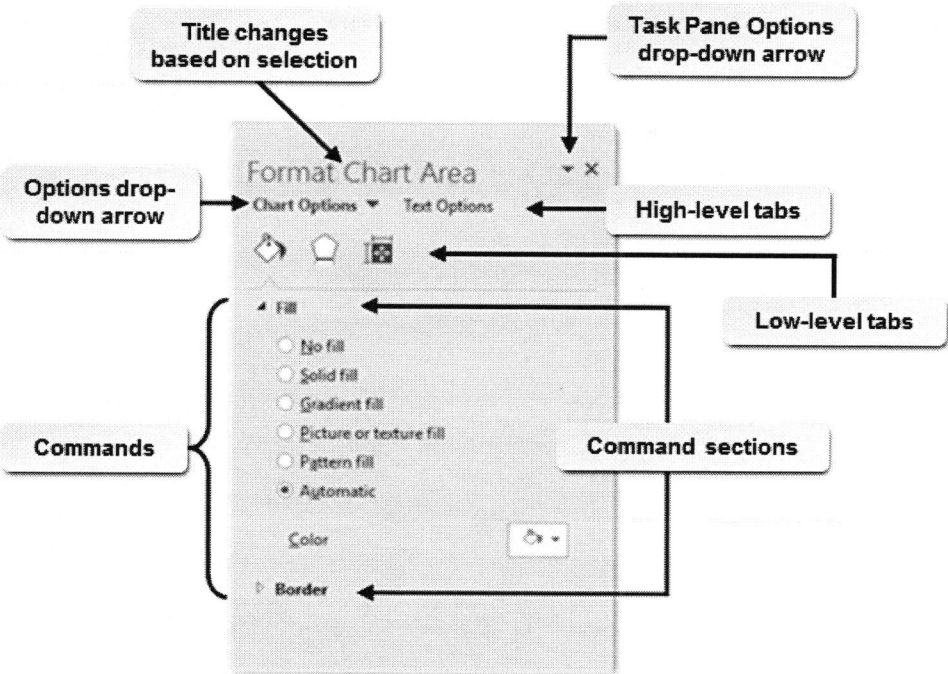

Figure 4-11: The Format task pane displays different sets of commands and options depending on which chart element you currently have selected.

The following table describes the various elements of the **Format** task pane.

Format Task Pane Element	Description
Title	Displays variations of the **Format** task pane's title depending on the chart element that is currently selected.
Task Pane Options drop-down arrow	Provides you with access to options for moving, resizing, or closing the **Format** task pane.
Options drop-down arrow	Opens a drop-down menu that enables you to select different chart elements for formatting purposes. This is essentially the same menu you can access by selecting the **Format→Current Selection→Chart Elements drop-down arrow** from the **Chart Tools** contextual tab. Changing the selection changes the task pane's title and the displayed tabs and commands.
High-level tabs	Divide the formatting commands into functional groups at the highest level. Essentially, these divide the formatting commands and options between object formatting tasks and text formatting tasks. If a chart element doesn't contain text, the **Format** task pane displays only a single option at this level of the hierarchy.
Low-level tabs	Divide the formatting commands and options at a more granular level than the high-level tabs. The low-level tabs available are dependent upon your current selection.
Command sections	You can expand or collapse these task-specific sections to access or hide the specific commands and options you will use to format chart elements.
Commands and options	Enable you to apply formatting options to the selected chart element.

The Chart Tools Buttons

Whenever you select a chart in Excel, Excel displays a set of three buttons near the top-right corner of the chart area. You can use these three buttons to quickly access some of the most commonly used commands for formatting and modifying Excel charts. Selecting any of these three buttons opens either a menu or a gallery containing commands or options for configuring the currently selected chart.

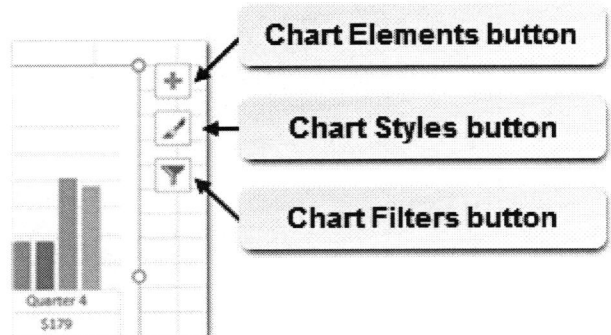

Figure 4–12: Use the chart tools buttons to quickly access common formatting and modification options.

The following table describes the commands or options available from each of the chart tools buttons.

Chart Tools Button	Selecting This Button
Chart Elements button	Opens a menu that enables you to toggle on or off, as well as modify various chart elements.
Chart Styles button	Opens a gallery providing you with quick access to various chart styles and color schemes.
Chart Filters button	Opens a menu that enables you to quickly toggle on or off the display of chart series, chart categories, or individual elements within either of these. From this menu, you can also toggle on or off the display of series labels and category labels.

The Select Data Source Dialog Box

You will use the **Select Data Source** dialog box to manage Excel chart data. From here, you can edit the entire dataset feeding the chart, or you can edit the data feeding any of the individual data series. You can also remove from or add back to the chart any of the individual data series, reorder how the data series appear on the chart, or switch the chart's X and Y axes. You can access the **Select Data Source** dialog box from the **Chart Tools** contextual tab by selecting **Design→Data→Select Data**.

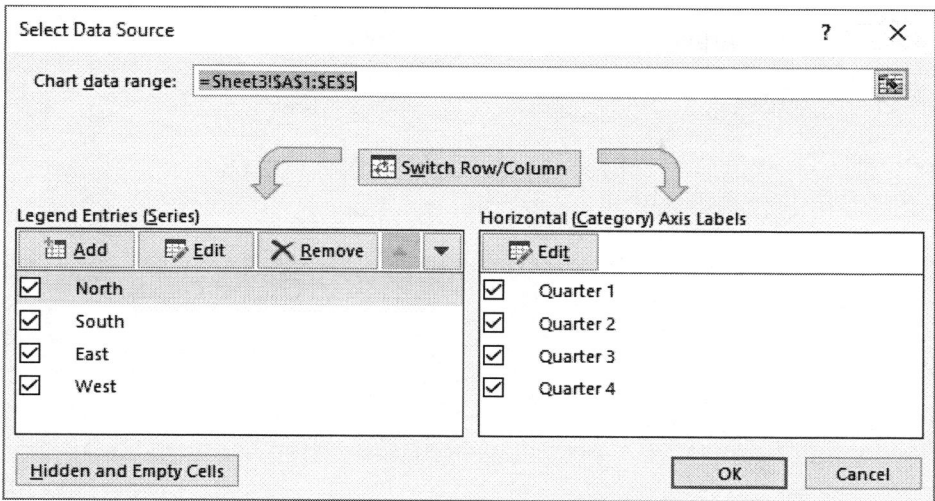

Figure 4–13: Use the Select Data Source dialog box to manage the data displayed by Excel charts.

Chart Animations

As previously mentioned, when you update the data associated with a chart, the chart itself also updates. In Excel 2016, these changes are animated to help worksheet developers and viewers get a clearer sense of how the changes affect the overall values and relationships in the chart. This functionality can also enable you to create dynamic, animated charts by using some of the add-ins available for Excel 2016.

 Access the Checklist tile on your CHOICE Course screen for reference information and job aids on How to Modify and Format Charts.

ACTIVITY 4-2
Modifying and Formatting Charts

Before You Begin

The workbook **My Annual Sales.xlsx** is open.

Scenario

As a marketing analyst, you have shared your initial charts with your manager. Your manager has suggested you modify and format these charts for a better presentation at the annual company meeting.

1. Change the layout of the clustered column chart on the Quarterly Sales worksheet.
   a) Select the **Quarterly Sales** worksheet and if necessary, select the clustered column chart.
   b) On the **Chart Tools** contextual tab, select **Design→Chart Layouts→Quick Layout** and then select **Layout 9** from the gallery.

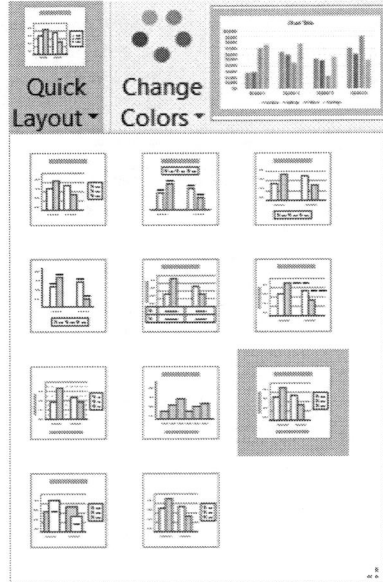

2. Modify the chart style of the Laptops line chart on the Sales Trends worksheet.
   a) Select the **Sales Trends** worksheet and if necessary, select the line chart.

b) On the **Chart Tools** contextual tab, select **Design→Chart Styles→More button** and from the gallery select **Style 12**.

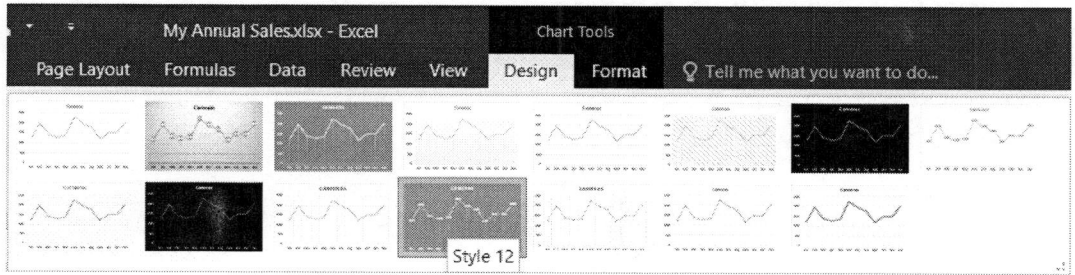

3. Change the chart type of the pie chart on the Sales Comparison worksheet to a 3-D pie chart.

   a) Select the **Sales Comparison** worksheet and if necessary, select the pie chart.
   b) On the **Chart Tools** contextual tab, select **Design→Type→Change Chart Type**.
   c) From the **Pie** category, in the **Change Chart Type** dialog box, on the **All Charts** tab, select the second variant **3-D Pie** and select **OK**.

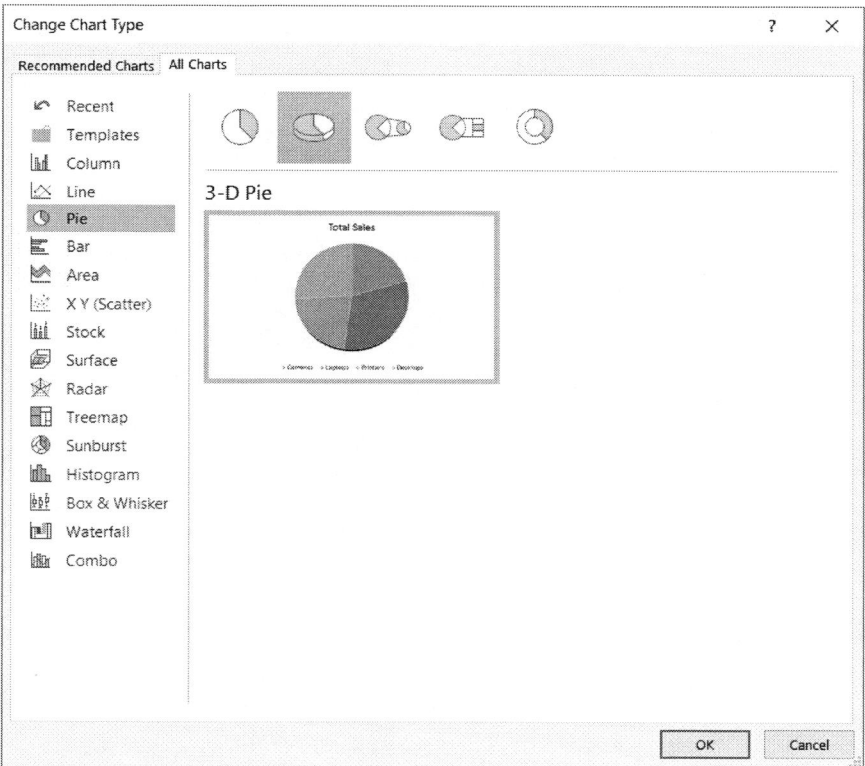

4. Apply a chart style to the pie chart.

   a) On the **Chart Tools** contextual tab, select **Design→Chart Styles→More button** and from the gallery select **Style 1**.

   b) Select the **Chart Elements** button and hover over **Data Labels**. Select the arrow that appears to the right and select **More Options** from the menu.

c) In the **Format Data Labels** task pane, in the **Label Options** section, select the **Percentage** check box and deselect the **Value** check box.

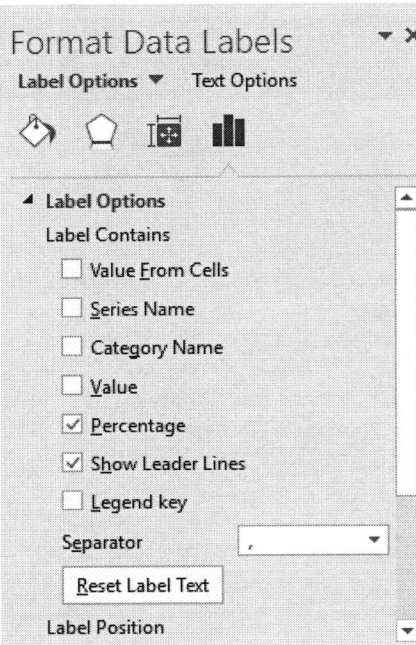

d) Close the **Format Data Labels** task pane.

5. Change the default titles on the column chart on the Quarterly Sales worksheet.

a) Select the **Quarterly Sales** worksheet and if necessary, select the clustered column chart.

b) On the **Chart Tools** contextual tab, select **Format→Current Selection→Chart Elements drop-down arrow** and select **Chart Title**.

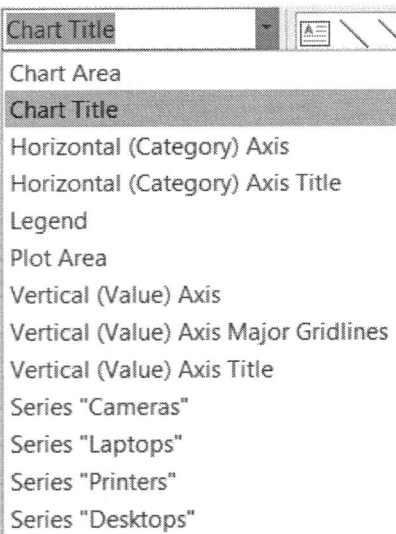

c) Select the **Formula Bar** and type *Quarterly Sales* and press **Enter**.

d) Select the **vertical Axis Title label** on the left side of the chart, type *Sales* and then press **Enter**.

 Note: You may notice that the text is entered in the **Formula Bar**.

e) Select the **horizontal Axis Title label** at the bottom of the chart, and type *2016* and then press **Enter**.

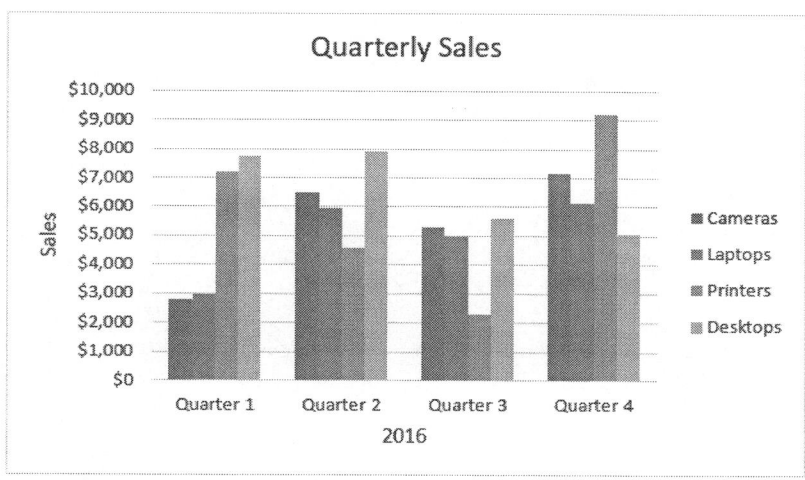

6. Move and resize the Quarterly Sales clustered column chart.

a) Point to the chart area surrounding the chart. Using the move pointer click and drag the chart so that the upper-left of the chart covers cell G3.

> **Note:** It is good practice to leave at least one row and one column of space around the edges of charts.

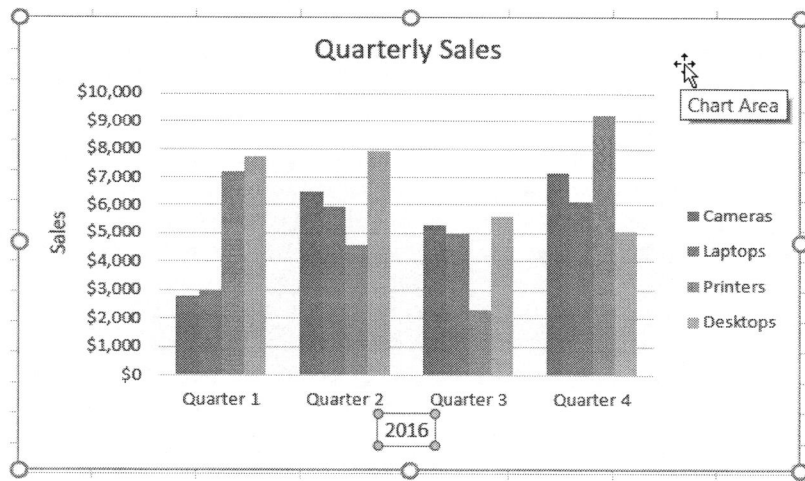

b) Point the cursor to the bottom-right resize handle until the mouse changes to a resize pointer.
c) Click and drag to enlarge the chart to cover cell P20.

7. Save the workbook and keep the file open.

TOPIC C

Use Advanced Chart Features

Have you ever needed to graphically display two widely different sets of data simultaneously? For example, you may wish to show how unit sales correlate to overall sales totals within the same chart. It's likely that the figures for total sales are much higher than they are for the number of units sold; after all, many items cost far more than a dollar these days. Putting both figures on the same chart would likely make at least one of the data series difficult to read. Or suppose you want to display future projections for your datasets on the same chart you display the data itself. Without the future data, how can you create chart elements that visually convey the information you wish to share? What if you have to create a lot of these charts? Does all of this mean a lot of extra data entry, calculation, and formatting?

Fortunately, Excel 2016 includes a wide range of advanced charting features that enable you to display widely varying sets of data together, include forecasting trends on your charts, and reuse highly stylized or formatted charts again and again. It almost goes without saying that this level of functionality means you can quickly make an impact on nearly any presentation without having to put a lot of time and effort into doing so.

Dual-Axis Charts

A dual-axis chart is, simply, a chart that displays two sets of information on the same chart. This can be in the form of a dual-Y-axis chart, which displays two data series simultaneously, or a dual-X-axis chart, which displays two sets of categories simultaneously. By far, dual-Y-axis charts are used more frequently than dual-X-axis charts. But dual-X-axis charts can be useful for particular types of charts, such as bubble charts or XY (scatter) charts. Excel supports dual-axis charts only for 2-D chart types; they do not work with 3-D chart types. Additionally, you can create a chart with a secondary X axis only if it already has a secondary Y axis.

The main advantage to dual-axis charts is the ability to not only display two different sets of data simultaneously, but also to format the different sets of data independently of each other. This means you can make the various data series easily visually distinguishable from each other and display them within the same amount of space using different scales. For example, you can simultaneously display unit sales figures, which may range in the thousands, with total sales figures, which could range in the billions of dollars for expensive equipment. Clearly the data that is expressed in billions of units would be far easier to see within the same Y axis scale than the data with figures in the thousands. In fact, those figures may not even be visible with such a drastic difference in scale. When you format one or more data series as a different chart type than the original data series, the chart is known as a *combo chart*. Excel 2016 automatically adjusts the scale of secondary Y axes when the data values for the series you use to create them are drastically different than the values in the remaining series. But, you must apply other visual formatting manually.

Figure 4–14: Dual-axis charts enable you to simultaneously display and independently format various sets of data within the same space.

Note: If you're interested in using your Excel charts in external applications, presentations, or other forms of media, access the LearnTO **Save an Excel Chart as a Picture** presentation from the **LearnTO** tile on the CHOICE course screen.

Access the Checklist tile on your CHOICE Course screen for reference information and job aids on How to Create a Dual-Axis Chart.

Forecasting

In addition to creating secondary axes to display various data series or categories simultaneously, Excel includes a chart feature that can help you forecast trends in your data. *Forecasting* is the process of using the trends that exist within past data to predict future outcomes. By its nature, forecasting can never be entirely accurate, as one can never precisely predict all possible future outcomes. As a general rule, the more you forecast out into the future, the less accurate your forecasts become.

Trendlines

In Excel, trendlines are chart elements that can graphically represent both the current trends that exist within your data and past or future forecasts of those trends. You can add trendlines to any of the following non-stacked, 2-D chart types: column, line, bar, area, stock, XY (scatter), and bubble. You can name and format trendlines to make them easier to view on charts or to adhere to organizational branding standards. To access the options for adding trendlines to your charts, select the desired chart to display the **Chart Tools** buttons, select the **Chart Elements** button, point the cursor at the **Trendlines** check box, and then select the arrow that appears to the right of it.

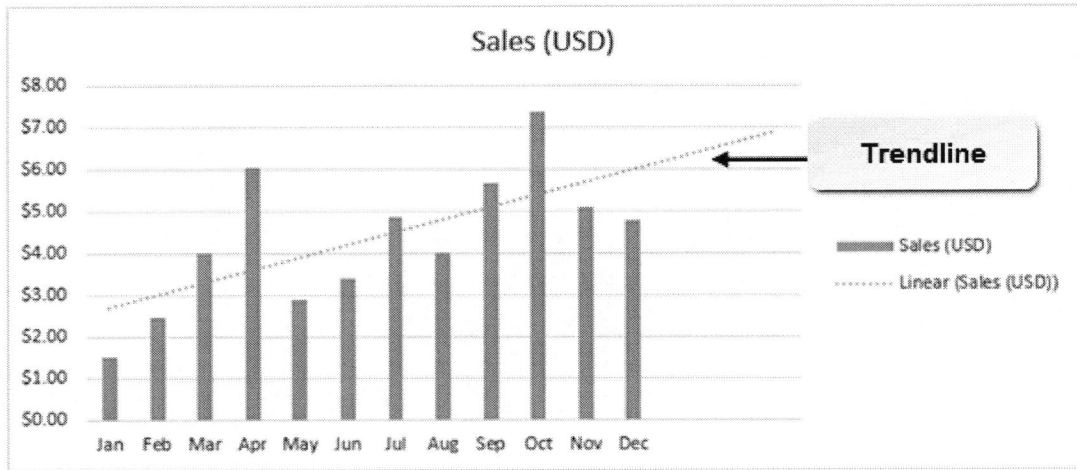

Figure 4–15: Trendline on an Excel chart.

Trendline Types

You can use different types of trendlines to display and forecast data trends depending on the type of data you wish to analyze. Excel provides you with six options for adding trendlines to your charts.

Trendline Type	Use This to Display or Forecast Data That
Exponential	Increases in rate of change at an ever-faster rate over time.
Linear	Is linear in nature. When you graph linear relationships, the resulting graph is a straight line that represents a trend that holds steady, or that increases or decreases by a steady rate.
Logarithmic	Has a rapidly increasing or decreasing rate of change that eventually levels out.
Polynomial	Fluctuates over time.
Power	Increases in rate of change at a steady rate over time.
Moving average	Fluctuates randomly over time. Use this type of trendline to smooth out random patterns of values to give viewers a sense of the overall average change in values over time.

The Format Trendline Task Pane

You will use the **Format Trendline** task pane to apply formatting and effects to your chart trendlines and to change the type of trendlines in your charts. You can access the **Format Trendline** task pane by selecting the desired trendline, and then, on the **Chart Tools** contextual tab, select **Format→Current Selection→Format Selection**.

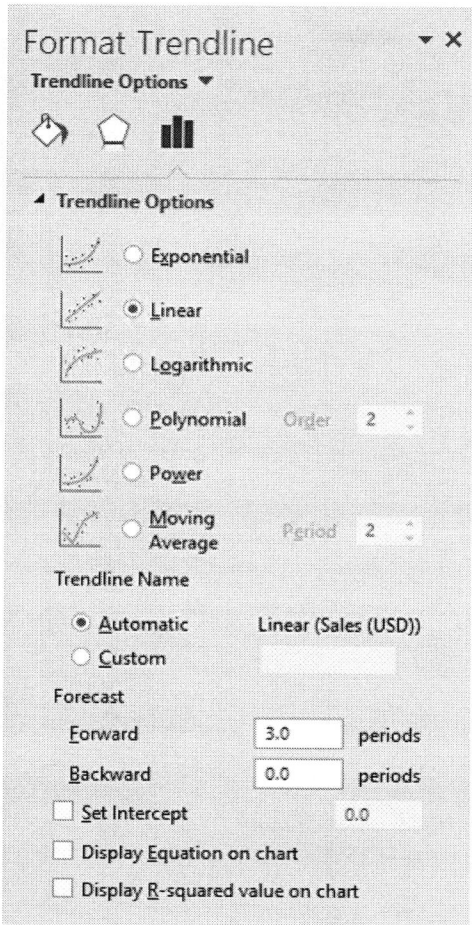

Figure 4–16: The Format Trendline task pane.

 Access the Checklist tile on your CHOICE Course screen for reference information and job aids on **How to Work with Trendlines.**

ACTIVITY 4–3
Creating a Dual–Axis Chart

Before You Begin
The workbook **My Annual Sales.xlsx** is open.

Scenario
In addition to the previous charts you have created, your manager has asked you to build some more complex charts. You have been provided with a workbook that contains the second and third quarter monthly totals and their percentage of total sales for the year thus far. Your manager has heard about combo charts and wants to display total sales on one axis and percentage of total sales on another. In addition, with only six months of recorded data, your manager would like to see a projection of what the next three months might look like. You decide to add a trendline to forecast this trend.

1. Create a combo chart from the monthly totals.
   a) Select the **Monthly Totals** worksheet.
   b) Select the range **A1:C7**.
   c) Select **Insert→Charts→dialog box launcher**.
   d) In the **Insert Chart** dialog box, select the **All Charts** tab and then select **Combo**.
   e) In the **Choose the chart type and axis for your data series** section, in the **% of Total Sales** row, select the check box for **Secondary Axis**.

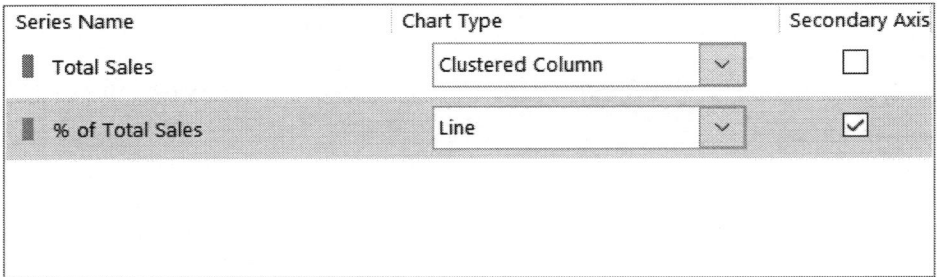

Choose the chart type and axis for your data series:

Series Name	Chart Type	Secondary Axis
Total Sales	Clustered Column	☐
% of Total Sales	Line	☑

f) Select **OK**.

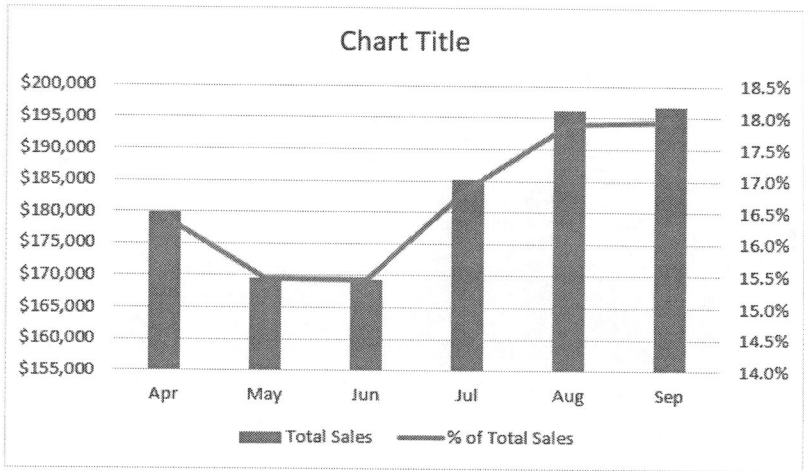

2. Modify the chart title and include axis titles for each Y axis.

a) Select the **Chart Elements** button ⊞ and hover over **Axis Titles**. Select the arrow that appears to the right and select **Primary Vertical** and **Secondary Vertical**.

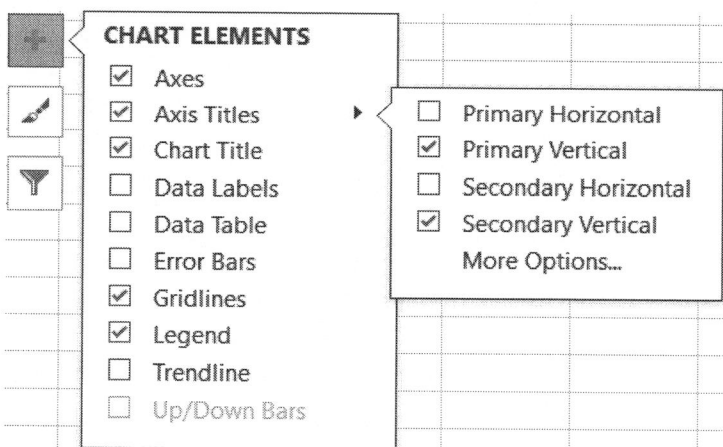

b) On the left side of the chart, select the **Vertical (Value) Axis Title**. Type **=** and select cell **B1**, then press **Enter**.

c) On the right side of the chart, select the **Secondary Vertical (Value) Axis Title**. Type **=** and select cell **C1**, then press **Enter**.

    d) Select the **Chart Title** and type *Monthly Totals* and then press **Enter**.

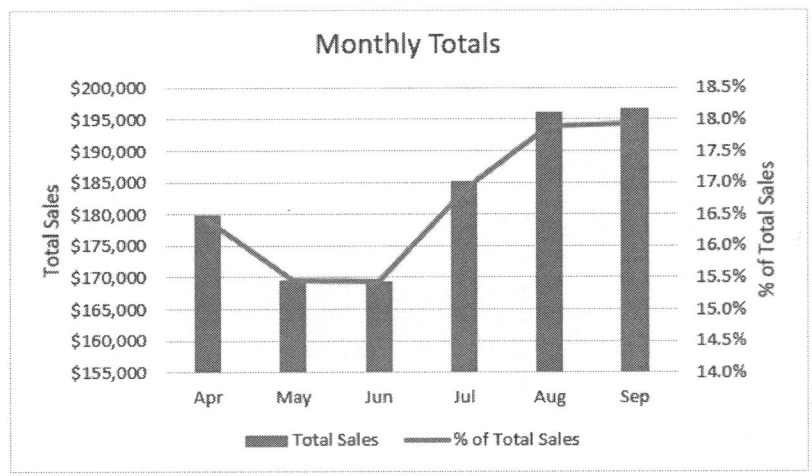

3. Add a trendline to the total sales series.

    a) On the **Chart Tools** contextual tab, select **Format→Current Selection→Chart Elements drop-down arrow** and select **Series "Total Sales"**.

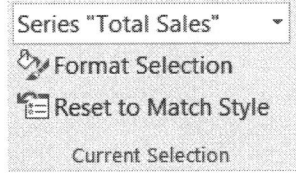

    b) Select the **Chart Elements** button ⊞ and hover over **Trendline**. Select the arrow that appears to the right and select **More Options**.

    c) In the **Format Trendline** task pane, verify that the **Trendline Options** high-level tab is selected and then, if necessary, select the **Trendline Options** low-level tab. 📊

    d) In the **Trendline Options** section, verify that **Linear** is selected. In the **Forecast** group, select the **Forward** text box, type *3* and then press **Enter**.

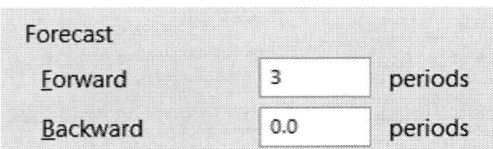

e) Verify that the trendline has been added to the chart, forecasting three periods forward.

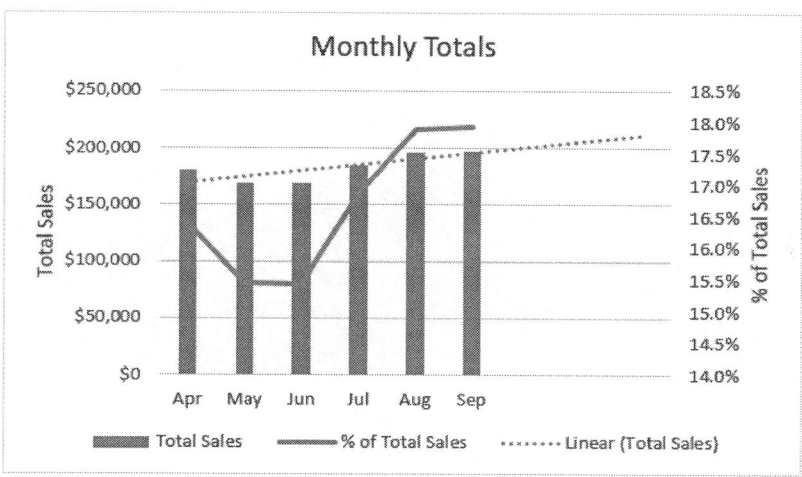

4. Save the workbook and keep the file open.

Chart Templates

Working with advanced charting features can require quite a bit of chart formatting and modification. And, it's likely you'll need to reuse at least some of your charts for multiple purposes, projects, or periods. So, you would certainly benefit from the ability to save all of the formatting and modification work that went into creating your charts for use in future workbooks. This can be especially helpful if you've painstakingly formatted chart elements to adhere to organizational branding guidelines and will frequently need to create charts that follow them. Fortunately, Excel provides you with the ability to save charts as chart templates that you can apply to other datasets in the same workbook or to datasets in other workbooks.

Like other Excel templates, a chart template is a type of file that stores a chart type and all of the associated formatting you've applied to it. The file extension for Excel 2016 chart templates is .crtx. Excel stores chart templates in a subfolder in the Microsoft **Templates** folder named **Charts**. Once saved, you can access chart templates from the **Templates** tab in either the **Insert Chart** dialog box or the **Change Chart Type** dialog box, just as you can any other chart type. This is true only if you save your chart templates in the **Charts** folder. Do not save chart templates in any other folder if you wish to access them from the dialog boxes.

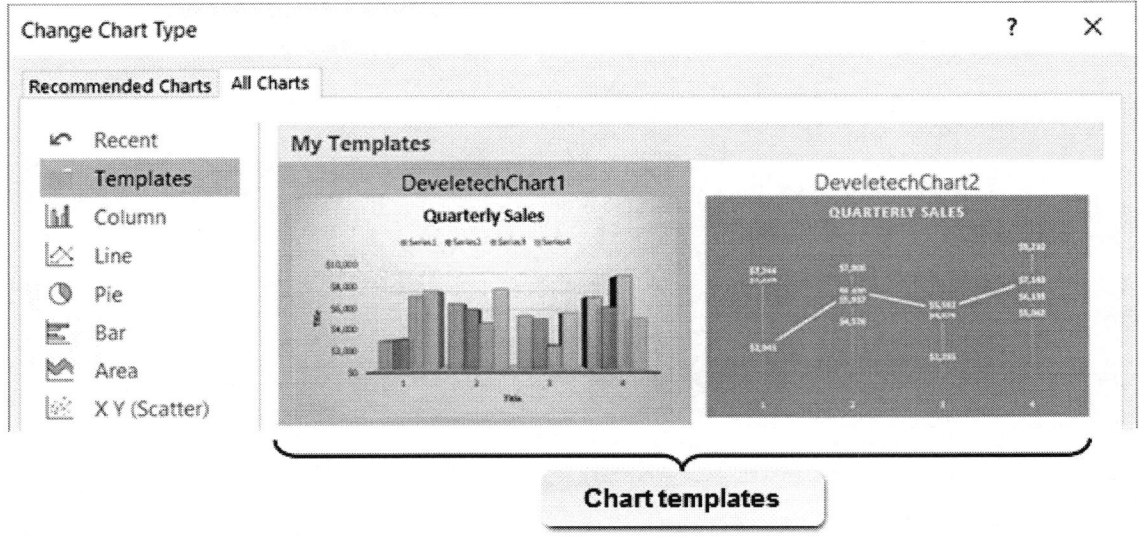

Figure 4-17: Chart templates available for use in the Change Chart Type dialog box.

 Access the Checklist tile on your **CHOICE** Course screen for reference information and job aids on **How to Create and Use Chart Templates.**

ACTIVITY 4-4
Creating a Chart Template

Before You Begin
The workbook **My Annual Sales.xlsx** is open.

Scenario
You like the look and feel of the chart you created to forecast monthly sales. You know that you'll be creating similar charts for other sales periods. Instead of creating and manually adding elements to your charts each time you create them, you decide to create a chart template from the chart that you can apply to future datasets.

---

1. Verify that you are on the Monthly Totals worksheet, and if necessary, select the Monthly Totals combo chart.

2. Save the chart as a template.
   a) Right-click the chart and then select **Save as Template**.
   b) In the **Save Chart Template** dialog box, ensure the **Charts** folder is selected.

    Note: Excel should automatically direct you to the **Charts** folder. The label <User> in the chart templates path image will be your user name. The **AppData** folder is typically a hidden system folder, so you will not see the folder browsing through File Explorer, although you can type AppData in the address path to go to that folder directly.

   « Users ><User>> AppData > Roaming > Microsoft > Templates > Charts

   c) In the **File name** field, type **Trendline Chart Template**.
   d) Verify the **Save as type** is **Chart Template Files(*.crtx)**, and then select **Save**.

3. Test the new chart template.
   a) Select the **Projected Sales** worksheet.
   b) Select the range **A1:C7**.
   c) Select **Insert→Charts→dialog box launcher**.
   d) In the **Insert Charts** dialog box, select the **All Charts** tab, and then select the **Templates** category.

e) In the **My Templates** section, select the **Trendline Chart Template** and select **OK**.

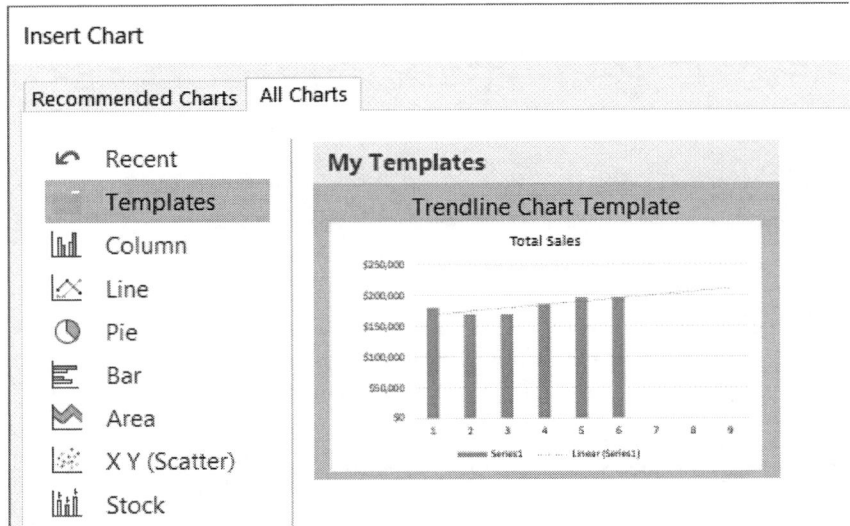

f) Verify that Excel created a dual-axis combo chart with a trendline.

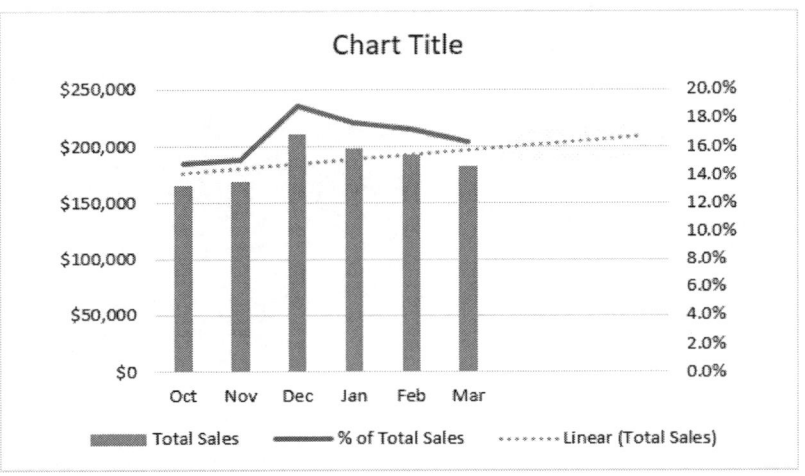

4. Save and close the workbook.

Summary

In this lesson, you presented your data graphically using charts. You did this by creating charts to display your data in various types. You initially learned to create basic charts like column, bar, line, and pie charts. You then learned to format and modify those charts along with the ability to build advanced charts such as combo charts, and to include trendlines making charts easier to read and interpret. Providing your audience members with a visual snapshot of your data enables them to quickly recognize trends in your raw data, make easy comparisons, and focus on your message.

What are a couple of reasons for which you anticipate including charts in your workbooks?

What uses will you have for Excel's advanced charting features in your current role?

 Note: Check your CHOICE Course screen for opportunities to interact with your classmates, peers, and the larger CHOICE online community about the topics covered in this course or other topics you are interested in. From the Course screen you can also access available resources for a more continuous learning experience.

5 | Using PivotTables and PivotCharts

Lesson Time: 1 hour, 30 minutes

Lesson Objectives

In this lesson, you will analyze data with PivotTables, PivotCharts, slicers, and timelines. You will:

- Create a PivotTable.

- Analyze PivotTable data.

- Present data with PivotCharts.

- Filter data using timelines and slicers.

Lesson Introduction

You've already seen the way Microsoft® Office Excel® 2016 functions and how features such as sorting, filtering, and summary functions can help you drill down into your data to get answers to very specific questions. Although using these features is often a good option for attaining specific answers, these aren't necessarily the best options if you need to frequently change the questions you're asking of your data. To change the question you're asking when using functions, sorting, and filtering, you often need to rewrite functions, adjust criteria, or re-filter you data; sometimes, you even need to use several of these methods at the same time. You certainly could take this route, but it isn't the most efficient way to re-query your data to get the variety of answers you need. If you work in a high-paced, data-intensive environment, you simply may not have the time needed to recalculate every time a supervisor asks you a different question. You need something a little more dynamic.

Excel 2016 includes a powerful feature that enables you to ask any number of questions of your data; get detailed, specific answers; and do it all over again in just a matter of moments. By taking advantage of this functionality, you can get critical, time-sensitive organizational intelligence to the people who need it quickly, easily, and with a high-level of flexibility.

TOPIC A

Create a PivotTable

To take advantage of the functionality and flexibility of PivotTables, you must first understand how to create them. Although this is a relatively simple process, you must also know a bit about the type of data that works best for PivotTables. By taking a few moments to gain this foundational level of understanding, you'll be preparing yourself to create useful, effective PivotTables that you can use to analyze your raw data in incredibly fine detail.

Pivoting

Simply put, *pivoting*, in Excel, is a way to manipulate, rotate, or turn large amounts of data into a summarization of that data. You and your organization collect and track data for the express purpose of gaining insight and information from that data to make decisions. When you ask questions of your data, you get information about what products or services your customers prefer and which ones they do not. In this course, you have learned to create functions, sort, filter, summarize and subtotal data in order to gain perspective on your data. Pivoting enables you to view your data from a variety of new perspectives.

To pivot your data, Excel summarizes your values by row and column. Data that can be grouped, like company names, cities, states/provinces, product codes and names are good examples of items that can be used as row or column headings. Values are data that can be summarized, averaged, or calculated for a percentage. Examples of values include quantities, prices, and counts of values both numeric and text based. Take the following example: the raw data on the left contains a contiguous list of data and each row in that data, which can be called a record, identifies a unique entry to the list. When Excel pivots the raw data, the state/province data is grouped as row labels and the values of total sale are summarized. This provides a concise report of your data that can also be formatted, sorted, and filtered further to gain more insight. This report quickly answers the question of what are the total sales for each state/province.

 Note: As with filtering and sorting, pivoting does not affect your raw data; it only modifies your view of the data.

Here's a look at how the previous example would work in a worksheet. The list is a set of order transactions by various companies in different locations purchasing items with different quantities and price.

	A	B	C	D	E	F
1	Company	City	State/Province	Quantity	Unit Price	Total Sale
2	Affiliated Grocers	Las Vegas	NV	100	$14.00	$1,400.00
3	Affiliated Grocers	Las Vegas	NV	30	$3.50	$105.00
4	Associated Markets	New York	NY	10	$30.00	$300.00
5	Associated Markets	New York	NY	10	$53.00	$530.00
6	Associated Markets	New York	NY	10	$3.50	$35.00
7	Central Market Cooperative	Las Vegas	NV	15	$18.00	$270.00
8	Central Market Cooperative	Las Vegas	NV	20	$46.00	$920.00
9	Value Grocers	Portland	OR	30	$9.20	$276.00
10	Associated Markets	New York	NY	20	$9.20	$184.00
11	Go Shop Markets	Denver	CO	10	$12.75	$127.50
12	Market Save	Los Angelas	CA	200	$9.65	$1,930.00
13	Green Grains	Milwaukee	WI	17	$40.00	$680.00
14	Ponderay Foods	Memphis	TN	300	$46.00	$13,800.00
15	Value Grocers	Portland	OR	100	$12.75	$1,275.00
16	Family Food Stores	Chicago	IL	200	$2.99	$598.00
17	World Food	Boise	ID	300	$46.00	$13,800.00
18	Family Food Stores	Chicago	IL	10	$25.00	$250.00
19	Family Food Stores	Chicago	IL	10	$22.00	$220.00
20	Family Food Stores	Chicago	IL	10	$9.20	$92.00
21	Milburn Markets	Miami	FL	20	$3.50	$70.00
22	Milburn Markets	Miami	FL	50	$2.99	$149.50
23	Baldwin Baskets	Seattle	WA	25	$18.00	$450.00
24	Baldwin Baskets	Seattle	WA	25	$46.00	$1,150.00
25	Baldwin Baskets	Seattle	WA	25	$2.99	$74.75

Row Labels	Sum of Total Sale
CA	$2,550.00
CO	$2,905.50
FL	$4,644.75
ID	$13,800.00
IL	$2,272.50
NV	$2,695.00
NY	$4,949.00
OR	$4,683.00
TN	$15,432.50
UT	$3,786.50
WA	$2,410.75
WI	$8,007.50
Grand Total	**$68,137.00**

Pivoted Data

Original Data

Figure 5-1: Pivoted data provides sales totals at a glance.

PivotTables

A *PivotTable* is a dynamic Excel data object that enables you to analyze data by pivoting columns and rows of raw data without altering the raw data. PivotTables are effective for summarizing large volumes of data according to two or more criteria to return specific answers to your questions. PivotTables combine some of the most powerful and useful types of Excel functionality, such as sorting, filtering, summary functions, and subtotals, to give you an incredible level of control over how you view your data.

When you create a PivotTable, Excel enables you place it on the same worksheet as the original data, or you can insert it on a new worksheet. Once the PivotTable is created, you can re-pivot, re-sort, re-summarize, and re-filter your data any number of times without affecting the original dataset. In addition to pivoting columns and rows, you can nest columns and rows within one another to create a hierarchy, much as you do when using subtotals. You can expand or collapse levels of the hierarchy to view more or less detail in your PivotTables. And you can use any of the available summary functions to summarize your pivoted data for a variety of purposes. You can also create PivotTables out of either data in the same workbook, or data from other workbooks and external data sources.

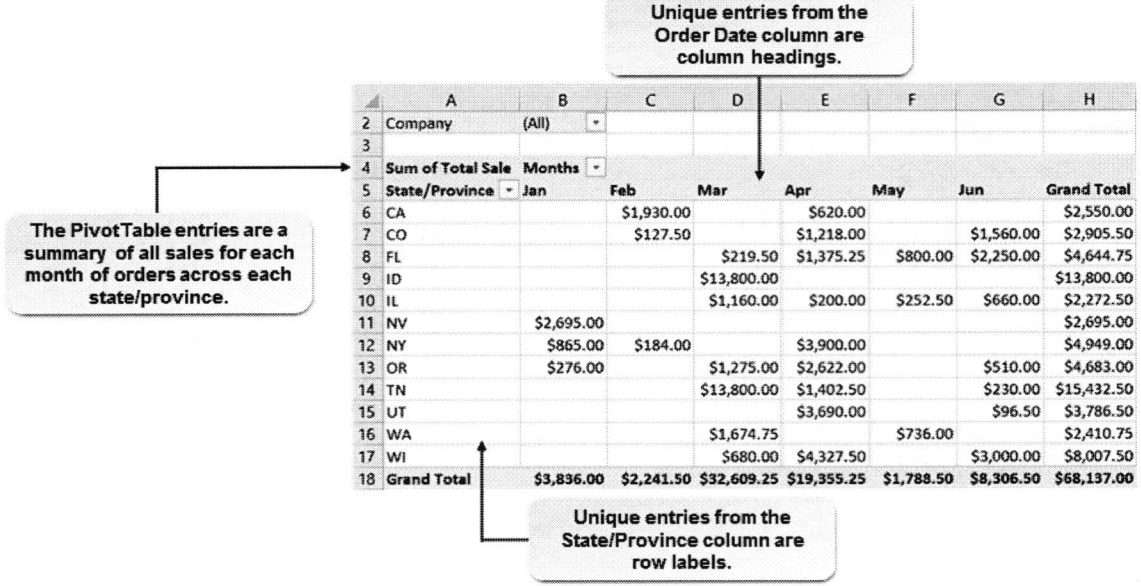

Figure 5-2: A PivotTable containing a hierarchy of raw data. In this example, Company, Total Sale, State/Province, and Months are all column labels in the original dataset.

Recommended PivotTables

A quick way to get started with PivotTables is to use Recommended PivotTables. When you use this feature, Excel determines PivotTable layouts based on your data. From this starting point, you can change the arrangement of fields in the PivotTable for additional analysis of your data. Recommended PivotTables is accessible from **Insert→Tables→Recommended PivotTables**.

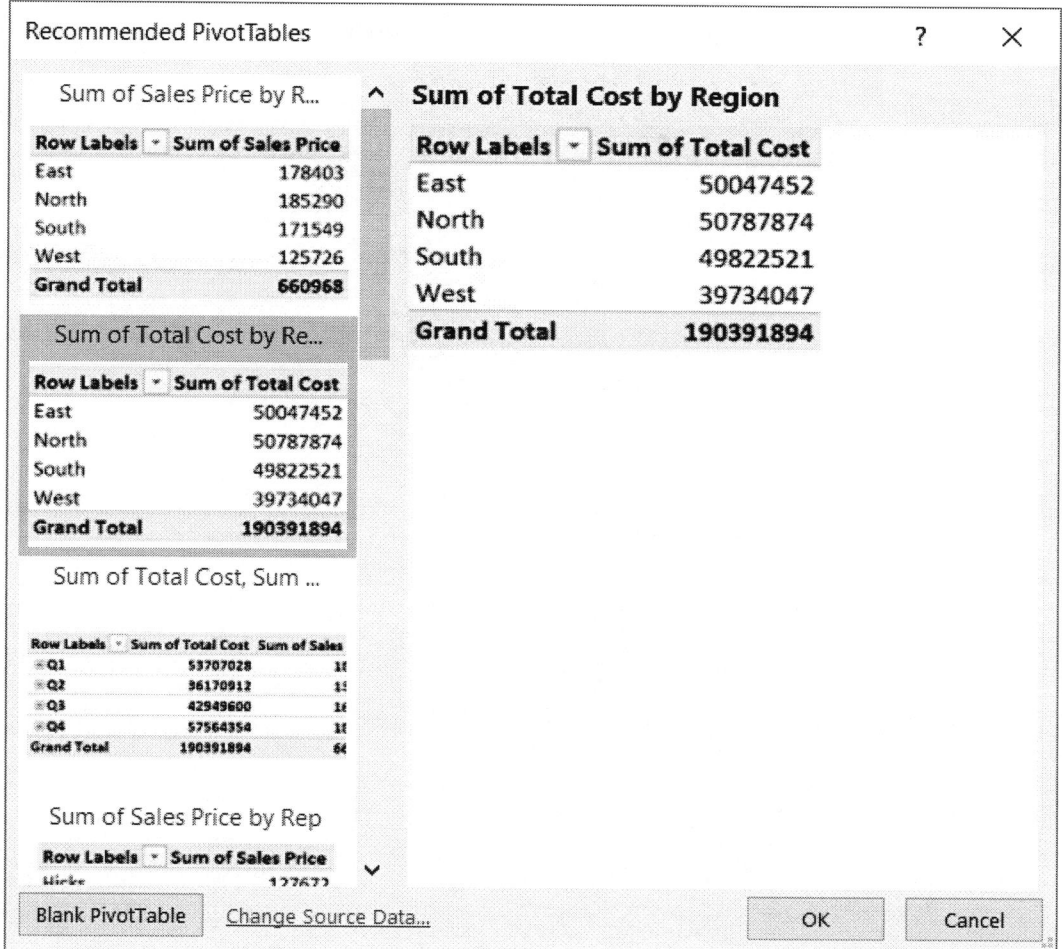

Figure 5-3: Examples of Recommended PivotTables.

Transactional Data

There is an extremely important consideration for you to keep in mind when creating and working with PivotTables: your data format. PivotTables are designed to work with, and work best with, raw *transactional data*. Transactional data is not summarized in any way, so it does not contain row labels, only column labels. Columns in a transactional dataset are also known as *fields*. The best way to visualize transactional data is to examine the root word "transaction." In a transactional dataset, each transaction, or *entry*, is located in its own separate row. To carry on the example from earlier of sales transactions at a variety of locations, each sale, regardless of when or where it took place, would be entered as an individual row of data. The dataset columns represent the specific elements of each transaction: date, time, location, amount, and so on.

In a summarized dataset, even a raw one, the data has already been compiled in some way and will have row labels as well as column labels. For example, you may have raw sales data for each sales rep in your organization. Because each rep has his or her own row of data, the dataset would likely contain the total of each person's sales, as opposed to each sale regardless of the rep. Although you can create PivotTables from summary data, they will never give you as much granular insight into your data as PivotTables created from transactional data.

	A	B	C	D	E	F	G	H	I
1	Date	Time	Store Number	Item Number	Quantity	Price	Sub Total	Tax	Total
2	1/4/2016	10:06:00 AM	S953	8293	11	$25.01	$275.16	5.0%	$288.92
3	1/5/2016	1:31:00 PM	S891	6754	18	$13.28	$239.11	6.5%	$254.66
4	1/5/2016	9:12:00 AM	S613	7669	25	$26.67	$666.74	6.5%	$710.08
5	1/6/2016	12:09:00 PM	S562	3633	19	$14.93	$283.73	6.0%	$300.75
6	1/6/2016	10:56:00 AM	S675	4311	29	$6.05	$175.58	4.5%	$183.48
7	1/6/2016	1:13:00 PM	S110	4964	14	$21.37	$299.13	5.0%	$314.08
8	1/7/2016	11:36:00 AM	S389	6839	5	$6.61	$33.07	5.0%	$34.73
9	1/8/2016	2:06:00 PM	S327	7225	19	$13.20	$250.88	5.5%	$264.68
10	1/8/2016	12:23:00 PM	S562	2081	11	$14.77	$162.44	6.5%	$173.00
11	1/11/2016	3:50:00 PM	S675	4486	29	$24.48	$709.82	7.0%	$759.50
12	1/12/2016	1:45:00 PM	S389	6566	9	$8.97	$80.70	7.0%	$86.35
13	1/12/2016	4:32:00 PM	S327	3511	14	$4.39	$61.44	6.0%	$65.13
14	1/13/2016	9:07:00 AM	S148	8497	24	$6.14	$147.39	6.0%	$156.24
15	1/13/2016	12:17:00 PM	S110	2190	19	$10.71	$203.56	5.5%	$214.76
16	1/13/2016	2:48:00 PM	S613	3452	22	$28.54	$627.91	5.0%	$659.30
17	1/13/2016	4:40:00 PM	S562	5662	30	$16.28	$488.30	5.0%	$512.72
18	1/14/2016	10:40:00 AM	S953	2567	12	$7.27	$87.21	7.0%	$93.31
19	1/15/2016	1:45:00 PM	S891	2934	6	$23.57	$141.39	6.0%	$149.88

Transactional Data

	A	B	C	D
1	Store Number	Avg Qty Sold	Avg Price	Total Sales
2	S110	16.5	$16.04	$264.66
3	S148	24.0	$6.14	$147.36
4	S327	16.4	$8.80	$144.32
5	S389	7.0	$7.79	$54.53
6	S562	20.0	$15.33	$306.60
7	S613	23.5	$27.61	$648.84
8	S675	29.0	$15.27	$442.83
9	S891	12.0	$18.42	$221.04
10	S953	11.5	$16.14	$185.61

Summarized Data

Figure 5–4: Transactional data shows each event, whereas summary data compiles it in some way.

 Note: It makes more sense to view your data as two types: values to summarize and values to group. Values of dates, times, quantity, price, etc. are good examples of values that can be summarized. Values of cities, states, companies, accounts, etc. are examples of values that can be grouped.

The Create PivotTable Dialog Box

You use the **Create PivotTable** dialog box to insert PivotTables into your worksheets. From here, you can select the desired dataset, include a reference to a named range or table, or select a connection to an external data source. You can also select a location for the PivotTable, which can be on the same worksheet as the dataset or on another worksheet in the same workbook. You can access the **Create PivotTable** dialog box by selecting **Insert→Tables→PivotTable**.

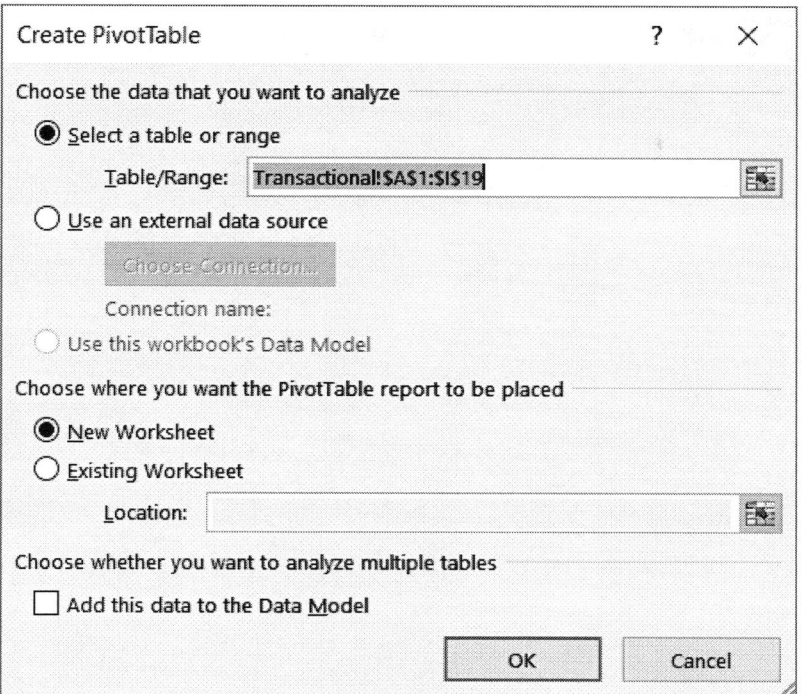

Figure 5-5: The Create PivotTable dialog box.

The PivotTable Fields Task Pane

Once you create a PivotTable, you will use the **PivotTable Fields** task pane to configure the PivotTable and perform data analysis tasks. Excel automatically opens the **PivotTable Fields** task pane when you insert a PivotTable in a worksheet. The top half of the pane, the **Choose fields to add to report** list, displays a list of all of the fields (columns) from the original dataset; Excel pulls the names for these from the column labels. The bottom half of the pane, the **Drag fields between areas below** section, displays a series of four areas that you use to configure the PivotTable. By dragging the various fields to the various areas, you configure the structure of the PivotTable and select the values upon which Excel performs calculations.

As PivotTables are, by default, dynamic, you can drag fields to the various areas of the **PivotTable Fields** task pane as necessary and your PivotTable will update automatically. You can move the fields around as often as you like, and you can include more than one field in each area. When you drag more than one field into the same area, Excel creates a hierarchy in the PivotTable with items on top of the area representing higher levels in the hierarchy. This works much like using subtotals and outlines in ranges.

Each field that you have dragged into an area displays a field drop-down arrow. This provides you with access to context menus and dialog boxes that enable you to configure your PivotTables further.

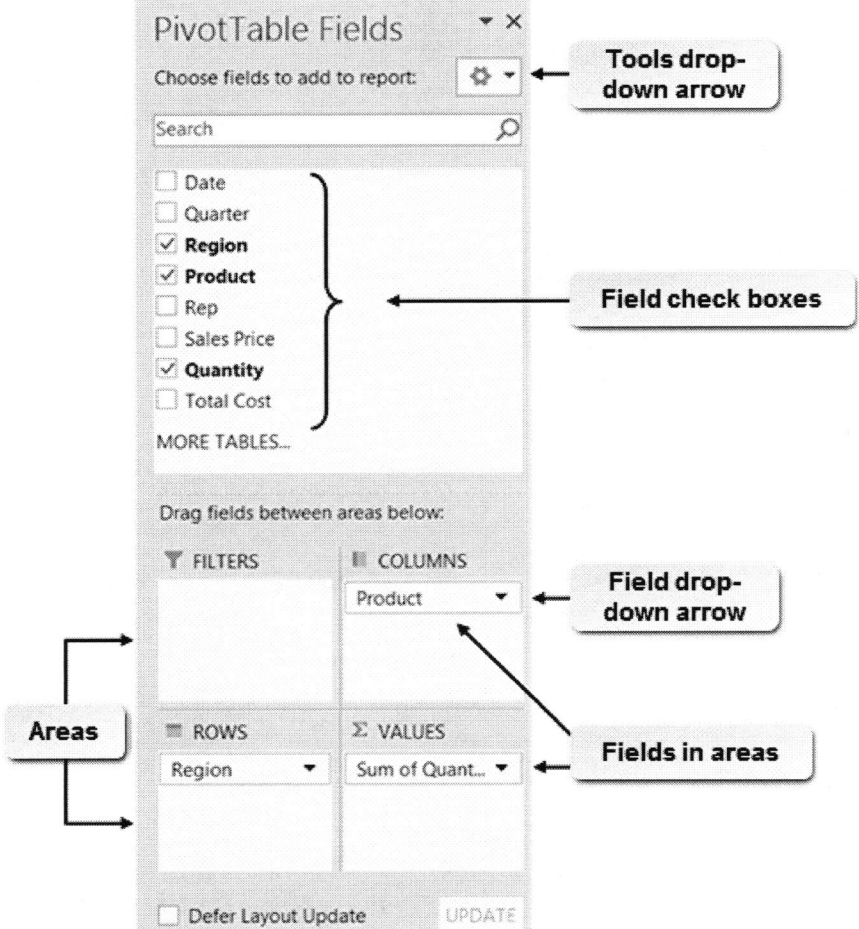

Figure 5-6: Use the elements of the PivotTable Fields task pane to configure the structure of PivotTables.

The following table provides a brief description of the various elements of the **PivotTable Fields** task pane.

PivotTable Fields Task Pane Element	Description
Tools drop-down arrow	Provides you with access to a menu that contains various preconfigured **PivotTable Fields** task pane layouts. Select from among these options to customize the **PivotTable Fields** task pane to suit your needs. From the **Tools** drop-down menu, you can also alter the order in which your fields appear within the **Choose fields to add to report** section of the **PivotTable Fields** task pane.
Field check boxes	These enable you to add or remove fields from the various areas. Checking a field's check box adds it to an area, whereas unchecking it removes the field from all areas. You have no control over where Excel places a field when you check its check box, so many users prefer to simply drag the fields to the desired areas.

PivotTable Fields Task Pane Element	Description
Field drop-down arrow	Selecting a field's drop-down arrow displays a context menu that provides you with various options for configuring your PivotTables. For example, you can move fields to another area (again, this can also be done simply by dragging the field to another area), move fields within a hierarchy, or access the **Field Settings** or **Value Field Settings** dialog boxes.
FILTERS area	Drag fields here to include field values as filter criteria for the PivotTable.
COLUMNS area	Drag fields here to create columns out of the unique entries in a field.
ROWS area	Drag fields here to create rows out of the unique entries in a field.
VALUES area	Drag fields here to have Excel perform calculations on or summarize their values.

 Note: To learn how to use field entries to filter your PivotTable data, access the LearnTO **Add a Report Filter to an Excel PivotTable** presentation from the **LearnTO** tile on the CHOICE course screen.

 Access the Checklist tile on your CHOICE Course screen for reference information and job aids on How to Create a PivotTable.

ACTIVITY 5-1
Creating a PivotTable

Data File

C:\091056Data\Using PivotTables and PivotCharts\Sales Data.xlsx

Before You Begin

Excel 2016 is open.

Scenario

As the sales manager, you need to track sales. Because Develetech's products are sold across many regions, you want to be able to analyze the sales data in a number of ways. You decide the best way to answer your questions now and in the future is to create a PivotTable.

1. In Excel, open the workbook **Sales Data.xlsx**.

2. Create a PivotTable from the data.
   a) Verify that cell **A1** is selected.
   b) Select **Insert→Tables→PivotTable**.
   c) In the **Create PivotTable** dialog box, in the **Choose the data that you want to analyze section**, verify that the **Select a table or range** option is selected.
   d) In the **Choose where you want the PivotTable report to be placed section**, verify that the **New Worksheet** option is selected and select **OK**.

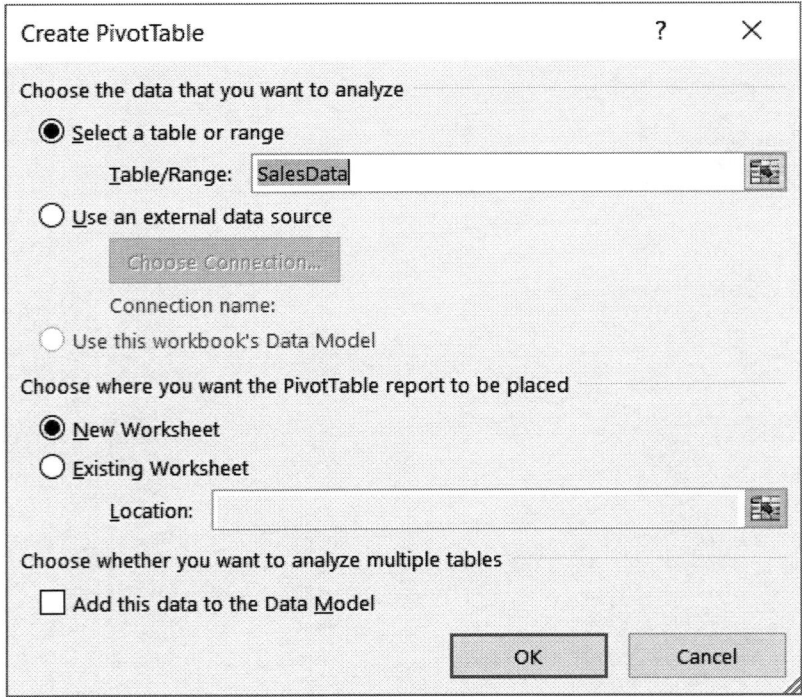

e) Observe that the PivotTable framework is created on a new worksheet.

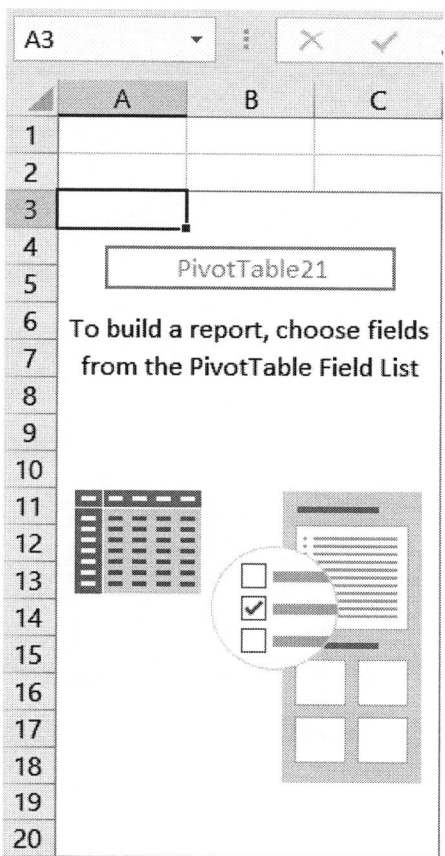

3. Build the PivotTable report.

   a) In the **PivotTable Fields** task pane, in the **Choose fields to add to report section**, select the check boxes for **Region** and **Total Sales**.

b) Verify that Excel builds a PivotTable on Sheet1 depicting the sum of total sales for each region.

 Note: Notice that Excel does not retain cell formatting from original data when creating PivotTable reports.

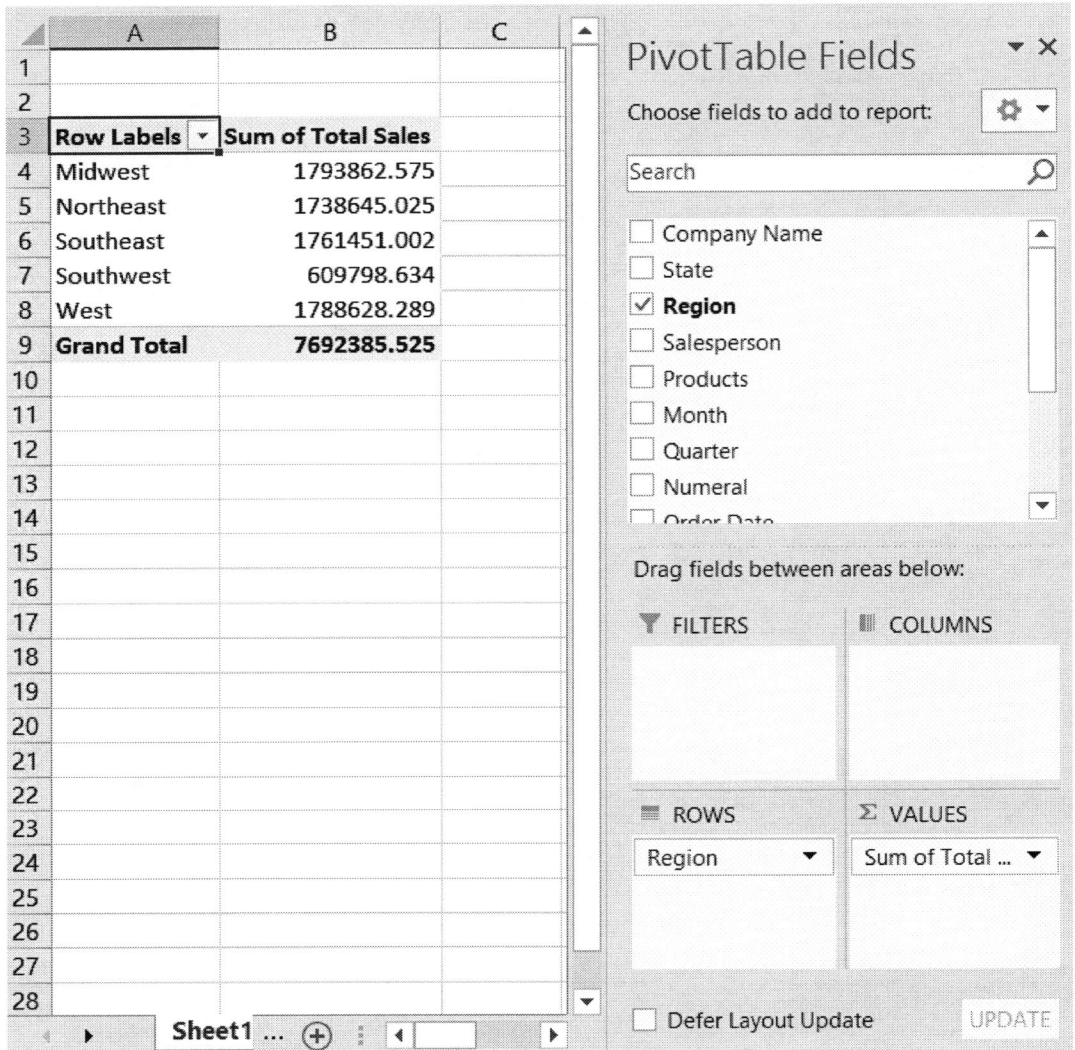

4. Create a Recommended PivotTable from the sales data.
   a) Select the **Data** worksheet and verify that cell **A1** is selected.
   b) Select **Insert→Tables→Recommended PivotTables**.

c) Examine the various PivotTable options in the **Recommended PivotTables** dialog box. Select the second variant, **Sum of Total Sales by Region** and select **OK**.

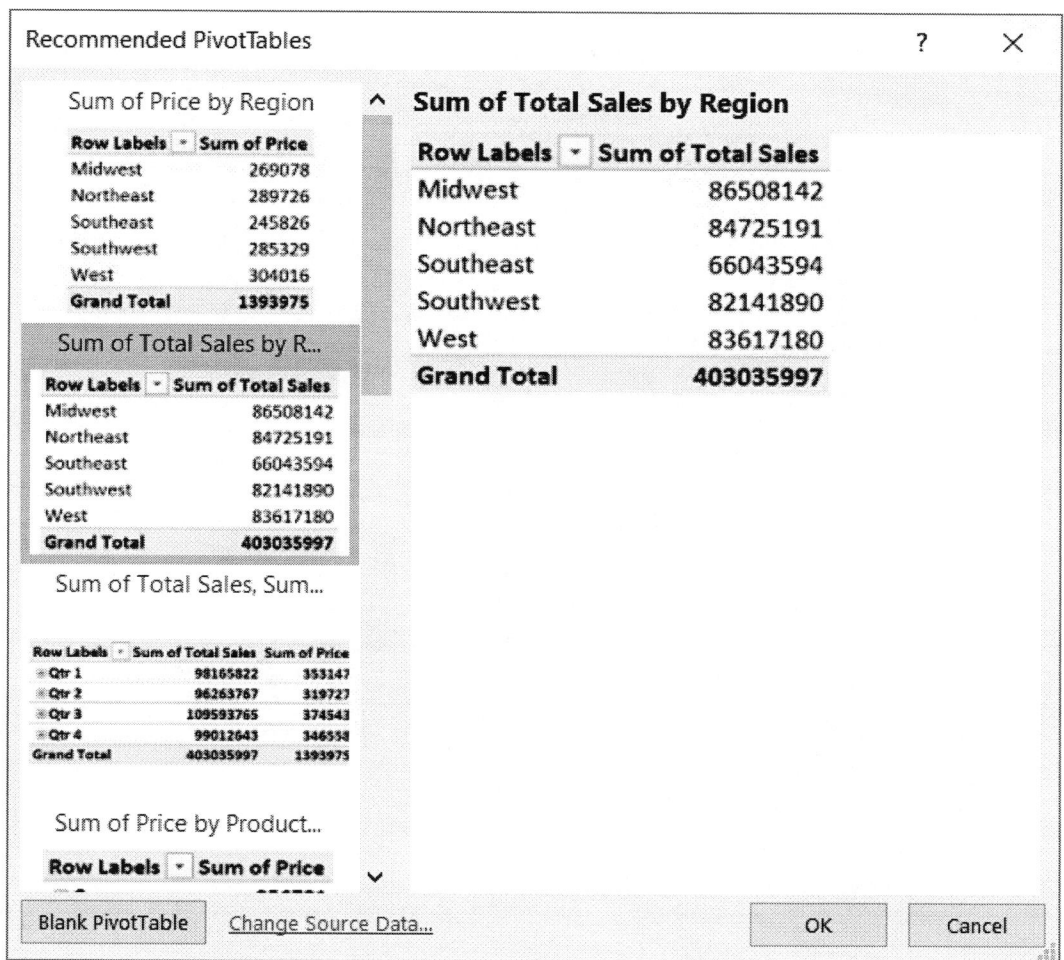

d) Verify that Sheet2 contains the new PivotTable.

 Note: This action builds the same PivotTable report on Sheet2 as the first PivotTable report on Sheet1. Recommended PivotTables are a good way to get started building your own PivotTable reports.

5. Modify the PivotTable on Sheet2 to include products.

   a) In the **PivotTable Fields** task pane, in the **Choose fields to add to report section**, select **Products**.

b) Verify the PivotTable is updated to include total sales for products in each region.

Row Labels	Sum of Total Sales
⊟ **Midwest**	**1793862.575**
Bluetooth speaker	135147.39
Camera	230618.7
Laptop	261654.975
Mobile phone	232967.454
Music player	110948.281
Printer	62843.715
Tablet computer	225452.5
Television	257996.06
Video game console	276233.5
⊟ **Northeast**	**1738645.025**
Bluetooth speaker	103351.65
Camera	278159.7
Laptop	260798.925
Mobile phone	243062.901
Music player	119938.615
Printer	57614.238
Tablet computer	190385
Television	232727.796
Video game console	252606.2

6. Save the workbook as *My Sales Data.xlsx* and keep the file open.

TOPIC B

Analyze PivotTable Data

Now that you have created your PivotTable, you're ready to dive right in and crunch the numbers to gain the organizational insight that can help you succeed. As with all Excel data analysis tasks, creating and configuring effective PivotTables is a matter of asking the right questions to glean the necessary information. When working with PivotTables, this all boils down to structure. You already know PivotTables enable you to reorganize and re-analyze your data as many times as necessary to get all of the answers you're looking for. But, how do you translate your questions into a PivotTable structure? Actually, it's relatively simple.

Excel 2016 provides you with a number of different tools and commands you can use to organize the structure of your PivotTables. Knowing how these tools work and understanding how PivotTable structure translates into actionable intelligence are the keys to getting the answers you seek.

Start with Questions, End with Structure

To create PivotTables that will be useful to you, begin by thinking about the types of questions you would like your raw data to answer. This is precisely that same type of initial analysis you perform when determining which functions or formulas to include in worksheets. The only difference here is that you will use your questions as a basis for organizing your PivotTables, not to enter a function or a formula. Once you've determined what question you want Excel to answer, you can begin to design your PivotTable's structure.

There are a couple of items to keep in mind before beginning this process. First, it's typically best to create rows and columns out of fields that have a fairly finite set of entries, such as sales reps, regions, or products; in other words, data that can be grouped easily. You may not, for example, find it very useful to create rows out of dates that occurred over a 10-year span of time as you could end up with thousands of rows of data. Second, you should create rows out of the field for which you are primarily interested in determining some fact, and create columns out of your secondary criterion. For example, if you want to know the total sales per product for each sales rep in your department, you would typically create rows out of sales reps (your primary concern) and columns out of the products (the items for which you are measuring performance). Then you would ask Excel to use the SUM function to total the sales for each rep per product.

Let's take a look at a simple example.

▲	A	B	C	D	E	F	G	H
1	Date	Quarter	Region	Product	Rep	Sales Price	Quantity	Total Cost
2	1/6/2015	Q1	East	Mobiles	Williams	$5,394	396	$2,136,024.00
3	1/7/2015	Q1	East	Television	Ortega	$7,858	433	$3,402,514.00
4	1/11/2015	Q1	East	Washing Machine	Hogan	$2,067	301	$622,167.00
5	1/11/2015	Q1	East	Computer	Jordan	$8,601	477	$4,102,677.00
6	1/11/2015	Q1	East	Printers	Hicks	$6,802	129	$877,458.00
7	1/13/2015	Q1	East	Desktops	Williams	$5,130	458	$2,349,540.00
8	1/13/2015	Q1	East	Cameras	Ortega	$5,314	241	$1,280,674.00
9	1/20/2015	Q1	East	Laptops	Hogan	$8,497	156	$1,325,532.00
10	1/20/2015	Q1	South	Mobiles	Jordan	$8,819	112	$987,728.00
11	1/22/2015	Q1	South	Television	Hicks	$9,029	125	$1,128,625.00
12	1/24/2015	Q1	South	Washing Machine	Williams	$5,047	448	$2,261,056.00
13	1/25/2015	Q1	South	Computer	Ortega	$1,628	412	$670,736.00
14	1/28/2015	Q1	South	Printers	Hogan	$6,872	418	$2,872,496.00
15	2/1/2015	Q1	South	Desktops	Jordan	$3,811	206	$785,066.00
16	2/1/2015	Q1	South	Cameras	Hicks	$8,905	396	$3,526,380.00
17	2/4/2015	Q1	South	Laptops	Williams	$8,482	234	$1,984,788.00
18	2/4/2015	Q1	North	Mobiles	Ortega	$7,041	116	$816,756.00
19	2/8/2015	Q1	North	Television	Hogan	$9,144	123	$1,124,712.00
20	2/9/2015	Q1	North	Washing Machine	Jordan	$1,523	101	$153,823.00

Figure 5-7: This is the beginning of a table with over 100 entries of sales data.

Now, here's a PivotTable created from the entire dataset that answers this question: What are the total sales for each sales rep by product?

Sum of Total Cost	Column Labels								
Row Labels	Cameras	Computer	Desktops	Laptops	Mobiles	Printers	Television	Washing Machine	Grand Total
Hicks	$7,949,172.00	$4,678,622.00	$5,138,844.00	$2,963,272.00	$855,800.00	$6,919,838.00	$4,994,039.00	$1,545,552.00	$35,045,139.00
Hogan	$4,827,284.00	$734,433.00	$1,581,792.00	$8,912,656.00	$1,694,940.00	$4,457,014.00	$1,965,124.00	$10,994,481.00	$35,167,724.00
Jordan	$3,824,510.00	$10,915,869.00	$1,513,386.00	$1,778,562.00	$3,016,773.00	$1,636,487.00	$1,191,907.00	$468,299.00	$24,345,793.00
Ortega	$11,450,564.00	$5,338,479.00	$1,314,469.00	$1,835,180.00	$1,809,148.00	$2,671,600.00	$12,611,304.00	$5,053,960.00	$42,084,704.00
Williams	$4,320,349.00	$2,427,265.00	$13,563,534.00	$6,033,342.00	$12,039,887.00	$5,389,276.00	$2,406,716.00	$7,568,165.00	$53,748,534.00
Grand Total	$32,371,879.00	$24,094,668.00	$23,112,025.00	$21,523,012.00	$19,416,548.00	$21,074,215.00	$23,169,090.00	$25,630,457.00	$190,391,894.00

Figure 5-8: Example of PivotTable showing total sales for each sales rep by product.

Notice that the sales reps are listed by row and the products are listed by column. The PivotTable returns the total sales, indicating the use of the SUM function, for each sales rep for each product.

Now, let's say you'd like Excel to answer the following question: How many of each product was sold in each region? As you are primarily concerned with what is happening on a per-region basis, you would put the regions in rows and keep the products in columns. Then you would ask Excel to total the quantity sold of each product in each region, indicating the use of the SUM function.

Sum of Quantity	Column Labels								
Row Labels	Cameras	Computer	Desktops	Laptops	Mobiles	Printers	Television	Washing Machine	Grand Total
East	1209	1190	1127	980	1349	856	1321	1162	9194
North	1165	1718	1115	696	992	1024	898	1106	8714
South	1150	1500	1176	915	839	1425	1035	1250	9290
West	1343	1113	1506	1297	1058	1124	1522	1249	10212
Grand Total	4867	5521	4924	3888	4238	4429	4776	4767	37410

Figure 5-9: Example of PivotTable showing number of each product sold by region.

Notice that the rows and columns in each of these examples represent two of the criteria on which you are analyzing the data. The values throughout the rest of the table represent the third criterion: The values you are asking Excel to calculate based on the other two criteria. This is the basic structure you will use to create most PivotTables. The three keys to structuring your PivotTables are to determine the question you want Excel to answer, to visualize the table you wish to create, and determine what calculation you want Excel to perform.

The PivotTable Tools Contextual Tab

The **PivotTable Tools** contextual tab displays commands and options that are specific to working with PivotTables. Similar to other contextual tabs, the **PivotTable Tools** contextual tab appears when you select a PivotTable and disappears when you select outside the PivotTable. The **PivotTable Tools** contextual tab contains two tabs: the **Analyze** tab and the **Design** tab.

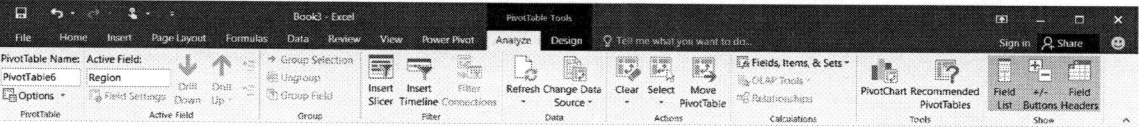

Figure 5-10: The Analyze tab.

The following table identifies the types of commands you will find in the various groups on the **Analyze** tab.

Analyze Tab Group	Contains Commands For
PivotTable	Accessing the **PivotTable Options** dialog box, which enables you to change global PivotTable settings. This group also displays the name of the currently selected PivotTable.
Active Field	Accessing the **Field Settings** and **Value Field Settings** dialog boxes, expanding or collapsing hierarchies in your PivotTables, and drilling down or up in PivotTables created from databases.
Group	Grouping various elements within a PivotTable and managing those groups.
Filter	Accessing and managing filtering commands and options.
Data	Refreshing PivotTable data when the source dataset has been updated, and for modifying the dataset that feeds PivotTables.
Actions	Clearing filtering, selecting elements of a PivotTable, and moving PivotTables in your workbooks.
Calculations	Configuring PivotTable calculations.
Tools	Creating PivotCharts and accessing recommended PivotTables.
Show	Toggling the display of PivotTable elements on or off.

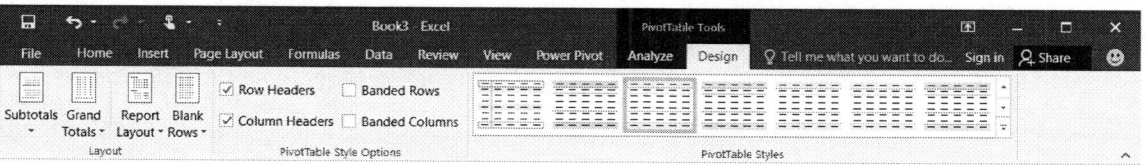

Figure 5-11: The Design tab.

The following table identifies the types of commands you will find in the various **Design** tab groups.

Design Tab Group	Contains Commands For
Layout	Toggling particular functionality on or off, and for modifying the overall layout of PivotTables.
PivotTable Style Options	Toggling the display of PivotTable elements on or off.
PivotTable Styles	Selecting and configuring PivotTable formatting options.

The Value Field Settings Dialog Box

When you select the drop-down arrow of a field in the **VALUES** area of the **PivotTable Fields** task pane, Excel provides you with access to the **Value Field Settings** dialog box. You will use the commands and options in the **Value Field Settings** dialog box to configure the calculations Excel performs on field data in PivotTables, and to configure how Excel displays the results of those calculations. The **Value Field Settings** dialog box is divided into two tabs: the **Summarize Values By** tab and the **Show Values As** tab.

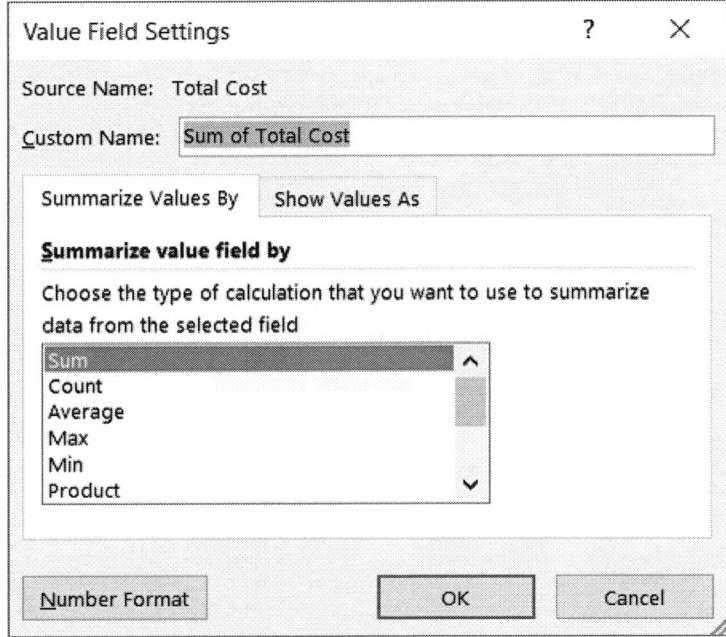

Figure 5–12: The Summarize Values By tab of the Value Field Settings dialog box.

The **Summarize Values By** tab enables you to select which function Excel uses to summarize the data in your PivotTables. The available functions here are the same as those available for creating subtotals and for summarizing table data. For example, you could use the SUM function to find the total of all values that meet the criteria outlined in the PivotTable rows and columns. Or, you could use the AVERAGE function to find the average values of the entries that meet the criteria.

 Note: The default summary function for numerical values is the SUM function. The default summary function for all other values is the COUNT function.

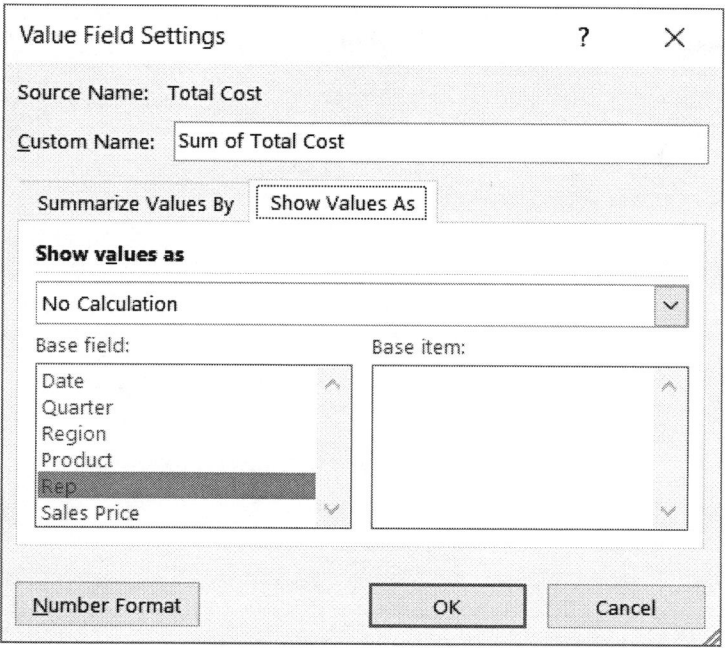

Figure 5-13: The Show Values As tab of the Value Field Settings dialog box.

The **Show Values As** tab provides you with access to options for how you wish to display your summarized PivotTable data. By default, the value here is **No Calculation**, which means the PivotTable will simply summarize your data according to the function selected on the **Summarize Values By** tab. You can also choose to have Excel display the summary data in a variety of other ways. For example, you may wish to show the summarized data as a percentage of the grand total or as a percentage of column or row totals. This could be helpful if you want to know what percentage of your total sales came from a particular region or which sales rep generated the highest percentage of your total or regional sales. Or, you may wish to show a relative comparison between values. For example, you may wish to see how far behind the sales leader other sales reps are in terms of total sales.

One other handy feature of the **Value Field Settings** dialog box is the **Number Format** button. Selecting this will open a scaled-down version of the **Format Cells** dialog box, which contains only the **Number** tab. Use this to change the cell formatting in your PivotTables to accommodate the various types of values you ask Excel to calculate.

Summarize and Show Combinations

Combining the options from the **Summarize Values By** tab and the **Show Values As** tab enables you to gain a deeper understanding of the information in your raw data. Here is a simple example that shows how the summary functions and the **Show Values As** tab options work together to give you new perspectives on your data. Take a look at this PivotTable that displays sales totals for sales reps per region. Here, the sales figures have been dragged to the **VALUES** area of the **PivotTable Fields** task pane, and the default SUM function and **No Calculation** option are selected.

Sum of Total Cost	Column Labels ▾				
Row Labels ▾	East	North	South	West	Grand Total
Hicks	$9,745,162.00	$12,860,316.00	$8,480,956.00	$3,958,705.00	$35,045,139.00
Hogan	$5,159,049.00	$6,402,120.00	$13,747,138.00	$9,859,417.00	$35,167,724.00
Jordan	$10,569,336.00	$5,483,362.00	$4,410,111.00	$3,882,984.00	$24,345,793.00
Ortega	$9,306,912.00	$12,367,815.00	$9,594,379.00	$10,815,598.00	$42,084,704.00
Williams	$15,266,993.00	$13,674,261.00	$13,589,937.00	$11,217,343.00	$53,748,534.00
Grand Total	$50,047,452.00	$50,787,874.00	$49,822,521.00	$39,734,047.00	$190,391,894.00

Figure 5–14: SUM function only.

Now take a look at how selecting the **% of Grand Total** option from the **Show Values As** tab changes your view of the data; the summary function is still the SUM function.

Sum of Total Cost	Column Labels ▾				
Row Labels ▾	East	North	South	West	Grand Total
Hicks	5.12%	6.75%	4.45%	2.08%	18.41%
Hogan	2.71%	3.36%	7.22%	5.18%	18.47%
Jordan	5.55%	2.88%	2.32%	2.04%	12.79%
Ortega	4.89%	6.50%	5.04%	5.68%	22.10%
Williams	8.02%	7.18%	7.14%	5.89%	28.23%
Grand Total	26.29%	26.68%	26.17%	20.87%	100.00%

Figure 5–15: % of Grand Total option.

Now, you can see what percentage of all sales is composed of each rep's sales in each region. Notice also that the grand totals for each row and for each column add up to 100 percent of all total sales. You now have a clear picture of which regions and which sales reps are generating your sales.

Now take a look at what happens when you change the summary function to the AVERAGE function and change the **Show Values As** tab option to **Difference From**. Here, all sales reps' sales averages are being compared to Hicks' sales, as this rep was the one selected in the **Value Field Settings**. You could, however, compare the values to any individual sales rep.

Average of Total Cost	Column Labels ▾				
Row Labels ▾	East	North	South	West	Grand Total
Hicks					
Hogan	-$532,324.50	-$1,076,366.00	$550,384.19	$242,750.88	-$221,193.40
Jordan	$369,390.00	-$1,229,492.33	-$783,476.81	-$18,930.25	-$465,188.96
Ortega	$158,986.00	-$376,555.29	$185,570.50	$362,273.50	$34,991.05
Williams	$788,833.00	-$189,920.14	$851,496.83	$412,491.63	$395,888.80
Grand Total					

Figure 5–16: Difference From option.

Notice that there are no values for Hicks, as this reps values are the ones the PivotTable is comparing the other values to. By looking at this PivotTable, you can see how far behind or ahead of the this rep all other reps are in terms of average regional and overall sales. Here, you see that, Hicks is between the highest and lowest ranges in average total sales. Combining summary functions with the **Show Values As** options is an effective way to gain a deep, granular understanding of the information hidden in your raw data.

 Note: To explore further methods of manipulating your PivotTable data, access LearnTO **Customize the View of a PivotTable** and LearnTO **Enhance a PivotTable With Conditional Formatting** from the **LearnTO** tile on the CHOICE course screen.

The GETPIVOTDATA Function

Once you have a PivotTable report, you may wish to extract a small portion or generate a summary of that data if the PivotTable is large. Fortunately, Excel provides the GETPIVOTDATA function as a way to show data from a PivotTable elsewhere in Excel. For example, you may have configured a PivotTable to show product sales for your regions and someone asks you what the laptop sales were in the Southwest region. While you can look at the PivotTable and determine the answer, you can also use the GETPIVOTDATA function to show this answer in a report on another worksheet.

Syntax: =GETPIVOTDATA(data_field, pivot_table, [field1, item1, field2, item2], ...)

Description: Use the GETPIVOTDATA to retrieve data from a PivotTable report provided that the data is visible in the report.

Required arguments:

- **data_field**: The name, enclosed in quotation marks, for the data field that contains the data that you want to retrieve. For example, "Total Sales".
- **pivot_table**: A reference to any cell, range of cells, or named range of cells in a PivotTable report. This information is used to determine which PivotTable report contains the data that you want to retrieve.

Optional arguments:

- **field1, item1, field2, item2**: One to 126 pairs of field names and item names that describe the data that you want to retrieve. The pairs can be in any order. Field names and names for items other than dates and numbers are enclosed in quotation marks. For example, the pairing of the **Region** field and the item **Southwest** as "Region","Southwest", and the pairing of the **Products** field and the item **Laptop** as "Products","Laptop".

In the following example, the GETPIVOTDATA function entered in B16 retrieves the total sales for the laptops in the Southwest region.

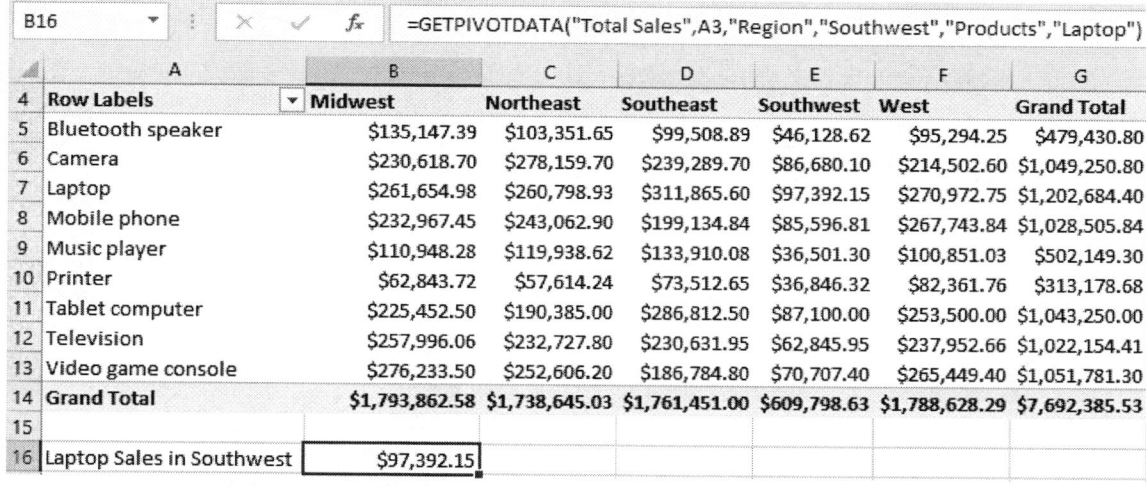

B16	▼ : ✕ ✓ *fx*	=GETPIVOTDATA("Total Sales",A3,"Region","Southwest","Products","Laptop")					
	A	B	C	D	E	F	G
4	Row Labels ▼	Midwest	Northeast	Southeast	Southwest	West	Grand Total
5	Bluetooth speaker	$135,147.39	$103,351.65	$99,508.89	$46,128.62	$95,294.25	$479,430.80
6	Camera	$230,618.70	$278,159.70	$239,289.70	$86,680.10	$214,502.60	$1,049,250.80
7	Laptop	$261,654.98	$260,798.93	$311,865.60	$97,392.15	$270,972.75	$1,202,684.40
8	Mobile phone	$232,967.45	$243,062.90	$199,134.84	$85,596.81	$267,743.84	$1,028,505.84
9	Music player	$110,948.28	$119,938.62	$133,910.08	$36,501.30	$100,851.03	$502,149.30
10	Printer	$62,843.72	$57,614.24	$73,512.65	$36,846.32	$82,361.76	$313,178.68
11	Tablet computer	$225,452.50	$190,385.00	$286,812.50	$87,100.00	$253,500.00	$1,043,250.00
12	Television	$257,996.06	$232,727.80	$230,631.95	$62,845.95	$237,952.66	$1,022,154.41
13	Video game console	$276,233.50	$252,606.20	$186,784.80	$70,707.40	$265,449.40	$1,051,781.30
14	Grand Total	$1,793,862.58	$1,738,645.03	$1,761,451.00	$609,798.63	$1,788,628.29	$7,692,385.53
15							
16	Laptop Sales in Southwest	$97,392.15					

Figure 5–17: The GETPIVOTDATA Function.

 Access the Checklist tile on your **CHOICE** Course screen for reference information and job aids on **How to Analyze PivotTable Data.**

ACTIVITY 5-2
Analyzing PivotTable Data

Before You Begin
The workbook **My Sales Data.xlsx** is open.

Scenario
You are pleased with the PivotTable reports you have created. You now want to see what other information you can glean from the PivotTable. You decide to see if you can answer the following questions:

- What are 4th quarter sales?
- What is the total sales for each quarter by region?
- What are the total sales for each region by product?

---

1. Modify the PivotTable report on Sheet1 to answer the question, What are the 4th quarter sales values?
   a) Select **Sheet1** and verify that the PivotTable is selected.
   b) In the **PivotTable Fields** task pane, in **Choose fields to add to report**, drag & drop **Quarter** to the **FILTERS** area.
   c) Verify that **Quarter** is in cell **A1** and a filter is in cell **B1**.
   d) Select the drop-down arrow in cell **B1** and select **Quarter 4** and then select **OK**.
   e) Verify that Quarter 4 total sales are **1,842,121.272**.

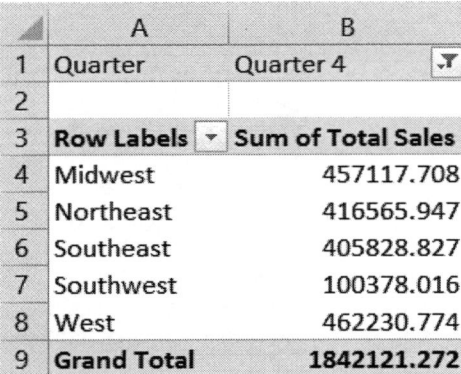

	A	B
1	Quarter	Quarter 4
2		
3	**Row Labels** ▾	**Sum of Total Sales**
4	Midwest	457117.708
5	Northeast	416565.947
6	Southeast	405828.827
7	Southwest	100378.016
8	West	462230.774
9	**Grand Total**	**1842121.272**

2. Clear the filter from Quarter and modify the PivotTable report to answer the question, What are the total sales by region for each quarter?
   a) Select the **AutoFilter** drop-down arrow in cell **B1** and select **All** and then select **OK**.
   b) In the **PivotTable Fields** task pane, in the **Drag fields between areas below** section, drag & drop **Quarter** to the **COLUMNS** area.

c) Verify that the PivotTable report updates to show you total sales for each region by quarter.

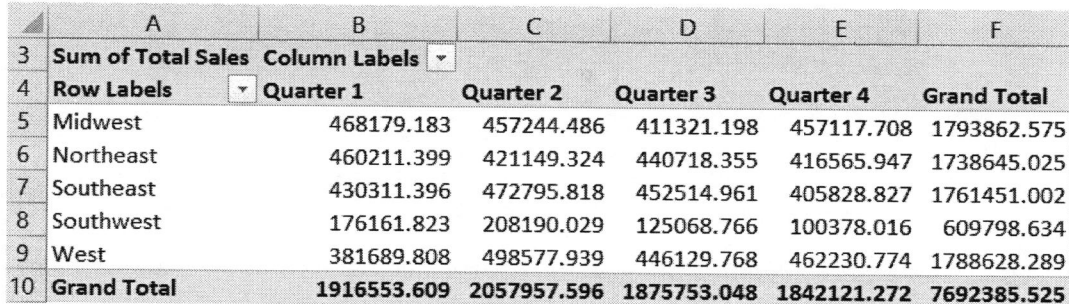

	A	B	C	D	E	F
3	**Sum of Total Sales**	**Column Labels**				
4	**Row Labels**	**Quarter 1**	**Quarter 2**	**Quarter 3**	**Quarter 4**	**Grand Total**
5	Midwest	468179.183	457244.486	411321.198	457117.708	1793862.575
6	Northeast	460211.399	421149.324	440718.355	416565.947	1738645.025
7	Southeast	430311.396	472795.818	452514.961	405828.827	1761451.002
8	Southwest	176161.823	208190.029	125068.766	100378.016	609798.634
9	West	381689.808	498577.939	446129.768	462230.774	1788628.289
10	**Grand Total**	**1916553.609**	**2057957.596**	**1875753.048**	**1842121.272**	**7692385.525**

3. Modify the PivotTable on Sheet2 to answer the question, What are the total sales for each region by product?

a) Select **Sheet2** and verify that the **PivotTable** is selected.

b) In the **PivotTable Fields** task pane, in the **Drag fields between areas below** section, drag & drop **Products** to the **COLUMNS** area.

c) Verify that the PivotTable report updates to show you regional sales for each product.

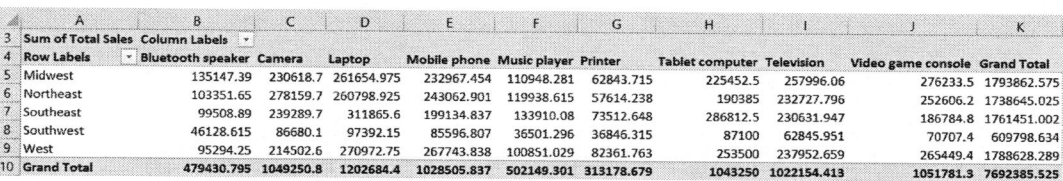

	A	B	C	D	E	F	G	H	I	J	K
3	Sum of Total Sales	Column Labels									
4	Row Labels	Bluetooth speaker	Camera	Laptop	Mobile phone	Music player	Printer	Tablet computer	Television	Video game console	Grand Total
5	Midwest	135147.39	230618.7	261654.975	232967.454	110948.281	62843.715	225452.5	257996.06	276233.5	1793862.575
6	Northeast	103351.65	278159.7	260798.925	243062.901	119938.615	57614.238	190385	232727.796	252606.2	1738645.025
7	Southeast	99508.89	239289.7	311865.6	199134.837	133910.08	73512.648	286812.5	230631.947	186784.8	1761451.002
8	Southwest	46128.615	86680.1	97392.15	85596.807	36501.296	36846.315	87100	62845.951	70707.4	609798.634
9	West	95294.25	214502.6	270972.75	267743.838	100851.029	82361.763	253500	237952.659	265449.4	1788628.289
10	Grand Total	479430.795	1049250.8	1202684.4	1028505.837	502149.301	313178.679	1043250	1022154.413	1051781.3	7692385.525

4. Modify the formatting of the PivotTable report.

a) In the **PivotTable Fields** task pane, in the **Drag fields between areas below** section, in the VALUES area, select the **Sum of Total Sales** drop-down arrow and select **Value Field Settings**.

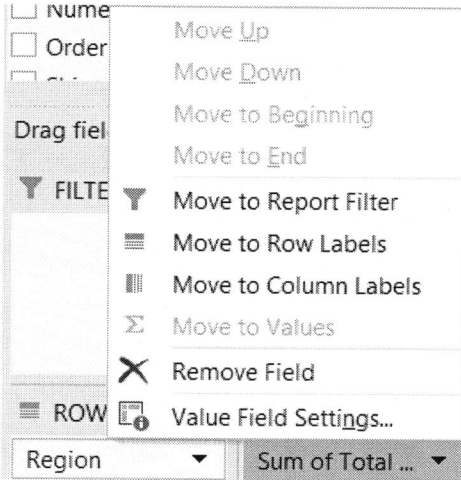

b) In the **Value Field Settings** dialog box, select **Number Format**.

c) In the **Format Cells** dialog box, on the **Number** tab, from the **Category** list box, select **Currency**.

d) In the **Decimal places** spin box type *0*, and then select **OK**.

e) In the **Value Field Settings** dialog box, select **OK**.

f) Verify the PivotTable updated the total sales values with the currency format.

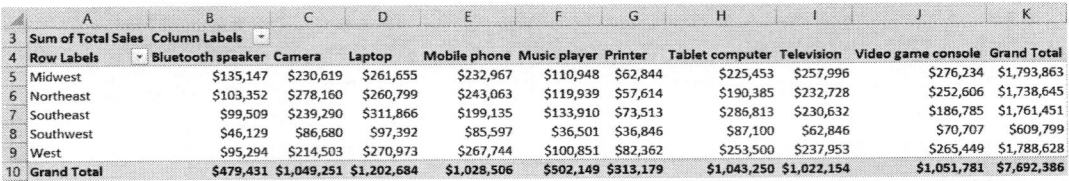

	A	B	C	D	E	F	G	H	I	J	K
3	Sum of Total Sales	Column Labels									
4	Row Labels	Bluetooth speaker	Camera	Laptop	Mobile phone	Music player	Printer	Tablet computer	Television	Video game console	Grand Total
5	Midwest	$135,147	$230,619	$261,655	$232,967	$110,948	$62,844	$225,453	$257,996	$276,234	$1,793,863
6	Northeast	$103,352	$278,160	$260,799	$243,063	$119,939	$57,614	$190,385	$232,728	$252,606	$1,738,645
7	Southeast	$99,509	$239,290	$311,866	$199,135	$133,910	$73,513	$286,813	$230,632	$186,785	$1,761,451
8	Southwest	$46,129	$86,680	$97,392	$85,597	$36,501	$36,846	$87,100	$62,846	$70,707	$609,799
9	West	$95,294	$214,503	$270,973	$267,744	$100,851	$82,362	$253,500	$237,953	$265,449	$1,788,628
10	Grand Total	$479,431	$1,049,251	$1,202,684	$1,028,506	$502,149	$313,179	$1,043,250	$1,022,154	$1,051,781	$7,692,386

5. Sort the **Grand Total** values in smallest to largest order.
   a) Select one of the **Grand Total** values in column **K**.
   b) Select **Home→Editing→Sort & Filter→Sort Smallest to Largest**.
   c) Verify that the Grand Totals are sorted in smallest to largest order.

Grand Total
$609,799
$1,738,645
$1,761,451
$1,788,628
$1,793,863
$7,692,386

6. Save the workbook and keep the file open.

TOPIC C

Present Data with PivotCharts

Although PivotTables provide you with an amazing array of options for analyzing your data, they have one downfall in common with other worksheet data: they can be difficult to read. You know you can convert the data in your worksheet ranges and tables into visually appealing, easy-to-interpret charts. You also know that doing so makes it easier for your audience to gather meaning from all of that data with just a glance. Wouldn't it be nice if you could do the same with PivotTable data?

The good news is that Excel 2016 provides you with a quick and easy way to translate your PivotTable data into charts just as you can do with your other data. Taking the time to familiarize yourself with this functionality will provide you with all of the benefits of Excel charts when it comes to presenting the data you analyze by using PivotTables.

PivotCharts

Like standard Excel charts, *PivotCharts* are graphical representations of numeric values and relationships among those values. The main difference is simply that PivotCharts are linked to PivotTable data, whereas standard charts are linked to either a range of data or a table. As with charts, when you alter the data in a PivotTable, PivotCharts update automatically to reflect the changes. As you drag fields from one area to another, update the PivotTable data, and modify the summary function and **Show Values As** options, your PivotCharts will dynamically change to reflect the changes in the PivotTable.

Excel provides you with many of the same options for formatting your PivotCharts, including the ability to change chart types, as it does with charts. And, the same considerations apply for deciding which chart type to select and which chart elements you should include in your PivotCharts. You use the **Insert Chart** dialog box to create PivotCharts from PivotTables. To create a PivotChart, you can access the **Insert Chart** dialog box from the **Charts** group on the **Insert** tab, or by selecting **Analyze→Tools→PivotChart** from the **PivotTable Tools** contextual tab.

	A	B	C	D	E	F
3	**Sum of Total Cost**	**Column Labels**				
4	**Row Labels**	**East**	**North**	**South**	**West**	**Grand Total**
5	Hicks	$9,745,162.00	$12,860,316.00	$8,480,956.00	$3,958,705.00	$35,045,139.00
6	Hogan	$5,159,049.00	$6,402,120.00	$13,747,138.00	$9,859,417.00	$35,167,724.00
7	Jordan	$10,569,336.00	$5,483,362.00	$4,410,111.00	$3,882,984.00	$24,345,793.00
8	Ortega	$9,306,912.00	$12,367,815.00	$9,594,379.00	$10,815,598.00	$42,084,704.00
9	Williams	$15,266,993.00	$13,674,261.00	$13,589,937.00	$11,217,343.00	$53,748,534.00
10	**Grand Total**	**$50,047,452.00**	**$50,787,874.00**	**$49,822,521.00**	**$39,734,047.00**	**$190,391,894.00**

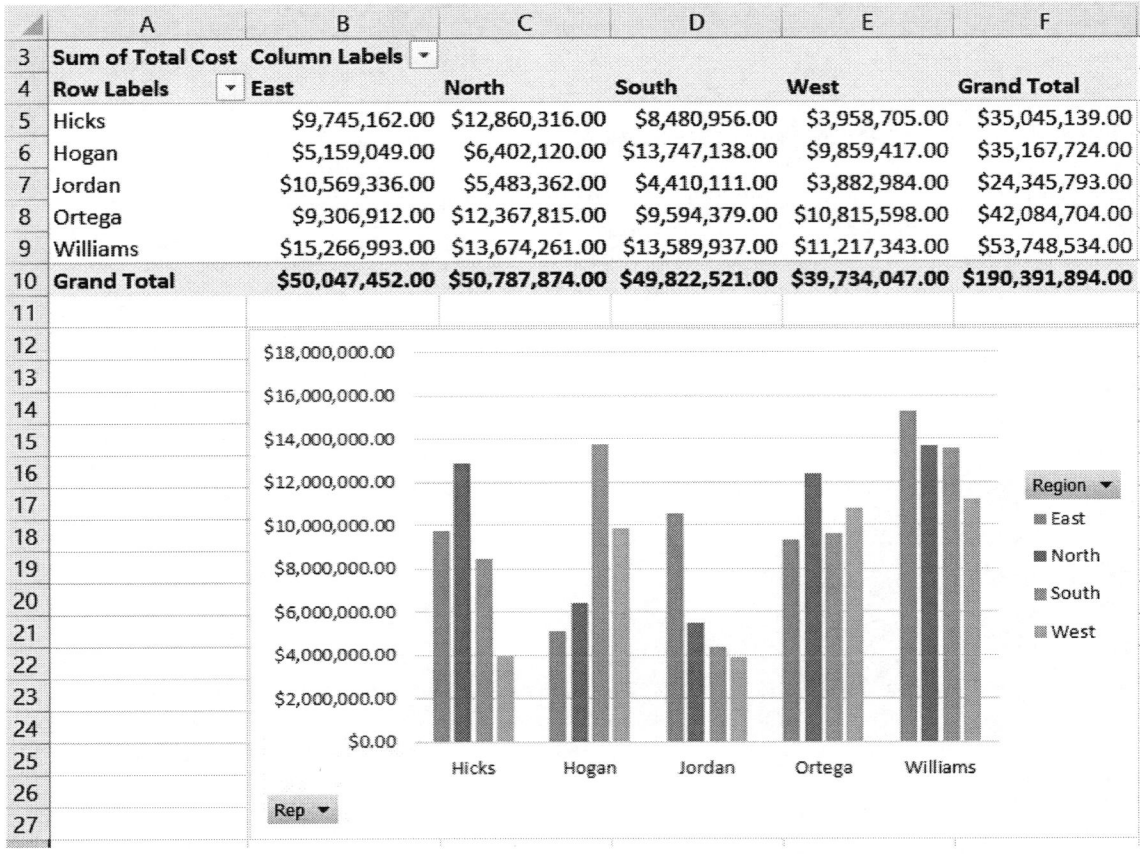

Figure 5-18: A PivotChart and its associated PivotTable.

The PivotChart Fields Task Pane

When you select a cell within a PivotTable, Excel displays the **PivotTable Fields** task pane. Likewise, when you select a PivotChart or a PivotChart element, Excel displays the **PivotChart Fields** task pane. These task panes are essentially the same. The only notable difference is that, on the **PivotChart Fields** task pane, the **ROWS** area appears as the **AXIS (CATEGORIES)** area and the **COLUMNS** area appears as the **LEGEND (SERIES)** area. Functionally, the two task panes are virtually identical.

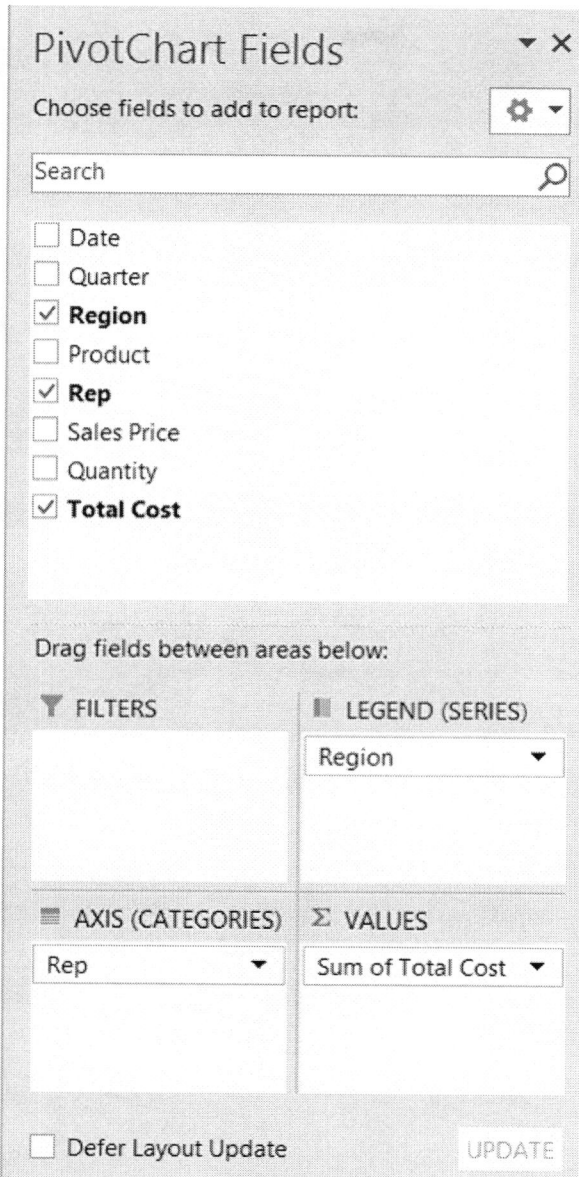

Figure 5-19: The PivotChart Fields task pane.

PivotChart Filters

One of the added benefits of PivotCharts is that they include their own set of filters, which are linked to the filters on the associated PivotTable. These filters correspond to the fields you drag to the **COLUMNS** and **ROWS** areas in the **PivotTable Fields** task pane (or the corresponding areas in the **PivotChart Fields** task pane), and they display the same filter and sorting options available on the PivotTable. Whether you filter or sort your data by using the options on the PivotTable or the options on the PivotChart, Excel updates both objects simultaneously. By right-clicking the PivotChart filters, you have access to the same context menus that open when you select fields in the various areas at the bottom of the **PivotTable Fields** task pane or the **PivotChart Fields** task pane.

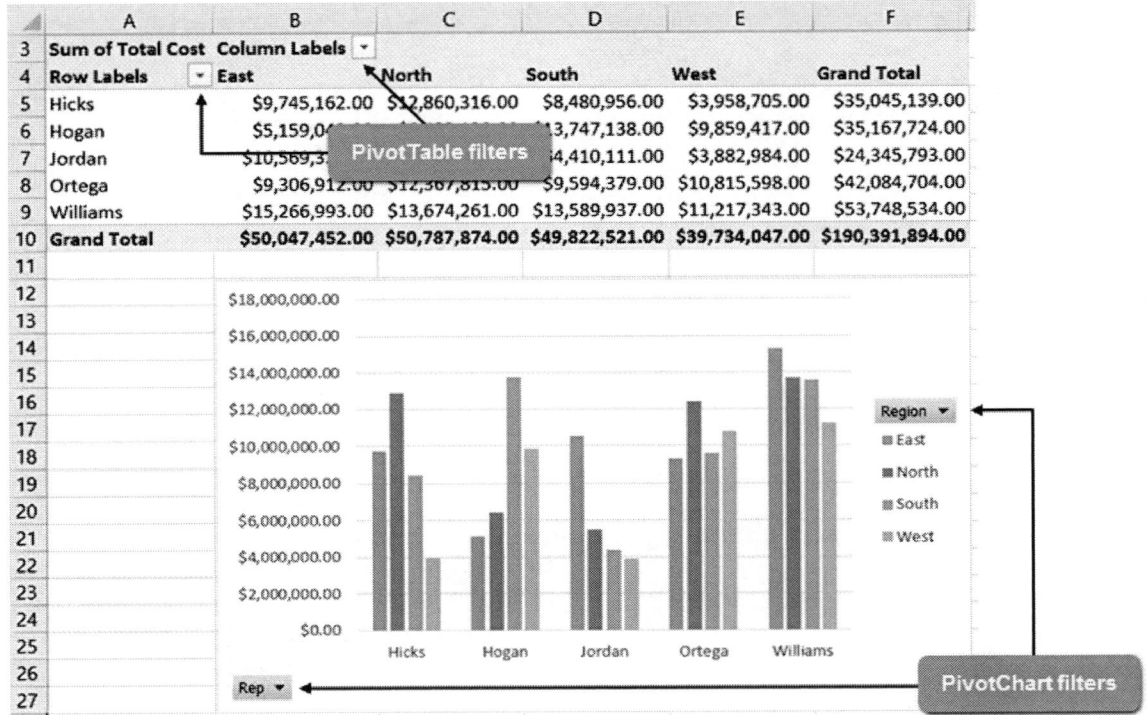

Figure 5–20: Changes made with either the PivotTable filters or the PivotChart filters reflected in both objects.

 Access the Checklist tile on your CHOICE Course screen for reference information and job aids on How to Create and Work with a PivotChart.

ACTIVITY 5-3
Presenting Data with PivotCharts

Before You Begin
The workbook **My Sales Data.xlsx** is open.

Scenario
You are pleased with the modifications you have made to the PivotTable reports you have created. You know that when you present this data to management they will want to see the data represented visually. You decide to create a PivotChart from one of your PivotTable reports.

1. Create a PivotChart from the PivotTable on Sheet1.
   a) Select **Sheet1** and verify that the PivotTable is selected.
   b) On the **PivotTable Tools** contextual tab, select **Analyze→Tools→PivotChart**.
   c) In the **Insert Chart** dialog box, on the **All Charts** tab, verify that the **Column** chart category is selected and select the fourth subtype, **3-D Clustered Column** and select **OK**.
   d) Verify that a 3-D clustered column chart depicts total sales for each region by quarter.

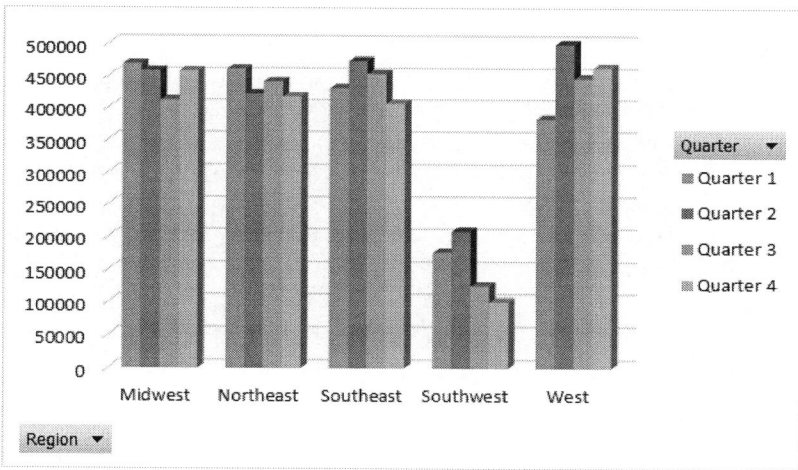

2. Examine the Southwest region, as you can see the total sales in this region are lower than in other regions.
   a) On the **PivotChart**, select the **Region** field button drop-down arrow and deselect **(Select All)**. Select **Southwest**, and then select **OK**.

b) You see that there is a decline in sales after the second quarter in the Southwest region.

 Note: When filtering is applied to a PivotChart, the same filtering is applied to the PivotTable.

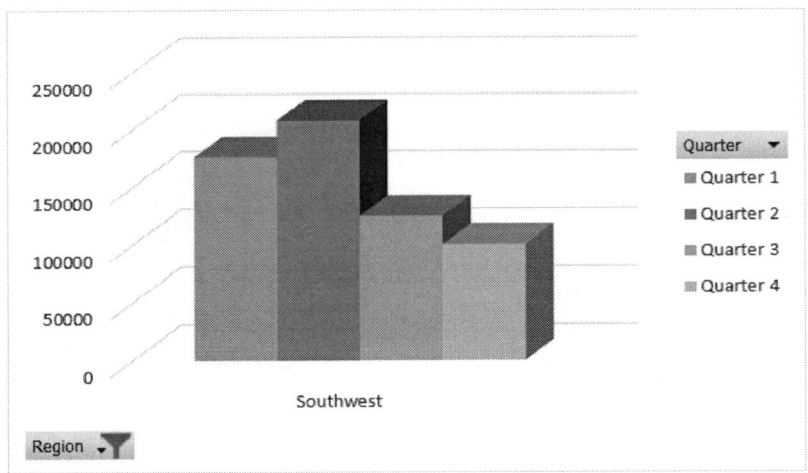

3. Create an additional PivotChart for the PivotTable on Sheet2 in order to examine the product sales for the Southwest.

   a) Select **Sheet2** and verify that the PivotTable is selected.
   b) On the **PivotTable Tools** contextual tab, select **Analyze→Tools→PivotChart**.
   c) In the **Insert Chart** dialog box, on the **All Charts** tab, verify that the **Column** chart category is selected and select the fourth subtype, **3-D Clustered Column** and select **OK**.
   d) Move the PivotChart next to the PivotTable, as necessary.
   e) On the **PivotTable**, select the **Row Labels AutoFilter** drop-down arrow in cell **A4** and deselect **(Select All)**. Select **Southwest**, and then select **OK**.
   f) Verify that the filtering of the PivotTable updated the PivotChart to display total sales of products in the Southwest region. You can see that sales of music players and printers are low in this region.

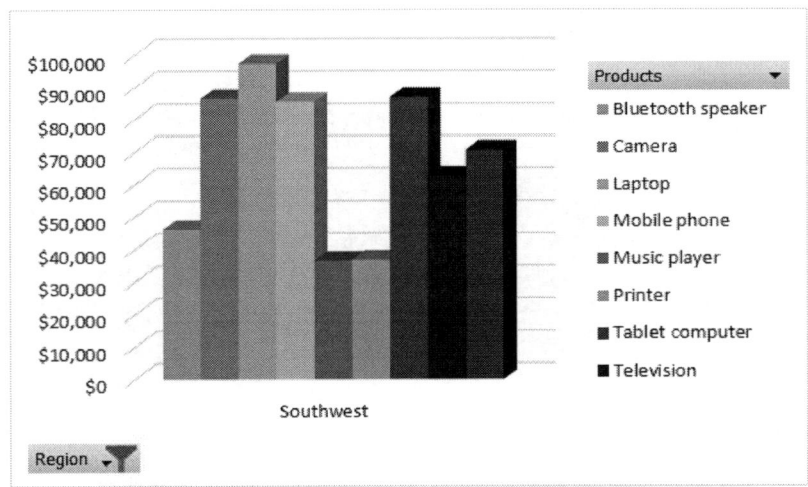

4. Modify the design of the PivotChart and explore details of the Southwest region.

   a) Select **Sheet1** and select the PivotChart, if necessary.
   b) On the **PivotChart Tools** contextual tab, select **Design→Chart Styles→Style 8**.

Note: You may have to select the **More** button on the **Chart Styles** gallery.

c) Double-click any column of the PivotChart.

d) In the **Show Detail** dialog box, select **State** and select **OK**.

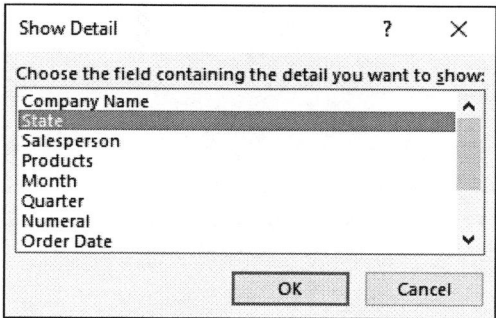

e) Move the PivotChart next to the PivotTable, as necessary.

f) Observe that the PivotChart and PivotTable are updated with the states in the Southwest region.

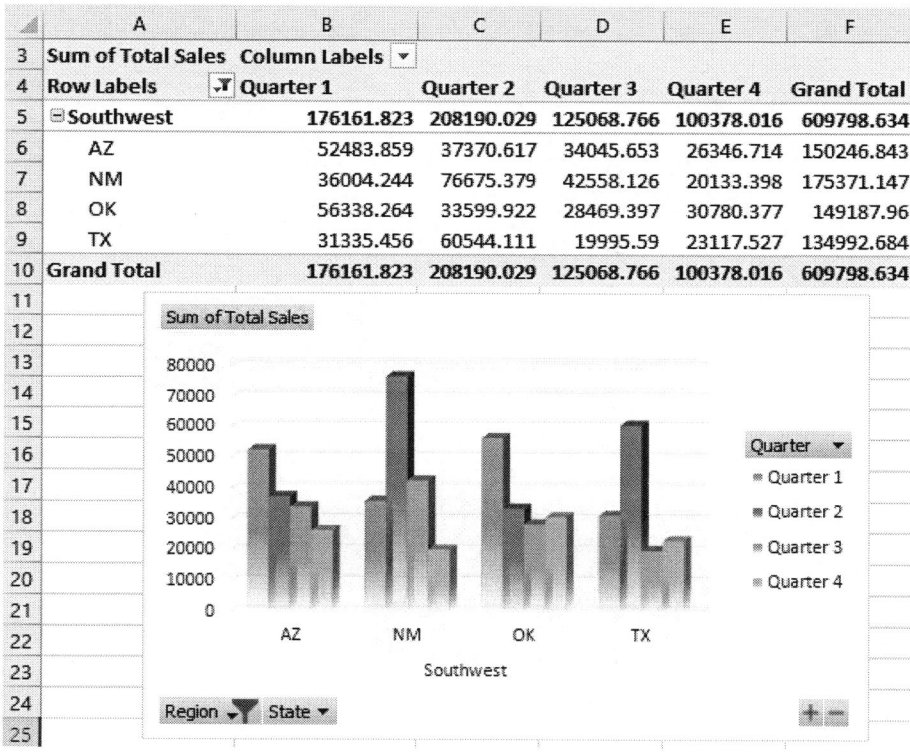

5. Save the workbook and keep the file open.

TOPIC D

Filter Data by Using Timelines and Slicers

The ability to filter your PivotTables enables you to drill down into your raw data to view the fine detail that lies within. As you likely have many questions to ask of your data, it can quickly become tedious to have to open drop-down menus, determine what items are filtered out, clear the filtering, and then re-filter your data to find the next answer. This is especially true if data analysis is one of your key functions. If you fall into this category of Excel users, you'll likely appreciate the ability to quickly and easily re-filter your PivotTables on any number of fields. In addition, the ability to quickly view the filters applied to the current dataset could come in handy if you're returning to a worksheet after having not worked in it for a while.

In short, you need some type of tool that gives you a high level of control over PivotTable filtering; one that is easy to work with and easy to interpret regardless of how many filters you apply to your PivotTables. Excel 2016 includes such a tool. Gaining an understanding of how this feature works will give you a greater level of control over your PivotTable filtering and the peace of mind of knowing that you have filtered your data in precisely the manner you meant to.

Slicers

Slicers are PivotTable filtering tools that you can link to various PivotTables in your worksheets. You can create a slicer out of any of the fields associated with a PivotTable, and then use those slicers to filter each field by any of its unique entries. Although a slicer is typically associated with a single PivotTable, you can link slicers to multiple PivotTables; this is typically done for PivotTables that are associated with the same raw dataset. This can be handy, for example, if you want to create multiple versions of the same PivotTable, create a unique structure for each to answer various questions about your data, and then filter them by the same criteria simultaneously.

Each unique value in a field appears as a separate button on the associated slicer. By default, slicer buttons appear highlighted in blue when the filter is inactive, meaning the associated value will appear in the PivotTable. When the filter is active, meaning the value has been removed from the PivotTable, the button appears white. When you first create a slicer, all filters are inactive, so all of the buttons are highlighted in blue. Selecting a slicer button activates all of the other filters, meaning only the value you selected will appear in the table. This may, at first, seem counterintuitive, but it makes sense when you think about it in this way: selecting a button displays the associated value in a PivotTable. To select multiple slicer buttons simultaneously, enable the **Multi-Select** button or press and hold down **Ctrl** while making your selections. Selecting the **Clear Filter** button deactivates all filters on a slicer, meaning all values will appear in the PivotTable.

 Note: As PivotTables and their associated PivotCharts are connected, any filtering you apply to one using slicers applies to both automatically.

Slicer buttons may also appear slightly grayed-out. Excel does this when some active filter has removed the associated values from view. Grayed-out slicer buttons are inactive, as you cannot filter on values that do not appear in the PivotTable. Clearing the filter that is suppressing the values from view will reactivate the associated slicer button(s).

The default slicer formatting is blue and white, but you can customize the display of slicers to match your worksheet formatting. You can place slicers anywhere on your worksheets or resize them as you like. You can even place copies of slicers in multiple locations. The original slicer and the copies remain linked, so whatever you do to one affects the others. This is true only of filtering tasks, not visual formatting.

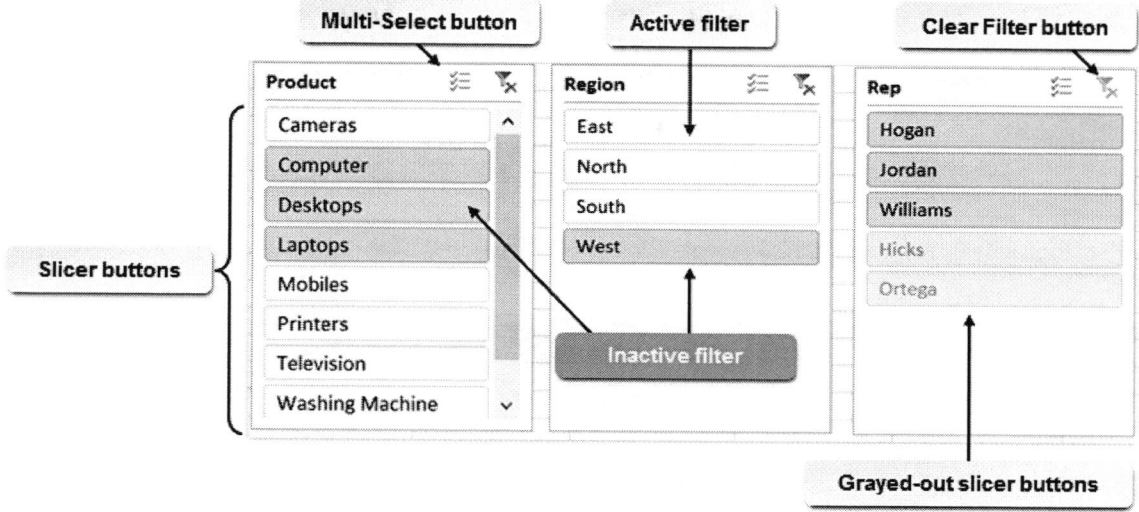

Figure 5-21: Use slicers to quickly and easily apply multiple filters to your PivotTables.

The Insert Slicers Dialog Box

You use the **Insert Slicers** dialog box to create slicers out of the various fields in your PivotTables. Each field appears as a check box option in the dialog box. To create a slicer out of a particular field, check the associated check box. You can access the **Insert Slicers** dialog box on the **PivotTable Tools** contextual tab by selecting **Analyze→Filter→Insert Slicer**.

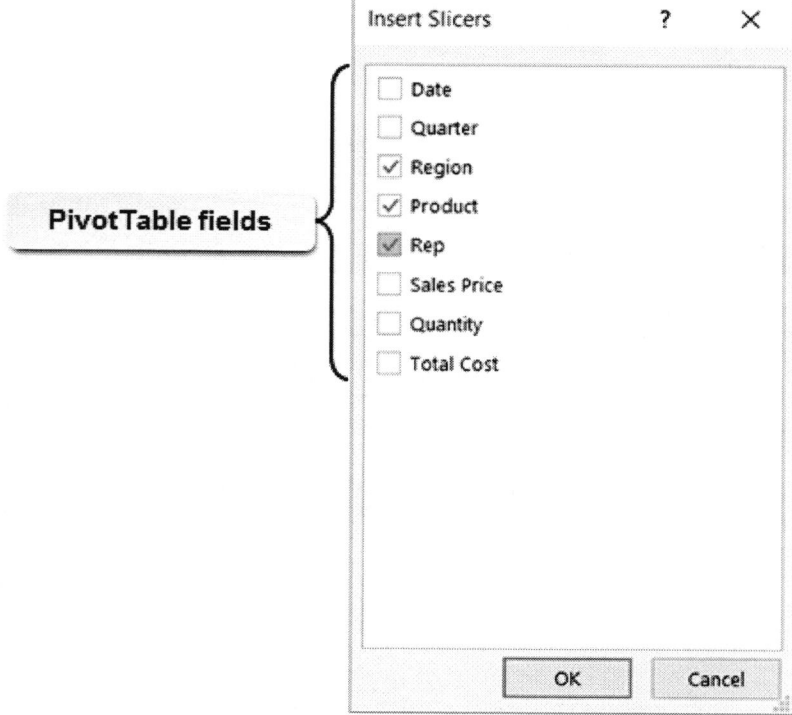

Figure 5-22: The Insert Slicers dialog box enables you to create slicers out of any PivotTable field.

The Slicer Tools Contextual Tab

You can access the commands you will use to work with PivotTable slicers on the **Slicer Tools** contextual tab. The **Slicer Tools** contextual tab appears when you select a slicer and disappears when you select any non-slicer object. It contains only a single tab: the **Options** tab.

If you select multiple slicers simultaneously, some of the commands on the **Slicer Tools** contextual tab remain active and others become deactivated. For example, you can typically resize or apply formatting to multiple slicers at the same time, but you can only manage slicer connections one at a time.

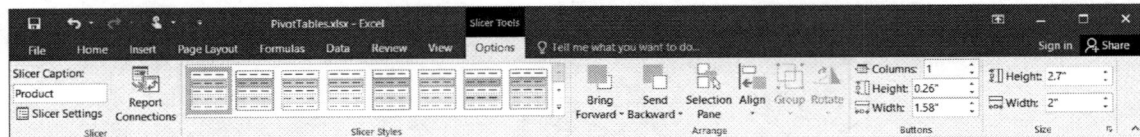

Figure 5-23: The Slicer Tools contextual tab.

The following table describes the types of commands you will find in the command groups on the **Slicer Tools** contextual tab.

Slicer Tools Contextual Tab Group	Contains Commands For
Slicer	Renaming slicers, accessing slicer options, and managing slicer connections to PivotTables.
Slicer Styles	Applying formatting to slicers.
Arrange	Configuring the arrangement of slicers on screen. You can use the commands in this group to order slicers from front to back, align slicers with other objects, group slicers, and rotate the display of slicers.
Buttons	Modifying the size and alignment of slicer buttons. Changes you make here can also affect the size of the slicers themselves.
Size	Modifying the size of slicers. Changes you make here can also affect the display of slicer buttons.

The Report Connections Dialog Box

You can use the **Report Connections** dialog box to manage slicer connections. All PivotTables that are associated with the same raw dataset can share slicers. These *shared slicers* affect all PivotTables that share them, so what you filter in one PivotTable is filtered in all PivotTables that share the slicer. It is important to note that PivotTables that are associated with the same raw dataset do not have to share slicers. You can create unique slicers for each one that filters the same fields independently. It is only the slicers that you connect to multiple PivotTables that will affect them all simultaneously. You can access the **Report Connections** dialog box from the **Slicer Tools** contextual tab by selecting **Options→Slicer→Report Connections**. The name of the field associated with the currently selected slicer appears in the **Report Connections** dialog box's title bar.

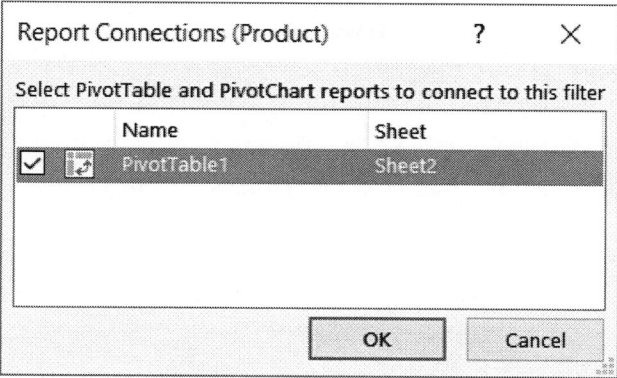

Figure 5-24: Use the Report Connections dialog box to manage slicer connections.

Timelines

As with slicers, *timelines* are PivotTable filtering tools that you can link to various PivotTables in your worksheets. You can create a timeline out of any date field associated with a PivotTable, and then use timelines to filter by any of its unique date entries. Although a timeline is typically associated with a single PivotTable, you can link timelines to multiple PivotTables; this is typically done for PivotTables that are associated with the same raw dataset. Use the **Report Connections** dialog box to associate a timeline with more than one PivotTable. From the **Timeline Tools** contextual tab, select **Options→Timeline→Report Connections**.

 Note: As PivotTables and their associated PivotCharts are connected, any filtering you apply to one using timelines applies to both automatically.

The default timeline formatting is blue and white, but you can customize the display of timelines to match your worksheet formatting. You can place timelines anywhere on your worksheets or resize them as you like.

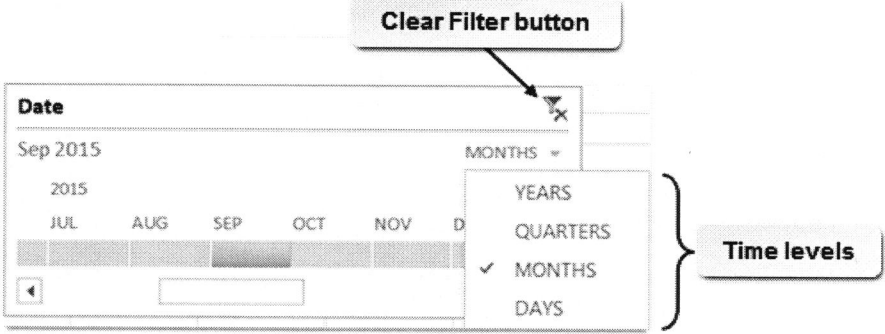

Figure 5-25: Use timelines to quickly and easily apply date filters to your PivotTables.

The Insert Timelines Dialog Box

You use the **Insert Timelines** dialog box to create a timeline out of the date fields in your PivotTables. Each field appears as a check box option in the dialog box. To create a timeline out of a particular field, check the associated check box. You can access the **Insert Timelines** dialog box from the **PivotTable Tools** contextual tab by selecting **Analyze→Filter→Insert Timelines**.

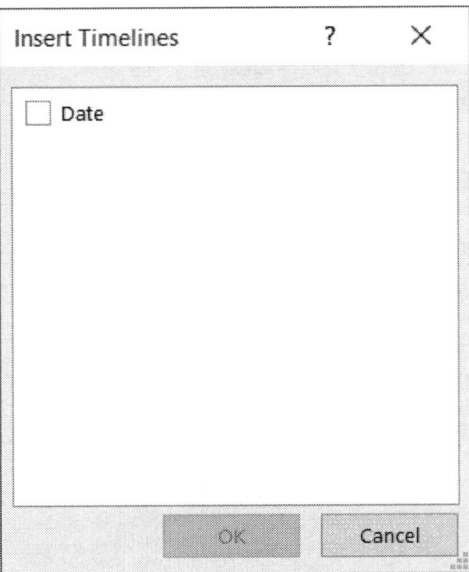

Figure 5-26: The Insert Timelines dialog box enables you to create a timeline out of any PivotTable date field.

The Timeline Tools Contextual Tab

You can access the commands you will use to work with PivotTable timelines on the **Timeline Tools** contextual tab. The **Timeline Tools** contextual tab appears when you select a timeline and disappears when you select any non-timeline object. It contains only a single tab; the **Options** tab.

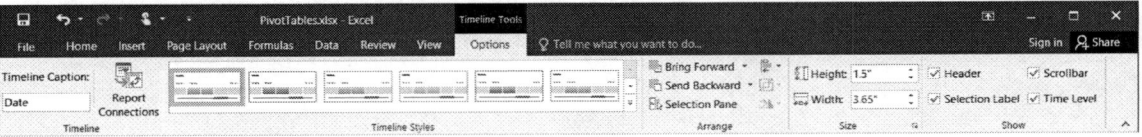

Figure 5-27: The Timeline Tools contextual tab.

The following table describes the types of commands you will find in the command groups on the **Timeline Tools** contextual tab.

Timeline Tools Contextual Tab Group	Contains Commands For
Timeline	Renaming a timeline and managing timeline connections to PivotTables.
Timeline Styles	Applying formatting to timelines.
Arrange	Configuring the arrangement of timelines on screen. You can use the commands in this group to order timelines from front to back, align timelines with other objects, and group timelines.
Size	Modifying the size of the timeline.
Show	Showing or hiding various elements on the timeline.

 Access the Checklist tile on your CHOICE Course screen for reference information and job aids on How to Insert and Work with Slicers and Timelines.

ACTIVITY 5-4
Filtering Data by Using Slicers and Timelines

Before You Begin
The workbook **My Sales Data.xlsx** is open.

Scenario
You are pleased with the modifications you have made to the PivotTable reports and the new PivotCharts you have created. You realize that the initial questions you asked to analyze your data were from your own perspective. In order to make the PivotTables and PivotCharts more flexible, you decide to create a timeline and insert slicers. This will enable you and anyone else to view sales data in many ways.

---

1. Insert a timeline to view fourth quarter sales values for the Southwest region.
   a) Verify that **Sheet2** is selected and move the PivotChart to clearly see the PivotTable, if necessary.
   b) Select the **PivotTable** and on the **PivotTable Tools** contextual tab, select **Analyze→Filter→Insert Timeline**.
   c) In the **Insert Timelines** dialog box, check **Order Date** and select **OK**.
   d) Move the timeline to clearly see all worksheet objects, if necessary.
   e) Select the **Time Level** drop-down arrow and select **Quarters**.

    Note: Excel groups months into quarters based on the calendar year.

   f) Select **Q4** of 2016 and verify that both the PivotTable and PivotChart update to show only Q4 values.

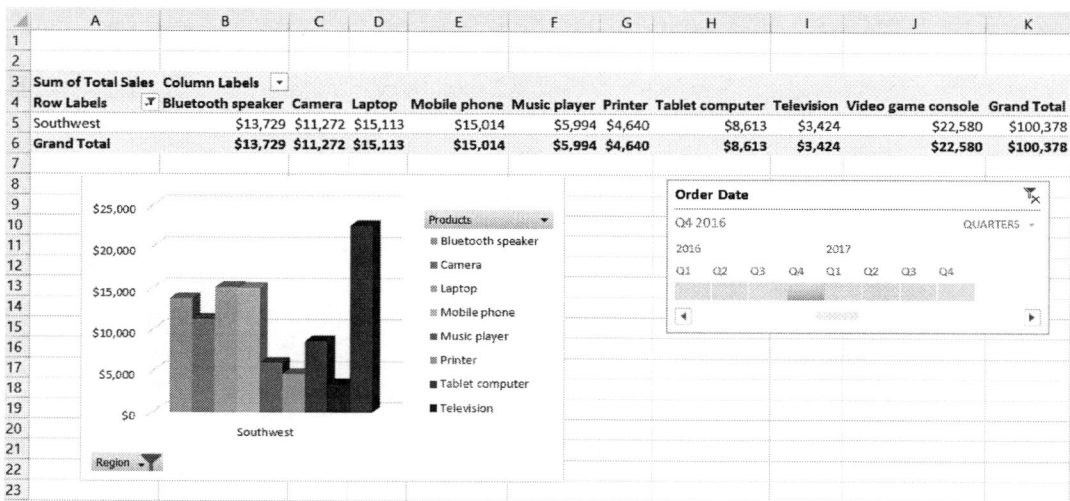

2. Insert slicers to filter the PivotTable and PivotChart.
   a) Select the **PivotTable**, if necessary, and on the **PivotTable Tools** contextual tab, select **Analyze→Filter→Insert Slicer**.
   b) In the **Insert Slicer** dialog box, check **Salesperson** and **State**, and then select **OK**.
   c) Move the **Salesperson** and **State** slicers as necessary to clearly see all worksheet objects.

---

3. Using the slicers, filter for sales in New Mexico and Texas for the salesperson Anderson.

   a) In the **State** slicer, select **Multi-Select**.
   b) Select **AZ** and **OK** to disable those states.

   c) In the **Salesperson** slicer, select **Anderson**.
   d) Verify the PivotTable and the PivotChart update to show total sales for Anderson in TX in Q4, noting that Anderson does not have sales in NM.

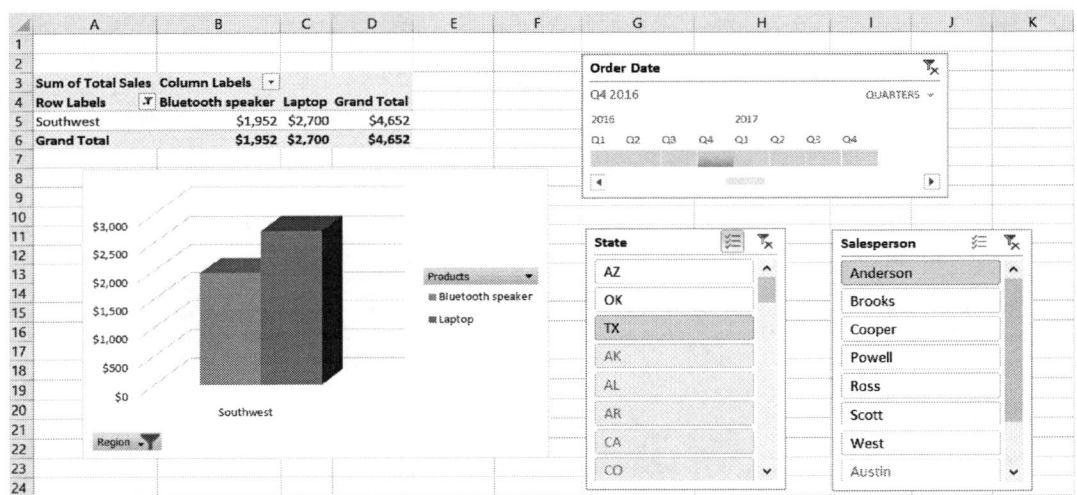

4. Save and close the workbook.

Summary

In this lesson, you used PivotTables, PivotCharts, slicers, and timelines to analyze and present your data. The ability to crunch and re-crunch your numbers, ask incredibly detailed questions of your data, present your results in an easily digestible manner, and do it all over again without affecting your raw data puts the power of information right in your hands. As the volume of data and the speed at which organizations generate it continues to grow, your ability to mine actionable intelligence from it becomes increasingly critical and can give you the competitive edge needed to succeed.

How do you see PivotTables and PivotCharts helping you with your regular tasks?

When might you use slicers?

 Note: Check your CHOICE Course screen for opportunities to interact with your classmates, peers, and the larger CHOICE online community about the topics covered in this course or other topics you are interested in. From the Course screen you can also access available resources for a more continuous learning experience.

Course Follow-Up

Congratulations! You have completed the *Microsoft® Office Excel® 2016: Part 2* course. You have learned how to use powerful functions to manipulate your data and to sort, filter, and query the data to summarize it in meaningful ways. In addition, you have created tables, applied conditional formatting and created charts to show data in a visual way. And finally, you learned how to create PivotTables and PivotCharts as a way to continually analyze your data from many viewpoints.

To gain a competitive edge in today's market, decision makers need to have a keen understanding of what's happening within their organizations. They need to be able to ask specific questions and get specific answers even when sifting through massive amounts of data. Becoming proficient at engaging your data in an ongoing dialogue to find these answers means you'll be able to provide the decision makers within your organization with the intelligence they need to keep you ahead of the competition. The more you know about Excel's analysis tools and formula and function syntax, the better you'll be able to analyze and examine your raw data to find the nuanced patterns and opportunities that could mean the difference between running with the pack and staying one step ahead of everyone else.

What's Next?

Microsoft® Office Excel® 2016: Part 3 is the next course in this series. In that course, you will build upon the skills you have acquired by working with multiple worksheets and workbooks, use lookup functions and formula auditing to troubleshoot your workbooks and fix errors, and to share and protect workbooks from unwanted changes. You will also learn to automate Excel functions, create sparklines and map data, as well as to forecast future data. You are also encouraged to explore Excel further by actively participating in any of the social media forums set up by your instructor or training administrator through the **Social Media** tile on the CHOICE Course screen.

A | Microsoft Office Excel 2016 Exam 77-727

Selected Logical Operations courseware addresses Microsoft Office Specialist (MOS) certification skills for Microsoft® Office Excel® 2016. The following table indicates where Excel 2016 skills that are tested on Exam 77-727 are covered in the Logical Operations Excel 2016 series of courses.

Objective Domain	Covered In
1. Create and Manage Worksheets and Workbooks	
1.1 Create Worksheets and Workbooks	
1.1.1 Create a workbook	Part 1
1.1.2 Import data from a delimited text file	Part 3
1.1.3 Add a worksheet to an existing workbook	Part 1
1.1.4 Copy and move a worksheet	Part 1
1.2 Navigate in Worksheets and Workbooks	
1.2.1 Search for data within a workbook	Part 1
1.2.2 Navigate to a named cell, range, or workbook element	Part 2, Topic 1-A
1.2.3 Insert and remove hyperlinks	Part 1
1.3 Format Worksheets and Workbooks	
1.3.1 Change worksheet tab color	Part 1
1.3.2 Rename a worksheet	Part 1
1.3.3 Change worksheet order	Part 1
1.3.4 Modify page setup	Part 1
1.3.5 Insert and delete columns or rows	Part 1
1.3.6 Change workbook themes	Part 1
1.3.7 Adjust row height and column width	Part 1
1.3.8 Insert headers and footers	Part 1
1.4 Customize Options and Views for Worksheets and Workbooks	
1.4.1 Hide or unhide worksheets	Part 1
1.4.2 Hide or unhide columns and rows	Part 1
1.4.3 Customize the Quick Access Toolbar	Part 1

Objective Domain	Covered In
1.4.4 Change workbook views	Part 1
1.4.5 Change window views	Part 1
1.4.6 Modify document properties	Part 1
1.4.7 Change magnification by using zoom tools	Part 1
1.4.8 Display formulas	Part 3
1.5 Configure Worksheets and Workbooks for Distribution	
1.5.1 Set a print area	Part 1
1.5.2 Save workbooks in alternative file formats	Part 1; Part 3
1.5.3 Print all or part of a workbook	Part 1
1.5.4 Set print scaling	Part 1
1.5.5 Display repeating row and column titles on multipage worksheets	Part 1
1.5.6 Inspect a workbook for hidden properties or personal information	Part 3
1.5.7 Inspect a workbook for accessibility issues	Part 3
1.5.8 Inspect a workbook for compatibility issues	Part 1
2. Manage Data Cells and Ranges	
2.1 Insert Data in Cells and Ranges	
2.1.1 Replace data	Part 1
2.1.2 Cut, copy, or paste data	Part 1
2.1.3 Paste data by using special paste options	Part 1
2.1.4 Fill cells by using AutoFill	Part 1
2.1.5 Insert and delete cells	Part 1
2.2 Format Cells and Ranges	
2.2.1 Merge cells	Part 1
2.2.2 Modify cell alignment and indentation	Part 1
2.2.3 Format cells by using Format Painter	Part 1
2.2.4 Wrap text within cells	Part 1
2.2.5 Apply number formats	Part 1
2.2.6 Apply cell formats	Part 1
2.2.7 Apply cell styles	Part 1
2.3 Summarize and Organize Data	
2.3.1 Insert sparklines	Part 3
2.3.2 Outline data	Part 2, Topic 2-D
2.3.3 Insert subtotals	Part 2, Topic 2-D
2.3.4 Apply conditional formatting	Part 2, Topics 3-B, 3-C; Part 1

Objective Domain	Covered In
3. Create Tables	
3.1 Create and Manage Tables	
3.1.1 Create an Excel table from a cell range	Part 2, Topic 3-A
3.1.2 Convert a table to a cell range	Part 2, Topic 3-A
3.1.3 Add or remove table rows and columns	Part 2, Topic 3-A
3.2 Manage Table Styles and Options	
3.2.1 Apply styles to tables	Part 2, Topic 3-A
3.2.2 Configure table style options	Part 2, Topic 3-A
3.2.3 Insert total rows	Part 2, Topic 3-A
3.3 Filter and Sort a Table	
3.3.1 Filter records	Part 2, Topic 2-B
3.3.2 Sort data by multiple columns	Part 2, Topic 2-A
3.3.3 Change sort order	Part 2, Topic 2-A
3.3.4 Remove duplicate records	Part 2, Topic 3-A
4. Perform Operations with Formulas and Functions	
4.1 Summarize Data by Using Functions	
4.1.1 Insert references	Part 1
4.1.2 Perform calculations by using the SUM function	Part 1
4.1.3 Perform calculations by using MIN and MAX functions	Part 1
4.1.4 Perform calculations by using the COUNT function	Part 1
4.1.5 Perform calculations by using the AVERAGE function	Part 1
4.2 Perform Conditional Operations by Using Functions	
4.2.1 Perform logical operations by using the IF function	Part 2, Topic 1-C
4.2.2 Perform logical operations by using the SUMIF function	Part 2, Topic 1-C
4.2.3 Perform logical operations by using the AVERAGEIF function	Part 2, Topic 1-C
4.2.4 Perform statistical operations by using the COUNTIF function	Part 2, Topic 1-C
4.3 Format and Modify Text by Using Functions	
4.3.1 Format text by using the RIGHT, LEFT, and MID functions	Part 2, Topic 1-E
4.3.2 Format text by using the UPPER, LOWER, and PROPER functions	Part 2, Topic 1-E
4.3.3 Format text by using the CONCATENATE function	Part 2, Topic 1-E
5. Create Charts and Objects	

Objective Domain	Covered In
5.1 Create Charts	
5.1.1 Create a new chart	Part 2, Topic 4-A
5.1.2 Add additional data series	Part 2, Topic 4-B
5.1.3 Switch between rows and columns in source data	Part 2, Topic 4-B
5.1.4 Analyze data by using Quick Analysis	Part 2, Topic 4-A
5.2 Format Charts	
5.2.1 Resize charts	Part 2, Topic 4-B
5.2.2 Add and modify chart elements	Part 2, Topic 4-B
5.2.3 Apply chart layouts and styles	Part 2, Topic 4-B
5.2.4 Move charts to a chart sheet	Part 2, Topic 4-A
5.3 Insert and Format Objects	
5.3.1 Insert text boxes and shapes	Part 2, Appendix E, Topic A
5.3.2 Insert images	Part 2, Appendix E, Topic A
5.3.3 Modify object properties	Part 2, Appendix E, Topic B
5.3.4 Add alternative text to objects for accessibility	Part 2, Topics 3-A, 4-B, Appendix E

B | Microsoft Office Excel 2016 Expert Exam 77–728

Selected Logical Operations courseware addresses Microsoft Office Specialist (MOS) certification skills for Microsoft® Office Excel® 2016. The following table indicates where Excel 2016 skills that are tested on Exam 77–728 are covered in the Logical Operations Excel 2016 series of courses.

Objective Domain	Covered In
1. Manage Workbook Options and Settings	
1.1. Manage Workbooks	
1.1.1 Save a workbook as a template	Part 1
1.1.2 Copy macros between workbooks	Part 3
1.1.3 Reference data in another workbook	Part 3
1.1.4 Reference data by using structured references	Part 2, Topic 3-A
1.1.5 Enable macros in a workbook	Part 3
1.1.6 Display hidden ribbon tabs	Part 1
1.2 Manage Workbook Review	
1.2.1 Restrict editing	Part 3
1.2.2 Protect a worksheet	Part 3
1.2.3 Configure formula calculation options	Part 2, Topic 1-B
1.2.4 Protect workbook structure	Part 3
1.2.5 Manage workbook versions	Part 1
1.2.6 Encrypt a workbook with a password	Part 3
2. Apply Custom Data Formats and Layouts	
2.1 Apply Custom Data Formats	
2.1.1 Create custom number formats	Part 1
2.1.2 Populate cells by using advanced Fill Series options	Part 1
2.1.3 Configure data validation	Part 3
2.2 Apply Advanced Conditional Formatting and Filtering	

Objective Domain	Covered In
2.1.1 Create custom conditional formatting rules	Part 2, Topic 3-B
2.2.2 Create conditional formatting rules that use formulas	Part 2, Topic 3-C
2.2.3 Manage conditional formatting rules	Part 2, Topic 3-B
2.3 Create and Modify Custom Workbook Elements	
2.3.1 Create custom color formats	Part 1
2.3.2 Create and modify cell styles	Part 1
2.3.3 Create and modify custom themes	Part 1
2.3.4 Create and modify simple macros	Part 3
2.3.5 Insert and configure form controls	Part 3
2.4 Prepare a Workbook for Internationalization	
2.4.1 Display data in multiple international formats	Part 3
2.4.2 Apply international currency formats	Part 3
2.4.3 Manage multiple options for +Body and +Heading fonts	Part 3
3. Create Advanced Formulas	
3.1 Apply Functions in Formulas	
3.1.1 Perform logical operations by using AND, OR, and NOT functions	Part 2, Topic 1-C
3.1.2 Perform logical operations by using nested functions	Part 2, Topic 1-C
3.1.3 Perform statistical operations by using SUMIFS, AVERAGEIFS, and COUNTIFS functions	Part 2, Topic 1-C
3.2 Look Up Data by Using Functions	
3.2.1 Look up data by using the VLOOKUP function	Part 3
3.2.2 Look up data by using the HLOOKUP function	Part 3
3.2.3 Look up data by using the MATCH function	Part 3
3.2.4 Look up data by using the INDEX function	Part 3
3.3 Apply Advanced Date and Time Functions	
3.3.1 Reference the date and time by using the NOW and TODAY functions	Part 2, Topic 1-D
3.3.2 Serialize numbers by using date and time functions	Part 2, Topic 1-D
3.4 Perform Data Analysis and Business Intelligence	
3.4.1 Import, transform, combine, display, and connect to data	
3.4.2 Consolidate data	Part 3
3.4.3 Perform what-if analysis by using Goal Seek and Scenario Manager	Part 3
3.4.4 Use cube functions to get data out of the Excel data model	Part 3
3.4.5 Calculate data by using financial functions	Part 2, Appendix D

Objective Domain	Covered In
3.5 Troubleshoot Formulas	
3.5.1 Trace precedence and dependence	Part 3
3.5.2 Monitor cells and formulas by using the Watch Window	Part 3
3.5.3 Validate formulas by using error checking rules	Part 3
3.5.4 Evaluate formulas	Part 3
3.6 Define Named Ranges and Objects	
3.6.1 Name cells	Part 2, Topic 1-A
3.6.2 Name data ranges	Part 2, Topic 1-A
3.6.3 Name tables	Part 2, Topic 3-A
3.6.4 Manage named ranges and objects	Part 2, Topic 1-A
4. Create Advanced Charts and Tables	
4.1 Create Advanced Charts	
4.1.1 Add trendlines to charts	Part 2, Topic 4-C
4.1.2 Create dual-axis charts	Part 2, Topic 4-C
4.1.3 Save a chart as a template	Part 2, Topic 4-C
4.2 Create and Manage PivotTables	
4.2.1 Create PivotTables	Part 2, Topic 5-A
4.2.2 Modify field selections and options	Part 2, Topics 5-A, 5-B
4.2.3 Create slicers	Part 2, Topic 5-D
4.2.4 Group PivotTable data	Part 2, Topic 5-B
4.2.5 Reference data in a PivotTable by using the GETPIVOTDATA function	Part 2, Topic 5-B
4.2.6 Add calculated fields	Part 3
4.2.7 Format data	Part 2, Topic 5-B
4.3 Create and Manage PivotCharts	
4.3.1 Create PivotCharts	Part 2, Topic 5-C
4.3.2 Manipulate options in existing PivotCharts	Part 2, Topic 5-C
4.3.3 Apply styles to PivotCharts	Part 2, Topic 5-C
4.3.4 Drill down into PivotChart details	Part 2, Topic 5-C

C | Microsoft Excel 2016 Common Keyboard Shortcuts

The follow table lists common keyboard shortcuts you can use in Microsoft® Office Excel® 2016.

Function	Shortcut
Switch between worksheet tabs, from left to right.	**Ctrl+PgDn**
Switch between worksheet tabs, from right to left.	**Ctrl+PgUp**
Select the region around the active cell (requires there to be content in the surrounding cells).	**Ctrl+Shift+*** or **Ctrl+*** (from the number pad)
Select the cell at the beginning of the worksheet or pane.	**Ctrl+Home**
Select the cell at the end of the worksheet.	**Ctrl+End**
Select the cell at an edge of the worksheet.	**Ctrl+Arrow keys**
Insert the current time.	**Ctrl+Shift+:**
Insert the current date.	**Ctrl+;**
Display the **Insert** dialog box.	**Ctrl+Shift++**
Display the **Delete** dialog box.	**Ctrl+-**
Display the **Format Cells** dialog box.	**Ctrl+1**
Select the entire worksheet.	**Ctrl+A**
Apply or remove bold formatting.	**Ctrl+B**
Apply or remove italic formatting.	**Ctrl+I**
Copy the selected cells.	**Ctrl+C**
Cut the selected cells.	**Ctrl+X**
Paste copied content.	**Ctrl+V**
Display the **Find and Replace** dialog box.	**Ctrl+F**
Display the **Insert Hyperlink** or **Edit Hyperlink** dialog box.	**Ctrl+K**

Function	Shortcut
Create a new workbook.	**Ctrl+N**
Close an open workbook.	**Ctrl+W**
Display the **Open** tab on the **Backstage** view.	**Ctrl+O**
Display the **Print** tab on the **Backstage** view.	**Ctrl+P**
Save the file.	**Ctrl+S**
Repeat the last command or action, if possible.	**Ctrl+Y** or **F4** (when the insertion point is not in the **Formula Bar**)
Undo the last command or action.	**Ctrl+Z**
Redo the last undo.	**Ctrl+Y**
Enter data in a cell while keeping it the active cell.	**Ctrl+Enter**
Select all contiguously populated cells in a column from the selected cell to the end of the range.	**Ctrl+Shift+Up Arrow** or **Ctrl+Shift+Down Arrow**
Select all contiguously populated cells in a row from the selected cell to the end of the range.	**Ctrl+Shift+Right Arrow** or **Ctrl+Shift+Left Arrow**
Toggle among relative, absolute, and mixed references when the insertion point is in or next to a cell reference in the **Formula Bar**.	**F4**
Open the **Save As** dialog box.	**F12**
Activate the **Tell Me** text box.	**Alt+Q**

D | Financial Functions

Finance and accounting professionals are most likely to use Excel's financial functions. These specialized functions are useful for calculating a variety of financial values, such as payments, interest, and investment values over time. The following are overviews of some of the more commonly used financial functions not directly covered in the course.

 Note: These function overviews assume some prior knowledge of finance.

The FV Function

Syntax: =FV(rate, nper, pmt, [pv], [type])

Description: This function calculates the future value of an investment with fixed, periodic payments and a fixed interest rate. Here is a breakdown of the function's syntax.

Required arguments:

*   **rate**: The interest rate per period. As with some of the other financial functions, it's important to be specific about the period here. If the interest rate is 10 percent and payments are made monthly, the **rate** value should be 10 percent divided by 12, or 0.10/12. If payments are annual, the **rate** value would simply be 10 percent, or 0.10.
*   **nper**: The number of periods from now for which you wish to calculate the future value. Make sure the periods for this argument are the same as those used in the **rate** argument.
*   **pmt**: The payment made each period. For example, if you invest $200 a month from your paycheck toward a retirement investment for 20 years, the **pmt** value should be 200 and the **nper** value should be 240 (12 months × 20 years).

 Note: Although the **pmt** argument is considered to be required, that's not exactly true. You could also use the FV function to calculate the future value of a lump-sum investment. For example, if you put $10,000 in a fixed-rate investment, without making additional periodic contributions, you could simply enter **10000** in the **pv** argument, and leave the **pmt** argument blank. The FV function would then return the future value of that lump sum if it sat untouched in the same investment.

Optional arguments:

*   **pv**: The present value of the investment. Use this argument to determine the future value of a one-time, lump-sum investment into a fixed-rate asset. Or, you can use this in addition to the **pmt** argument to determine the future value of an investment in which you already have money, but plan to add to on a regular basis over time.
*   **type**: Designates when payments are made within a particular period. This argument can have one of two values: 0 or 1. A value of 0 indicates payments are made at the end of the given period; for example, the last day of the month. A value of 1 indicates payments are made at the beginning of the period; for example, the first day of the year. If you do not enter a value, Excel treats it as 0.

In the following example, assume the investor put $10,000 into an investment with an annual fixed-rate of return of 8 percent. Also assume the investor plans to contribute another $1,500 each month for 30 years with payments made at the end of each month.

	A	B	C	D	E
1	Rate	Period (years)	Monthly Contribution	Initial Investment	Future Value
2	8%	30	$1,500.00	$10,000.00	($2,359,800.06)

E2 formula: `=FV(A2/12,B2*12,C2,D2,1)`

The IPMT Function

Syntax: =IPMT(rate, per, nper, pv, [fv], [type])

Description: This function returns the interest payment due for a particular period on an investment or a loan with regular payments and a fixed interest rate. Here is a breakdown of the function's syntax.

Required arguments:

- **rate**: The interest rate per period. It's important to be specific about the payment period here. If your interest rate is 10 percent and payments are made monthly, the **rate** value should be 10 percent divided by 12, or 0.10/12. If payments are annual, the **rate** value would simply be 10 percent, or 0.10.
- **per**: The period for which you wish to calculate the interest. Take note that this is not a range of dates or a specific date, but rather the payment number itself. So if payments are monthly on a four-year investment, the **per** value will have to be somewhere between 1 and 48. If you're calculating the interest for the first month of year 2, the **per** value is 13.
- **nper**: The total number of payments for the investment. For example, if payments are monthly on a five-year investment, the **nper** value is 60. Literally, this is the number of payment periods for the duration of the investment.
- **pv**: The principal, or lump-sum, value. This is the present value of all remaining payments.

 Note: For all arguments in the IPMT function, use negative numbers for any money you must pay out, and use positive numbers for any money you take in.

Optional arguments:

- **fv**: The future value of the investment after all payments have been made. If you do not enter a value for the **fv** argument, Excel treats it as zero. This may be easier to think of in terms of a loan. Typically, you are interested in values associated with paying a loan off in full, so the final, or future, value is 0.
- **Type**: Designates when payments are due within a particular period. This argument can have one of two values: 0 or 1. A value of 0 indicates payments are due at the end of the given period; for example, the last day of the month. A value of 1 indicates payments are due at the beginning of the period; for example, the first day of the year. If you do not enter a value, Excel treats it as 0.

In the following example, how much interest a borrower would owe in the first month of the second year of a five-year, $10,000 loan is being calculated. Payments are due at the end of each month.

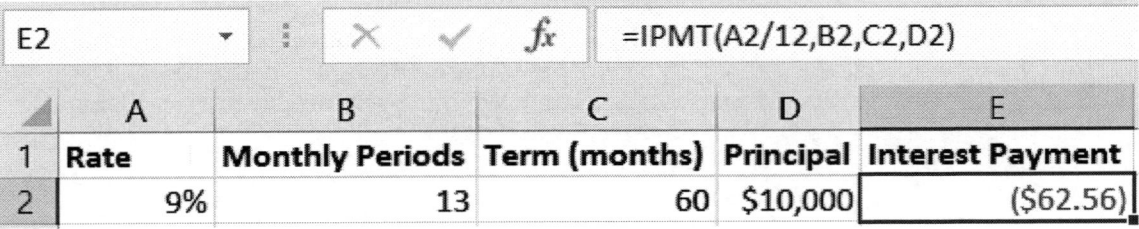

	A	B	C	D	E
1	Rate	Monthly Periods	Term (months)	Principal	Interest Payment
2	9%	13	60	$10,000	($62.56)

E2 formula: `=IPMT(A2/12,B2,C2,D2)`

If you were making the same calculation from the bank's perspective, you would have entered -$10,000 for the principal, as you would have paid the money out to the borrower. Excel would return $62.50, not -$62.50, because the interest payment would be owed to you from the borrower. The value **13** is entered for the **per** argument because the first month of the second year represents the 13th payment period.

The IRR Function

Syntax: =IRR(values, [guess])

Description: Returns the internal rate of return for a series of cash flows represented by the numbers in values. These cash flows do not have to be even, as they would be for an annuity. However, the cash flows must occur at regular intervals, such as monthly or annually. The internal rate of return is the interest rate received for an investment consisting of payments (negative values) and income (positive values) that occur at regular periods.

Required argument:

- **values**: An array or reference to cells that contain numbers for which you wan to calculate the internal rate of return.

Optional argument:

- **guess**: A number that you guess is close to the result of internal rate of return; 0.1 (10 percent) if omitted.

In the following example, cash flow has been recorded for five years including the initial cost of business. The internal rate of return is calculated over the first three years of business.

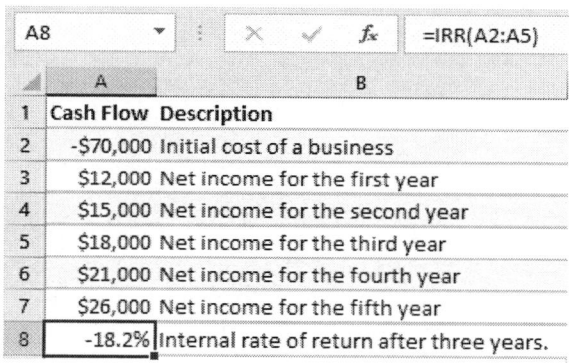

| A8 | ▾ | : | ✕ | ✓ | *fx* | =IRR(A2:A5) |

	A	B
1	**Cash Flow**	**Description**
2	-$70,000	Initial cost of a business
3	$12,000	Net income for the first year
4	$15,000	Net income for the second year
5	$18,000	Net income for the third year
6	$21,000	Net income for the fourth year
7	$26,000	Net income for the fifth year
8	-18.2%	Internal rate of return after three years.

The NPER Function

Syntax: =NPER(rate,pmt,pv,[fv],[type])

Description: Returns the number of periods for an investment based on periodic, constant payments and a constant interest rate.

Required arguments:

- **rate**: The interest rate per period.
- **pmt**: The payment made each period that cannot change over the life of the annuity.
- **pv**: The present value of the investment.

Optional arguments:

- **fv**: The future value, or a cash balance you want to attain after the last payment is made. If **fv** is omitted, it is assumed to be 0.
- **type**: The number 0 or omitted indicates payments are due at the end of the period, and 1 if the payments are due at the beginning of the period.

In the following example, the number of periods is calculated based on payments made at the beginning of each payment period with an annual interest rate of 12 percent, a payment of $100 per period with an initial payment of $1,000, and a future value of the investment of $10,000.

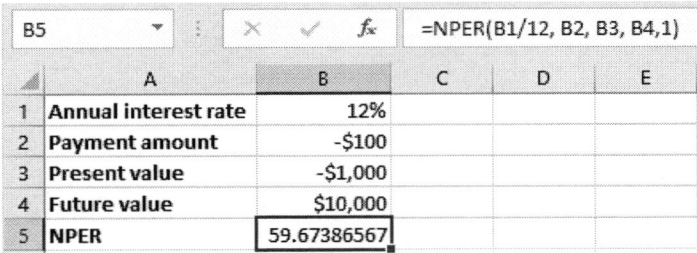

	A	B	C	D	E
	B5		*fx*	=NPER(B1/12, B2, B3, B4,1)	
1	Annual interest rate	12%			
2	Payment amount	-$100			
3	Present value	-$1,000			
4	Future value	$10,000			
5	NPER	59.67386567			

The NPV Function

Syntax: =NPV(rate, value1, [value2], ..., [value254])

Description: The NPV function calculates the net present value of an asset or an investment given the estimated or known future cash flows and the discount rate per period. In the function's syntax, **rate** is the discount rate per period, and the **value*X*** arguments represent the future cash flows. For this function, the cash flow, or **value** argument, period must be fixed and the cash flows must occur at the end of each period.

 Note: The NPV function does not take into account the initial cost of the investment, or the cash flow at Time 0. You must subtract this from the value returned by the NPV function manually to calculate the actual increase or decrease in net value from the investment.

In the following example, assume an annual discount rate of 9 percent and the given estimated cash flows.

	A	B	C	D	E
	B7		*fx*	=NPV(B1,B3:B6)	
1	Discount Rate	9%			
2	Initial Cost	-$100,000			
3	Cash Flow Yr. 1	$60,000			
4	Cash Flow Yr. 2	$40,000			
5	Cash Flow Yr. 3	$30,000			
6	Cash Flow Yr. 4	$25,000			
7	NPV	$129,589.21			

Notice that the initial cost is not included in the function; this is not factored in. To calculate the true NPV of the investment, you must subtract the initial cost of the investment from the value returned by the NPV formula. In this case, the NPV for the investment is $29,589.21.

The PMT function

Syntax: =PMT(rate, nper, pv, [fv], [type])

Description: This function calculates the payments for a loan with a fixed interest rate and fixed payment periods. You can use this function, for example, to calculate your payments for a fixed-rate mortgage, auto loan, or student loan. In the function's syntax, here are the required arguments: **rate** is the loan's fixed interest rate, **nper** is the total number of payments for the loan (for example, monthly payments for a three-year loan occur 36 times), **pv** is the present value (principal) of the loan. There are two optional arguments for the function: **fv** (future value of the loan) and **type**. The

fv argument is used to indicate the remaining balance on the loan at the end of the specified period. Typically, this will be zero (meaning the loan is fully paid off), which is the value if you omit this argument. If you want to calculate the payments to partially pay off the loan, use the **fv** argument to indicate how much should be left over once all of the payments are made. The **type** argument indicates whether the payment is due at the end of each payment period (indicated by a zero or by omitting the argument), or at the beginning of each pay period (indicated by a 1).

 Note: When using the PMT function, you must account for how often you plan to make payments when you enter the values for the **rate** and **nper** arguments. So, if the interest rate is 9 percent and you're making monthly payments for three years, the value for **rate** should be **.09/12**, and the value for **nper** should be **36**. If you make annual payments on the same loan, **rate** would be **.09** and **nper** would be **3**.

In the following example, you want to find the monthly payments for a five year loan for $50,000, with a fixed 5 percent interest rate.

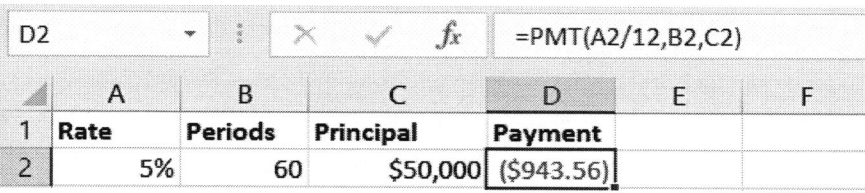

D2		▼ ⋮	✕ ✓ ƒx	=PMT(A2/12,B2,C2)		
	A	B	C	D	E	F
1	**Rate**	**Periods**	**Principal**	**Payment**		
2	5%	60	$50,000	($943.56)		

The PPMT Function

Syntax: =PPMT(rate, per, nper, pv, [fv], [type])

Description: The PPMT function calculates the amount owed against the principal for a particular period on an investment or a loan with regular payments and a fixed interest rate. The arguments for the PPMT function are exactly the same as those for the IPMT function. If you add the values returned for the same period of the same loan by the IPMT function and the PPMT function, you will calculate the total payment, less any fees, for the period.

Using the previous example, this is what the PPMT function would return for the principal payment due in the same period.

E2		▼ ⋮	✕ ✓ ƒx	=PPMT(A2/12,B2,C2,D2)	
	A	B	C	D	E
1	**Rate**	**Montlhy Periods**	**Term (months)**	**Principal**	**Interest Payment**
2	9%	13	60	$10,000	($145.02)

The PV Function

Syntax: =PV(rate, nper, pmt, [fv], [type])

Description: This function calculates the present value of a loan or an investment, based on a constant interest rate.

Required arguments:

- **rate**: The interest rate per period.
- **nper**: The total number of payment periods in an annuity.
- **pmt**: The payment made each period that cannot change over the life of the annuity.

Optional arguments:

- **fv:** The future value, or a cash balance you want to attain after the last payment is made. If fv is omitted, it is assumed to be 0.
- **type:** The number 0 or omitted indicates payments are due at the end of the period, and 1 if the payments are due at the beginning of the period.

In the following example, the present value of an annuity is calculated from an interest rate of 8 percent over 20 years with 12 payments each year, and a month end payment of $500.

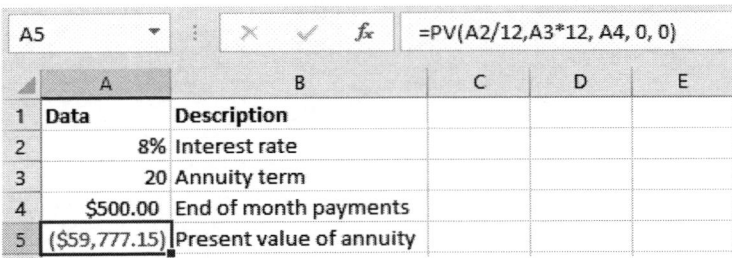

E | Working with Graphical Objects

Appendix Introduction

Although data is king in Microsoft® Office Excel® 2016, there are a number of reasons you may need to add graphical objects, outside of charts or PivotCharts, to your worksheets. You may want to simply enhance the visual appeal of your worksheets, or you may wish to include some type of "infographic" that simply can't be created with a chart. Perhaps you want to include your company logo in a visible location when sharing your screen with potential clients. Or, you may wish to include screenshots of relevant computer applications or websites when presenting related information.

Whatever the case, at some point you'll likely need to rely on graphical support for the data in your workbooks. Excel 2016 provides you with a number of tools for inserting, modifying, and even editing a variety of graphical objects that can enhance the visual appeal of a document and serve as interactive data objects. Understanding what these objects are, how they work, and how you can integrate them with your data can help you elevate your workbooks to a new level of sophistication.

TOPIC A

Insert Graphical Objects

Before you can use graphical objects to enhance the visual appeal of your workbooks or present your data with greater impact, you must first be able to insert them into your worksheets. Excel 2016 provides you with a variety of tools and commands that enable you to add numerous graphical objects to your worksheets. Understanding the differences among the types of graphical objects and the various methods for inserting them is a key first step in using graphical objects to enhance your workbooks.

Graphical Objects

There are six basic types of graphical objects that you can insert into your workbooks: pictures, clip art, shapes, SmartArt, WordArt, and screenshots. Each of these is suited to particular purposes. It's important to understand that these objects, much like charts, are separate objects that lie on top of worksheets; you do not insert them in cells. All of these graphical objects can be resized, modified, and moved. Some of them can also contain text or display the content of worksheet cells. You can access the commands for inserting most graphical objects in the **Illustrations** group on the **Insert** tab. You insert WordArt, however, by selecting **Insert→Text→WordArt**.

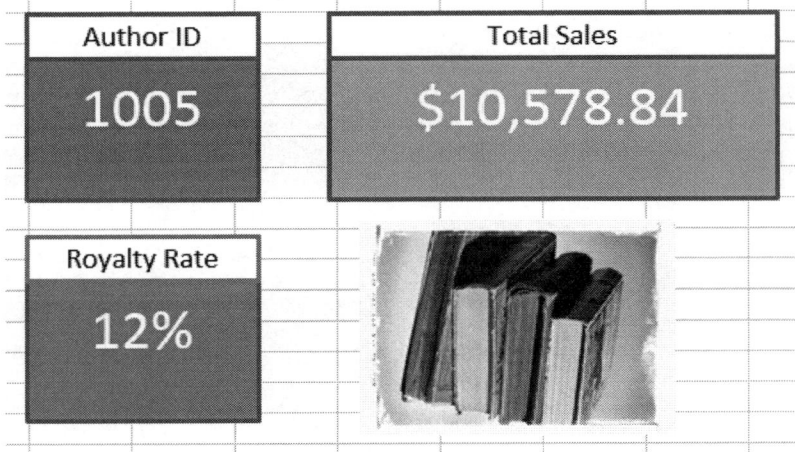

Figure E-1: Graphical objects enable you to add appeal to your worksheets and present data visually.

The following table describes each of the types of graphical objects in some detail.

Graphical Object Type	Description
Pictures	These are image files created outside of Excel, such as images from digital cameras, pictures downloaded from the web, or graphics and art saved as image files. Excel 2016 supports a variety of common image file formats.
Clip art	Simple artwork graphics or images that are available online, downloaded from **Office.com**. Clip art objects behave differently depending on the type of graphical object you select, but they are all still generically referred to as clip art.

Graphical Object Type	Description
Shapes	Simple graphical objects, such as circles, squares, rectangles, text callouts, and arrows that are generated within Excel and that you manually draw on your worksheets. Excel 2016 comes loaded with a wide variety of shapes. Shapes can also display text or the contents of worksheet cells.
SmartArt	Preconfigured graphics that you can use as graphical representations of textual content. You will typically use SmartArt to represent processes, procedures, cycles, or hierarchies. Common uses of SmartArt include creating organizational charts and representing sales or business cycles. As with shapes, you can use SmartArt to display text, but you cannot link cell content to SmartArt graphics.
WordArt	Preconfigured sets of text formatting that you can apply to the text in certain graphical objects. WordArt is customizable, but you cannot apply WordArt to text or data in worksheet cells; you can only apply it to text in graphical objects.
Screenshots	Images taken from the current display of your computer monitor. You capture these images directly within Excel, which can be of either entire windows or particular regions of your screen. Excel enables you to screen capture any currently open windows that are not minimized.

The Insert Picture Dialog Box

You will use the **Insert Picture** dialog box to insert images saved to your computer or network directories in your worksheets. From here, you can navigate to and select the image files you wish to insert. To access the **Insert Picture** dialog box, select **Insert→Illustrations→Pictures**.

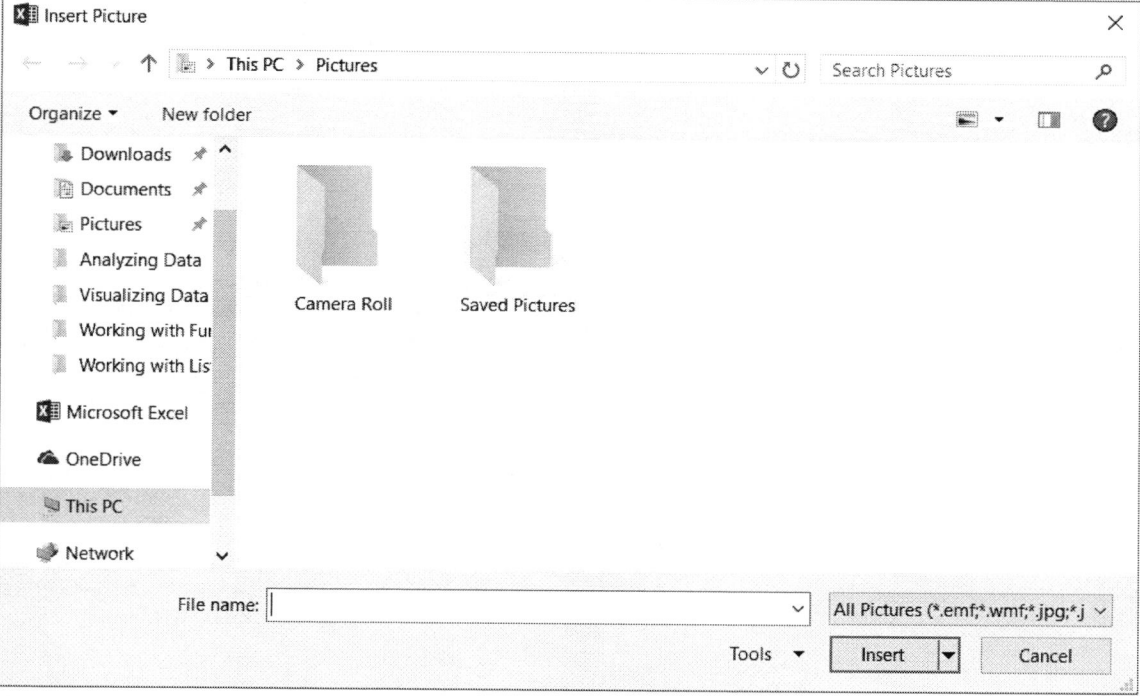

Figure E-2: The Insert Picture dialog box.

The Insert Pictures Window

You can use the **Insert Pictures** window to add online pictures including clip art images, also known as clips, to your worksheets. From here, you can search for and insert clips using Bing® Image Search on the web. Bing Image Search uses a copyright filter based on the Creative Commons licensing system. The **Insert Pictures** window displays a gallery of thumbnail images for the items that match your search query. You can also view a slightly larger preview of items returned in searches by selecting the magnifying glass icon that appears when you point the cursor at one of the thumbnail images. You can access the **Insert Pictures** window by selecting **Insert→Illustrations→Online Pictures**.

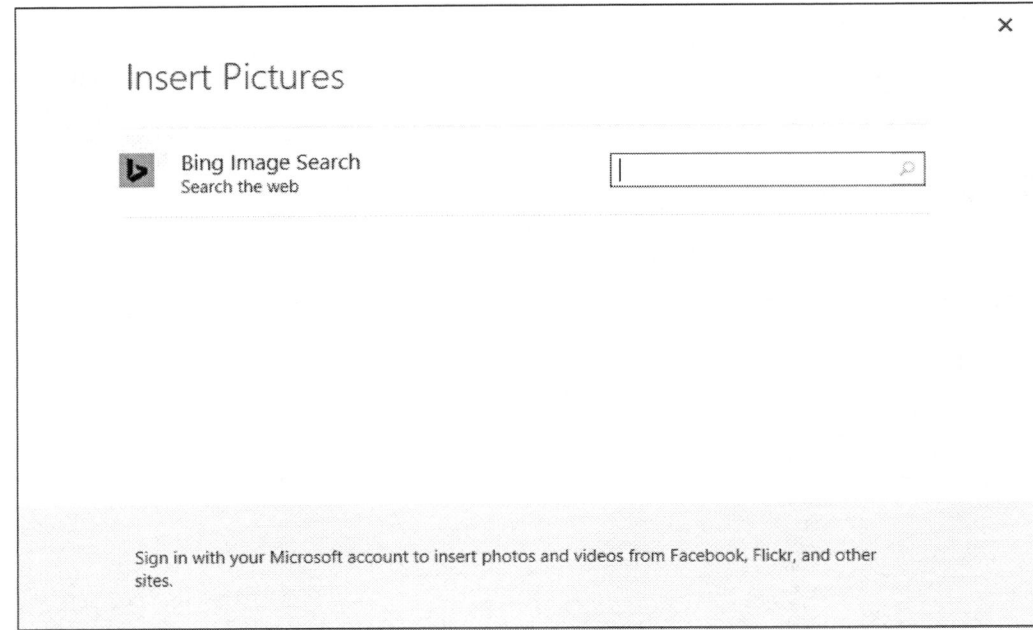

Figure E-3: Use the Insert Pictures window to search for, preview, and insert pictures and clips.

The Shapes Gallery

You will select the particular shapes you wish to add to your worksheets by using the **Shapes** gallery. The **Shapes** gallery is divided into a series of eight categories of related shape types. These include simple lines and arrows, basic geometric shapes, flowchart elements, and text callout boxes. Shapes you have recently used in your workbooks appear in the **Recently Used Shapes** section at the top of the **Shapes** gallery. You can access the **Shapes** gallery by selecting **Insert→Illustrations→Shapes**.

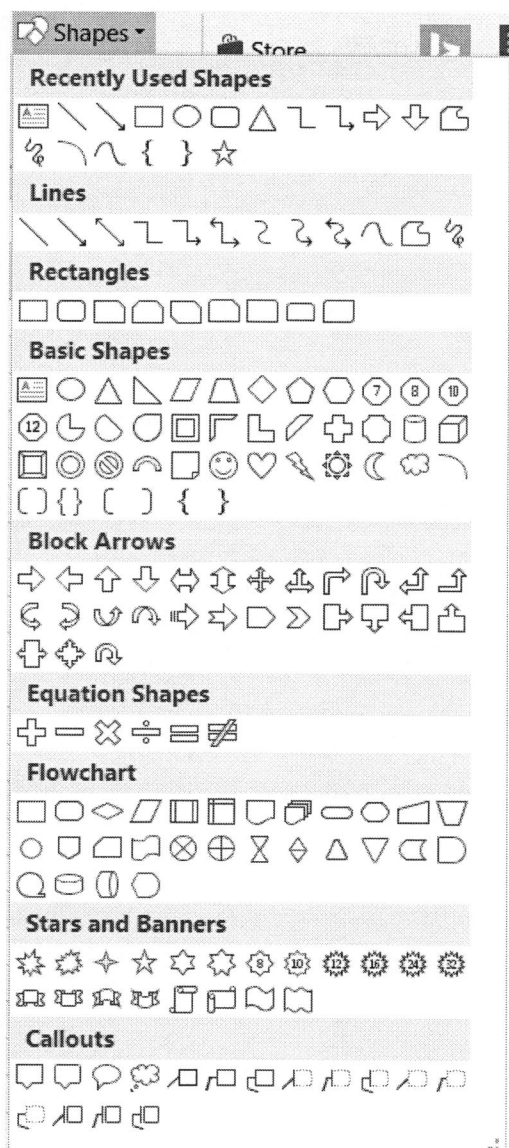

Figure E–4: The Shapes gallery.

The Take a Screenshot Command

The **Take a Screenshot** command enables you to capture an image from an open application on your computer. You can capture either an entire application window or a particular region of the screen. The screenshot tool enables you to screen capture open applications that are not minimized to the task bar. When you select the **Take a Screenshot** command, Excel opens the **Available Windows** gallery from which you can select an open application to capture. This method captures an image of the entire window of the selected application. To capture only a portion of the application window, select the **Screen Clipping** command from the bottom of the **Available Windows** gallery. Excel then activates the screen clipping tool, enabling you to select the particular region of your screen that you wish to capture. The screen clipping tool also enables you to capture screenshots of your desktop, which is not possible from the **Available Windows** gallery. You cannot capture an image of Excel from within Excel. You can access the screenshot tool by selecting **Insert→Illustrations→Take a Screenshot**.

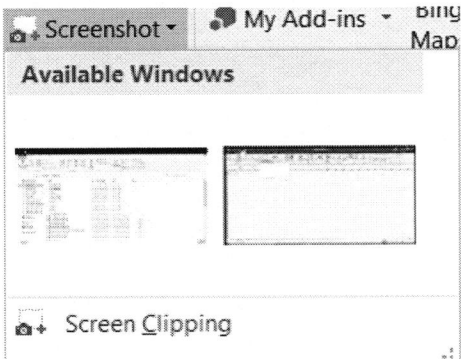

Figure E-5: The Take a Screenshot command.

Text Boxes

Technically speaking, text boxes are essentially the same as shapes. The main differences with text boxes are that they contain no formatting when you insert them, and they display an insertion point (cursor) when selected, indicating they are ready for you to enter text. Use text boxes to include additional information on your worksheets or to call attention to some fact or worksheet element. To insert a text box, select **Insert→Text→Text Box**.

	A	B	C	D	E	F
1						
2		Increase in sales for the Northeast region.				
3						

Figure E-6: A text box on an Excel worksheet.

WordArt

WordArt is a type of text formatting that you can apply to the text in certain graphical objects within Excel. By default, when you insert WordArt, Excel inserts it as a text box with the selected WordArt formatting applied to the text. You can, however, apply WordArt styles to some of the text in some other graphical objects, such as chart labels and text in shapes. Excel 2016 comes loaded with a small selection of preconfigured WordArt styles, and you can create custom WordArt styles. To insert a default WordArt text box, select **Insert→Text→WordArt**.

Figure E-7: WordArt formatting applied to the text in a text box.

 Access the Checklist tile on your CHOICE Course screen for reference information and job aids on How to Insert Graphical Objects.

TOPIC B

Modify Graphical Objects

Inserting graphical objects is a great way to enhance the visual appeal and impact of your workbooks. However, many of the raw images or basic shapes you insert may not suit your particular needs. For instance, you may need to ensure that all shapes adhere to your organization's branding guidelines. Or you may want to remove distracting background elements from images to focus your audience's attention on only the most important aspects of pictures. Whatever the reason, taking the time to gain the foundational knowledge needed to modify and edit your graphical objects will give you the flexibility you need to ensure that your images deliver the proper message and have the desired impact.

 Note: While there are no formal activities for this lesson, a sample data file has been provided to you so that you can practice adding shapes and connecting them to cell data in the **C:\091056Data\Appendix C** folder. Use the **graphic_objects.xlsx** file to practice adding, modifying, and connecting data to shapes; one has been included in the workbook as an example. You can also practice adding images or SmartArt as well. A sample solution file has been provided in the **C:\091056Data\Appendix C\solutions** folder.

Pictures and Drawings

There is an important distinction to understand before you modify the graphical objects in your workbooks. With the exception of SmartArt, although there are several types of graphical objects in Excel, Excel recognizes only two types of images in terms of editing and modifying graphical objects: pictures and drawings.

 Note: Although, technically, the individual elements of a SmartArt graphic are the same as shapes, SmartArt has a separate set of tools that you will use to modify your SmartArt graphics.

In terms of modifying graphical objects, Excel considers pictures, screenshots, and some clip art to be pictures, whereas it considers shapes, text boxes, and some other clips to be drawings. Each has its own unique set of tools for working with and modifying the various types of graphical objects.

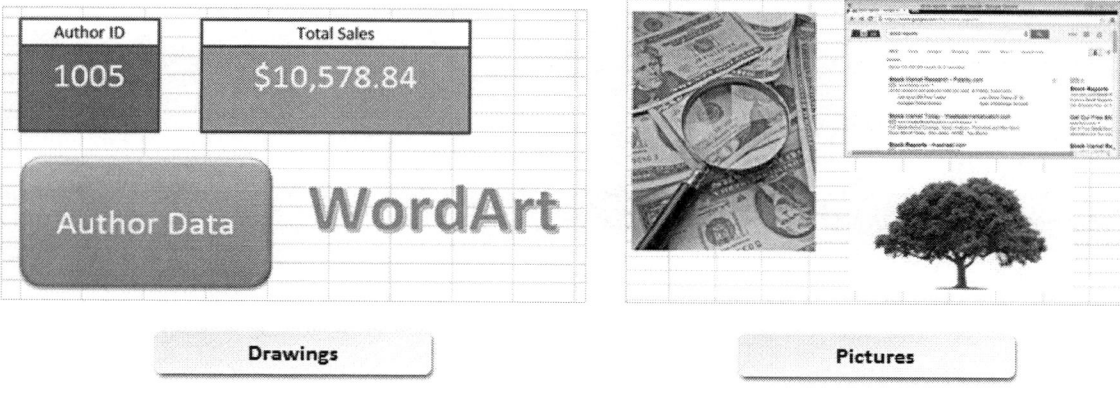

Figure E-8: Excel draws a distinction between drawings and pictures.

The Picture Tools Contextual Tab

Excel displays the **Picture Tools** contextual tab when you select a graphical object it considers to be a picture. The **Picture Tools** contextual tab contains only one tab, the **Format** tab, which displays the tools and commands you will use to edit, modify, and add effects to the pictures in your workbooks.

Figure E–9: The Picture Tools contextual tab.

The **Format** tab on the **Picture Tools** contextual tab is divided into four command groups. Each of these groups displays functionally related commands for working with pictures in Excel.

Format Tab Group	Contains Commands For
Adjust	Performing image-correction tasks, compressing the size of pictures, adding artistic effects to pictures, and removing picture backgrounds.
Picture Styles	Adding a variety of style elements to pictures, such as placing borders around them, adding drop shadows, and adding 3-D rotation and bevel effects.
Arrange	Changing the placement of pictures on worksheets, arranging multiple images front-to-back, grouping images together, and rotating images.
Size	Modifying the size of and cropping pictures.

The Image Editor

The **Adjust** group on the **Format** tab of the **Picture Tools** contextual tab contains a set of commands and tools sometimes referred to collectively as the image editor. These commands and tools enable you to perform image editing tasks, such as adjusting the brightness, contrast, or sharpness of a picture, that you might otherwise need a separate application to perform.

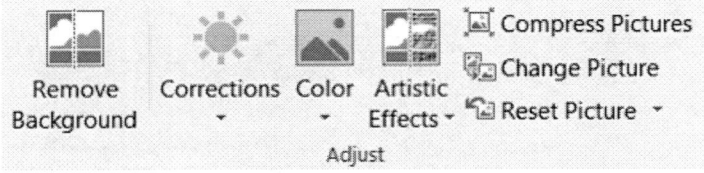

Figure E–10: The Adjust group's image editing tools.

The following table describes the type of image-correction and modification tasks you can perform by using the tools and commands available in the image editor.

Image Editor Command/ Tool	Use This To
Remove Background tool	Remove unwanted background elements from a picture. The **Remove Background** tool will attempt to guess at the main subject of an image and remove all other background elements. You can also manually select which regions of an image Excel will keep and which elements it will remove.
Corrections command	Adjust the sharpness, brightness, or contrast of an image.
Color command	Adjust the color tone or saturation of an image, recolor an image, or select a particular color to make transparent in an image.

Image Editor Command/ Tool	Use This To
Artistic Effects command	Apply a particular artistic effect to an image, such as making an image look like a pencil sketch, adding a blur effect, adding a pixelated effect, or turning a color image into a black-and-white image.
Compress Pictures command	Reduce the overall file size of your Excel workbook by compressing the images it contains.
Change Picture command	Replace a picture with another image file.
Reset Picture command	Remove any formatting changes you've made to a picture.

The Drawing Tools Contextual Tab

Excel displays the **Drawing Tools** contextual tab when you select a graphical object it considers to be a drawing. The **Drawing Tools** contextual tab contains only one tab, the **Format** tab, which displays the tools and commands you will use to edit, modify, and add effects to the drawings in your workbooks.

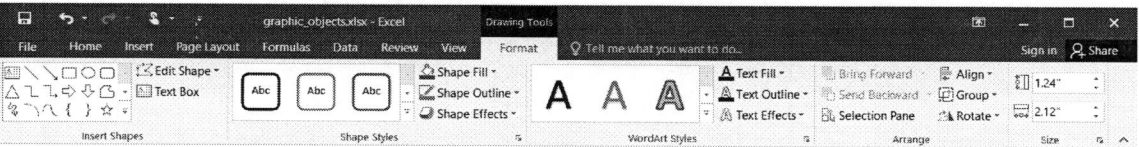

Figure E–11: The Drawing Tools contextual tab.

The **Format** tab on the **Drawing Tools** contextual tab is divided into five command groups. Each of these groups displays functionally related commands for working with drawings in Excel.

Format Tab Group	Contains Commands For
Insert Shapes	Inserting additional shapes, changing the outline (shape) of a shape, and inserting text boxes.
Shape Styles	Applying a variety of preconfigured or custom styles to drawings.
WordArt Styles	Applying a variety of preconfigured or custom styles to text you add to drawings.
Arrange	Changing the placement of drawings on worksheets, arranging multiple drawings front-to-back, grouping drawings together, and rotating drawings.
Size	Modifying the size of drawings.

The Selection Task Pane

Although you can use the commands on the **Picture Tools** or the **Drawing Tools** contextual tab to arrange images front-to-back on your worksheets, Excel 2016 includes a tool that makes doing so easier: the **Selection** task pane. The **Selection** task pane enables you to easily view the front-to-back order of graphical objects on your worksheets, view which objects are grouped together, change the order of objects and groups (and individual objects within groups), and hide from view or display any of the graphical objects on your worksheets.

It may not appear as such when objects are separated from each other, but all objects on a worksheet are arranged in a front-to-back order as if each exists on its own plane. This fact becomes evident, however, when you overlap objects onscreen. Objects that are in front of other objects will obscure the view of the objects behind them. Objects appear in the **Selection** pane from top to bottom as they appear on the worksheet from front to back. In other words, the object at the top of the **Selection** task pane is in front of all other objects on the worksheet.

When you group objects together, they behave as one independent object that you can move, arrange, resize, or modify collectively. You are, however, able to select individual objects within a group to perform modifications on them separate from the group. Grouped objects appear in the **Selection** task pane in a hierarchical fashion with the group existing at the same level as other independent objects, and the objects in the group appearing one level down in the hierarchy within the group.

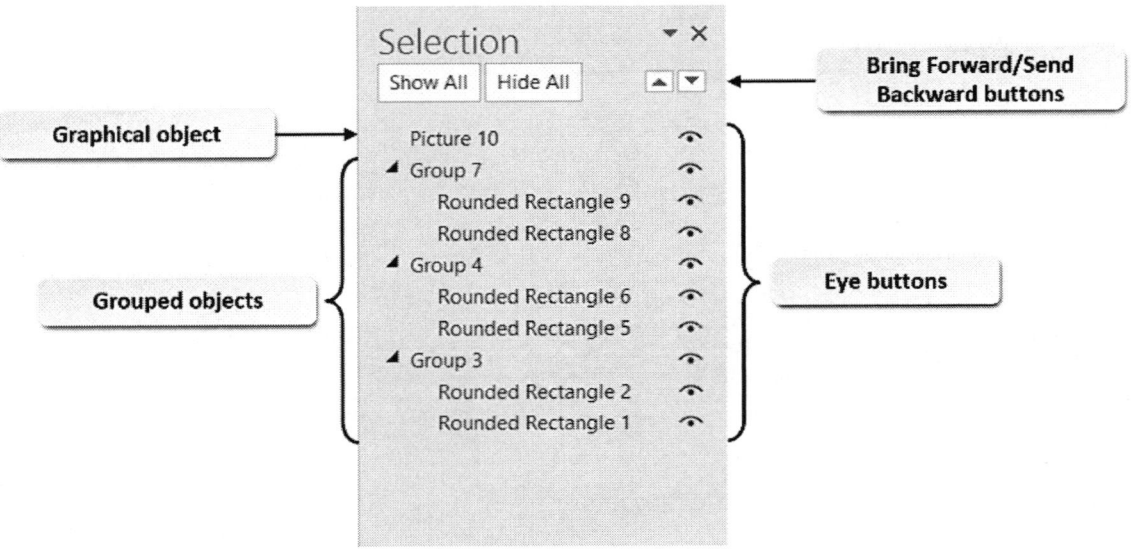

Figure E-12: The Selection task pane.

The following table describes the functions of the various elements of the **Selection** task pane.

Selection Task Pane Element	Description
Objects list	Displays the order of all objects and groups on a worksheet, as well as the order in which individual objects appear within a group.
Eye buttons	Enable you to hide or show any object or group.
Show All button	Turns on the display of all objects and groups on a worksheet.
Hide All button	Turns off the display of all objects and groups on a worksheet.
Bring Forward and **Send Backward** buttons	Enable you to move objects or groups up or down in the objects list, which changes their order on the worksheet.

The Format Shape and Format Picture Task Panes

Excel 2016 also provides you with access to two task panes that you can use to fine-tune the formatting and modification of your graphical objects: the **Format Shape** task pane and the **Format Picture** task pane. Like other task panes, these two task panes are organized into a hierarchical structure of tabs and expandable command sections, although the **Format Picture** task pane does not include high-level tabs as pictures can't contain text. You can access the **Format Shape** and the **Format Picture** task panes by selecting the dialog box launchers from the command groups in the **Picture Tools** and the **Drawing Tools** contextual tabs.

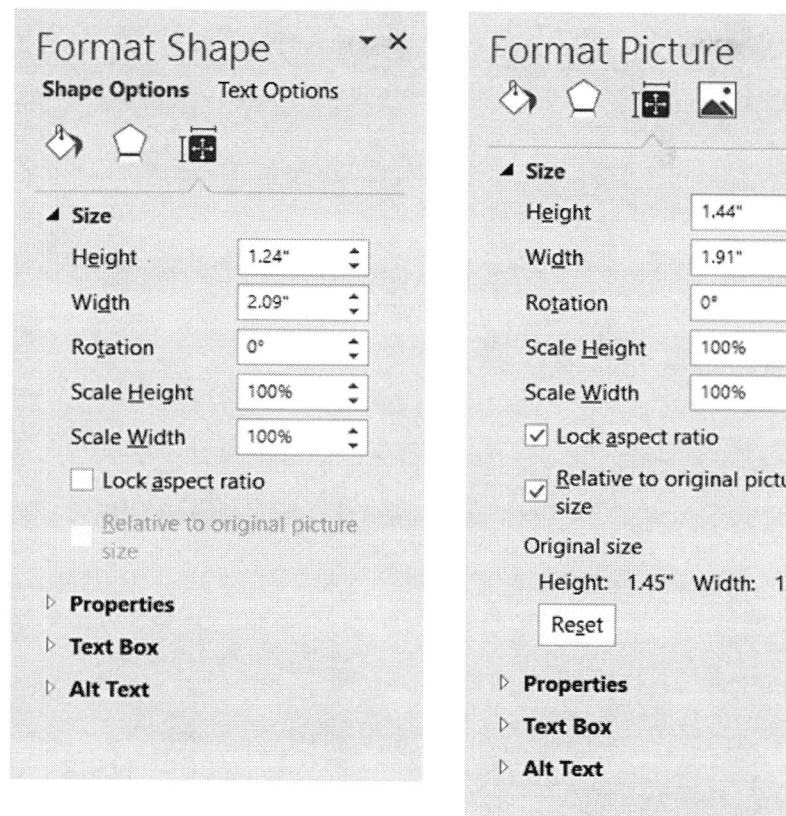

Figure E-13: Use the commands and the options available in the Format Shape and Format Picture task panes to work with the graphical objects on your worksheets.

Object Properties

As objects on an Excel worksheet don't exist within worksheet cells, it may seem odd that when you modify the size of or hide and unhide columns or rows, your objects move or resize along with the cells. This is actually a default setting that you can change using *object properties*. Configuring object properties enables you to control the behavior of objects on worksheets relative to the cells beneath them, whether or not objects print on printouts, and how worksheet protection affects the objects on your worksheets. You set object properties using the commands in the **Properties** command section on the **Size & Properties** tab of either the **Format Shape** or the **Format Picture** task pane.

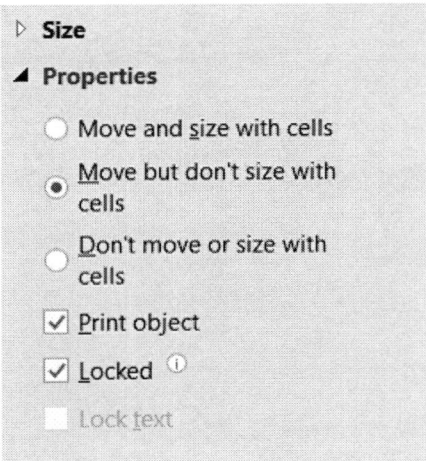

Figure E-14: Modify object properties to affect the behavior of objects relative to worksheet cells, when printing worksheets, and when applying worksheet protection.

The following table describes the various options in the **Properties** command section.

Object Property Option	Description
Move and size with cells radio button	This is the default property for objects in Excel 2016. With this option selected, objects on your worksheets will change size and position when you make adjustments to the cells beneath them.
Move but don't size with cells radio button	This option allows objects to move as you adjust cells beneath them, but maintains their current dimensions.
Don't move or size with cells radio button	This option enables you to make adjustments to the cells beneath worksheet objects without affecting either the placement or the size of the objects.
Print object check box	Determines whether or not objects will print on printed worksheets.
Locked check box	Protects objects from user changes if you have applied worksheet protection to the worksheet.
Lock text check box	Protects the text on objects from user changes if you have applied worksheet protection to the worksheet.

 Access the Checklist tile on your CHOICE Course screen for reference information and job aids on How to Modify Graphical Objects.

TOPIC C

Work with SmartArt

Creating complex graphical representations of textual information can be a daunting task. You must decide what shapes to include, how to size and format them, and how to arrange them on the graphic so they make sense. You may know what you would like to communicate, but be unsure of how to say it visually. So, how do you go about designing and building your graphic? Well, the good news is that you don't have to do all of the work yourself.

The SmartArt tools within Excel 2016 give you a vast array of options for creating graphics that are well-suited to a variety of needs. Understanding how to insert SmartArt into your workbooks and how to decide which layout to use will save you the effort of tirelessly adding and formatting individual shapes to create a complex graphic.

SmartArt Graphics

SmartArt graphics are visual representations of textual content that typically represent a process, a cycle, a hierarchy, or relationships. Excel 2016 contains eight different categories of SmartArt graphics that you can use to display a variety of textual information. In addition, you can download a number of other SmartArt templates from **Office.com**. Like other objects, SmartArt graphics are individual objects that can be moved, resized, arranged, and formatted in a variety of ways.

The following table describes some of the common uses for SmartArt graphics in the various SmartArt graphic categories.

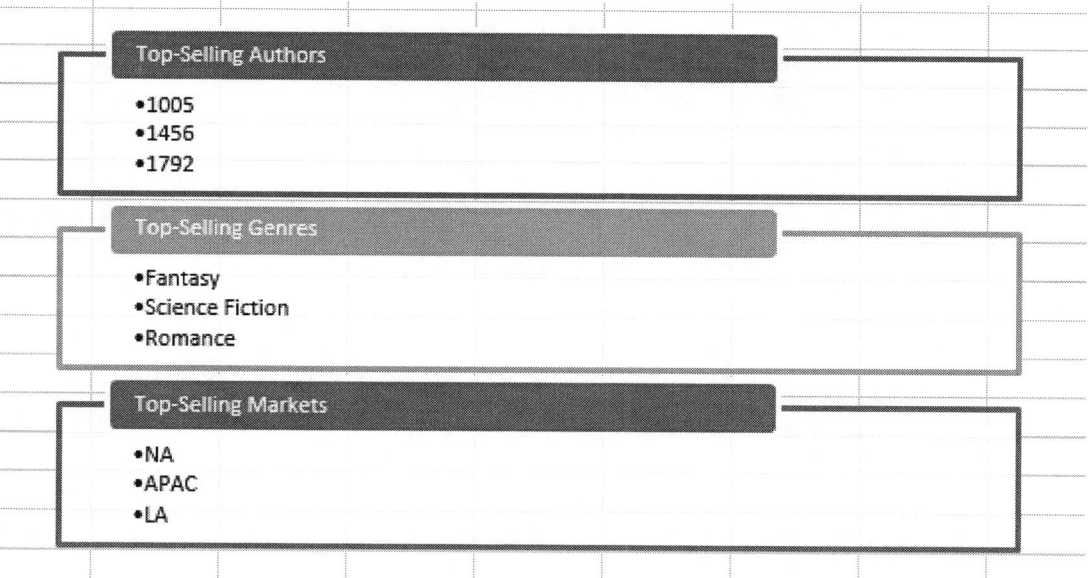

Figure E-15: A SmartArt graphic.

SmartArt Category	Is Used to Create Diagrams for Displaying
List	Information that does not need to be shown in sequential order. Lists are ideal for content such as bulleted lists.
Process	Information that needs to be shown in sequential order, such as a manufacturing process or a task procedure.

SmartArt Category	Is Used to Create Diagrams for Displaying
Cycle	A continuous process, such as an annual performance-review system or annual sales cycles.
Hierarchy	Steps in a decision process or an organizational chart.
Relationship	How various elements of a system interconnect with each other.
Matrix	How various elements of a system relate to the system as a whole.
Pyramid	How elements of varying degrees of importance or size relate, proportionally, to each other as part of the whole.
Picture	Content as a combination of text and graphics.

SmartArt Shapes

The individual elements of a SmartArt graphic are known as shapes. This can be a bit confusing as they share a name with the shapes you manually draw onto your Excel worksheets. Essentially, the individual elements of SmartArt are the same type of objects as shapes. But to differentiate the two, from this point forward, the term "shapes" will be used to refer to the objects you manually draw, and the elements of SmartArt graphics will be referred to as "SmartArt shapes."

It is the SmartArt shapes that display the text in SmartArt graphics. And, although they are typically formatted in much the same way as other SmartArt shapes in a SmartArt graphic, you can individually format, move, and resize them to suit your needs. Much as with grouped objects, to select a SmartArt shape, you first select the SmartArt graphic it is a part of, and then select the individual SmartArt shape you wish to interact with.

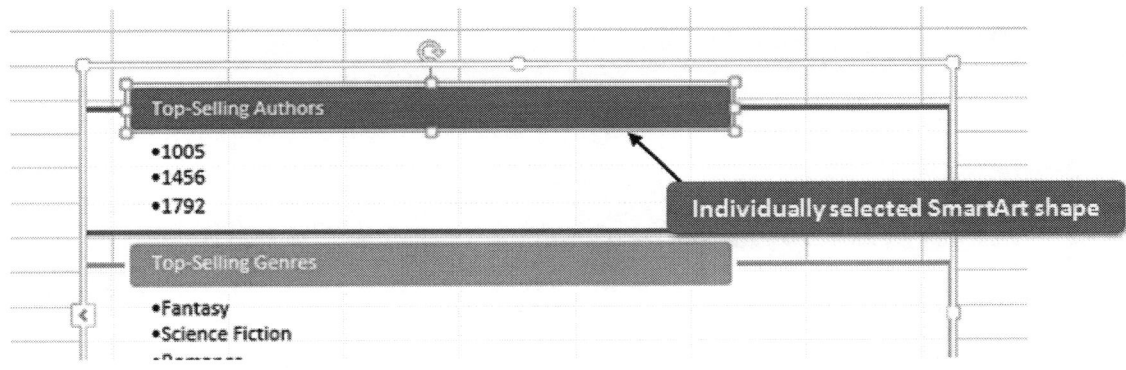

Figure E–16: A SmartArt shape.

The Choose a SmartArt Graphic Dialog Box

You will use the **Choose a SmartArt Graphic** dialog box to insert SmartArt graphics into your workbooks. The **Choose a SmartArt Graphic** dialog box is divided into a series of tabs that organize the available SmartArt graphics by category. As you select the various categories of SmartArt in the left pane, the dialog box displays the available SmartArt graphic layouts in the middle pane as thumbnail images. Selecting one of the thumbnail images displays a preview of the selected SmartArt layout along with a brief description of its common uses in the right pane. To display the **Choose a SmartArt Graphic** dialog box, select **Insert→Illustrations→Insert a SmartArt Graphic**.

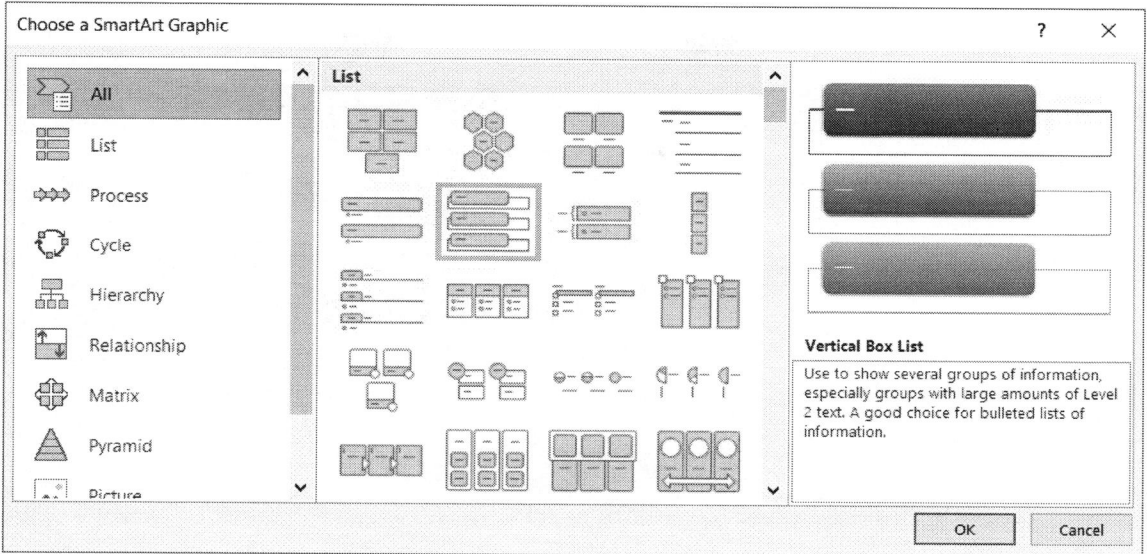

Figure E-17: The Choose a SmartArt Graphic dialog box.

The Text Pane

There are two methods you can use to add text to your SmartArt graphics. The first is to simply select the default text on the SmartArt shapes and then enter the text. The second method is to use the *Text pane*. With the **Text** pane open, you can still select the text placeholders directly in the SmartArt shapes to enter or edit text, but you can also place the insertion point in the various text placeholders within the **Text** pane to do the same.

Many SmartArt graphics are hierarchical in nature. This is especially beneficial when creating graphics for bullet list content and organizational charts. As such, Excel provides you with functionality to control and arrange the hierarchical relationships among the various bits of text in your SmartArt graphics. Once you enter text in the **Text** pane, pressing the **Enter** key will add a new text placeholder at the same hierarchical level, both in the **Text** pane and in the SmartArt graphic. You can also promote or demote text in the graphic's overall hierarchy. Depending on the particular SmartArt graphic you're working with, adding more lines of text may simply add bullet items within a SmartArt shape, or it may add new SmartArt shapes to contain the text. To open the **Text** pane, select the SmartArt graphic and then select the control.

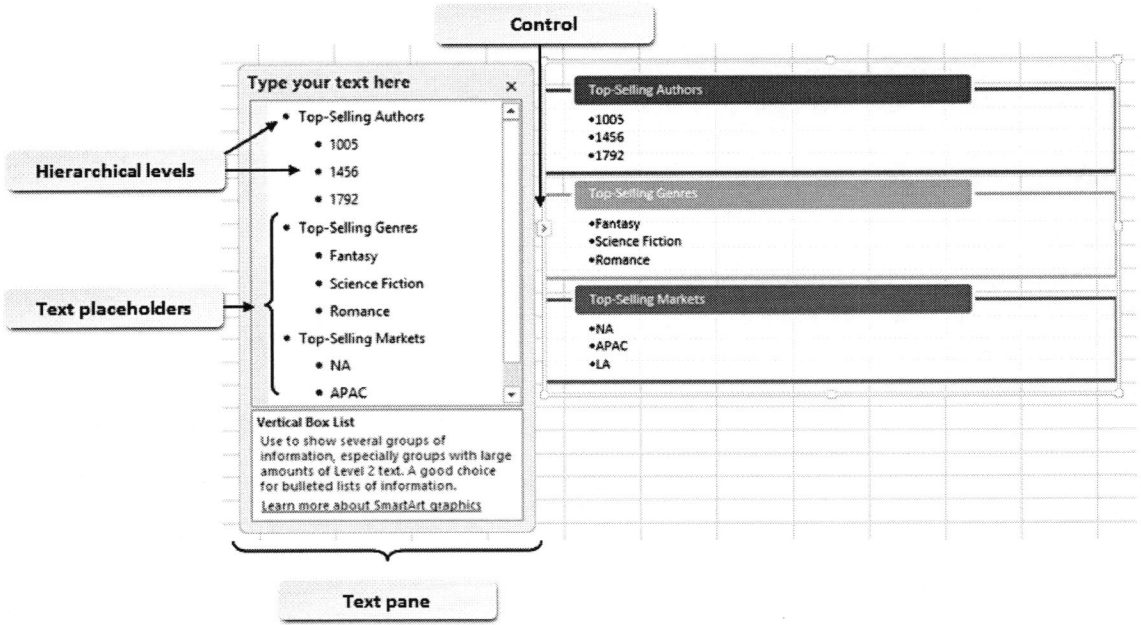

Figure E-18: The Text pane.

The SmartArt Tools Contextual Tab

You will find the commands and tools specific to working with and modifying SmartArt graphics on the **SmartArt Tools** contextual tab. The **SmartArt Tools** contextual tab is divided into two tabs: the **Design** tab and the **Format** tab. The **Design** tab contains the commands you will use to configure the overall structure of your SmartArt graphics, and to apply particular style elements to entire SmartArt graphics.

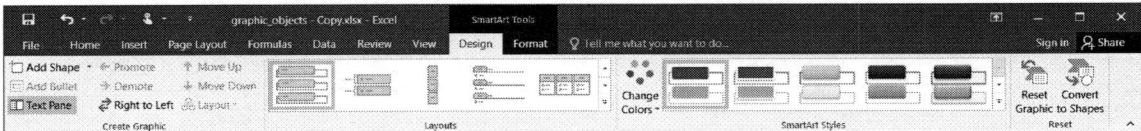

Figure E-19: The Design tab.

The **Design** tab on the **SmartArt Tools** contextual tab is divided into four command groups.

Design Tab Group	Contains Commands For
Create Graphic	Adding SmartArt shapes to SmartArt graphics, adding additional text panes to SmartArt shapes, and managing the hierarchical structure of SmartArt graphics.
Layouts	Modifying the overall layout of SmartArt graphics.
SmartArt Styles	Changing the overall color scheme of SmartArt graphics and applying stylistic elements, such as 3-D effects, beveling, and drop shadows, to SmartArt graphics.
Reset	Removing customization from SmartArt graphics and converting SmartArt graphics to standard Excel shapes.

The **Format** tab contains the commands you will use to apply formatting to the individual SmartArt shapes and their text within your SmartArt graphics.

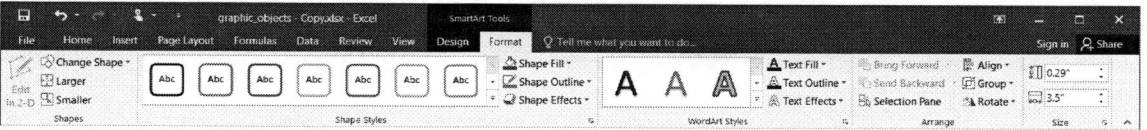

Figure E-20: The Format tab.

The **Format** tab on the **SmartArt Tools** contextual tab is divided into five functional groups.

Format Tab Group	Contains Commands For
Shapes	Changing the shape of and modifying the size of individual SmartArt shapes.
Shape Styles	Applying preconfigured or customized formatting to individual SmartArt shapes.
WordArt Styles	Applying preconfigured or customized formatting to the text within SmartArt shapes.
Arrange	Configuring the placement of, arranging, and rotating SmartArt shapes.
Size	Modifying the size of overall SmartArt graphics or individual SmartArt shapes.

 Access the Checklist tile on your CHOICE Course screen for reference information and job aids on How to Insert and Modify SmartArt.

F | Using Array Formulas

Appendix Introduction

In addition to the functions discussed in the course, Excel provides a type of function to help you easily reuse formulas throughout thousands of cells.

TOPIC A

Use Array Formulas

As you have used Excel for some time, you're likely well aware of the advantages of reusing formulas in worksheets. By copying a formula down a column or across a row, you save yourself the effort of manually typing the formula in each cell, or even of pasting the formula over and over again. This works well in smaller worksheets, but what if you had to drag a formula down a column with 10,000 rows? Although that would be much easier than manually typing a formula 10,000 times, this can still be awkward and time consuming. It seems there should be an easier way to perform a calculation on a large number of cells simultaneously.

Excel 2016 contains a powerful, yet largely underused, feature that enables you to perform tasks such as this, and a number of other seemingly complex computations, quickly, easily, and accurately: array formulas. Gaining a foundational understanding of how to use these powerful Excel formulas will open new doors to you, help you protect the integrity of your data, and generally make your Excel working life much easier.

Arrays

In order to understand how array formulas work, you'll need to know what an *array* is. An array, in the most basic sense, is simply a group of items. In Excel, an array is composed of the entries in a group of cells. An array can be made up of cell values from a single row or a single column, which are referred to as one-dimensional horizontal arrays and one-dimensional vertical arrays, respectively. An array can also include cell values from multiple rows or columns, in which case it is known as a two-dimensional array. You may be thinking that arrays sound exactly like ranges, and, in a sense, that's correct. The key difference between an array and a range is that an array is the representation of the values in a range in a computer's memory. Put another way, when an array formula acts upon a range, the range becomes an array. It is the range stored in the machine's memory so that the machine can perform calculations on it. It is important to keep in mind that arrays can also exist solely in a computer's memory without first being entered into cells.

 Note: You can store arrays by using defined names just as you can create named cells and ranges.

Array Formulas

Array formulas enable you to perform multiple calculations on cells in an array simultaneously. To illustrate the power and effectiveness of array formulas, consider the following image.

	A	B	C	D	E
1	Author	Sales	Rate	Commission	
2	Fred	$25,000.00	7.00%	$1,750.00	
3	Sally	$32,700.00	9.00%	$2,943.00	
4	Amy	$48,325.00	9.00%	$4,349.25	
5	Lauren	$75,456.00	9.00%	$6,791.04	
6	Bill	$103,210.00	12.00%	$12,385.20	
7	John	$5,978.00	7.00%	$418.46	
8					
9			Total	$28,636.95	
10					

Figure F–1: Example using formulas and functions.

Here, a formula has been entered in cell **D2** to multiply the author's sales by the commission rate. The formula was copied down the column from cell **D2** to cell **D7** and then the SUM function was used in cell **D9** to total the commission payments for all authors. This is likely the method you would have used in the same situation. However, imagine you were trying to do the same for a publishing company with 5,000 authors. It's easy to see how this could become quite a chore. Now, consider this example.

	A	B	C	D	E
1	Author	Sales	Rate		
2	Fred	$25,000.00	7.00%		
3	Sally	$32,700.00	9.00%		
4	Amy	$48,325.00	9.00%		
5	Lauren	$75,456.00	9.00%		
6	Bill	$103,210.00	12.00%		
7	John	$5,978.00	7.00%		
8					
9		Total Commissions Paid		$28,636.95	
10					

Figure F–2: Example using array formulas.

Here, the same total is reached, but without taking all of the extra steps as in the first example. So, how does one do this? By using array formulas. Here, Excel has been asked to multiply the figures in column **B** by the figures in column **C**, and then to add the products together and display the total in cell **D9**. And this was done by using a single formula. Let's take a closer look at how this works.

There are actually two general types of array formulas: *single-cell array formulas* and *multi-cell array formulas*. The aforementioned example illustrated the use of a single-cell array formula, but let's first look at multi-cell array formulas, as they may illustrate a little bit better how array formulas work.

Multi–Cell Array Formulas

As you may have guessed, you enter multi-cell array formulas in multiple cells, which yields multiple results for the calculation. Look back at the first example and consider the steps it took to calculate the commission payment for all authors. First, a simple multiplication formula was entered, and then it was dragged down so that it could be pasted into the remaining cells in the column. What if you didn't have to do that? Using multi-cell array formulas, you can calculate the commission payment for all authors at once, but you have to know how to tell Excel to do this.

Because array formulas work on arrays (stored values from ranges) instead of just single cells, you can enter a single array formula into all of the cells in the range **D2:D7** at once, and Excel will calculate the commission payment for all authors simultaneously. To do this, you would select the entire range **D2:D7** and then enter the following formula in the **Formula Bar**:

=B2:B7*C2:C7

Here, you're telling Excel to multiply the corresponding set of cells from each row together and place the associated results in the corresponding cells in the range **D2:D7**. But there's a catch: if you simply press **Enter** or **Tab** to enter the formula, Excel will calculate the result for the active cell only, leaving the others blank. To enter an array formula in worksheet cells, you must press **Ctrl +Shift+Enter**. For this reason, array formulas are often referred to as *Ctrl-Shift-Enter*, or CSE, formulas. When this array formula is entered properly, the worksheet will look like the following example.

D2	▼	:	✕	✓	*fx*	{=B2:B7*C2:C7}

◢	A	B	C	D	E
1	Author	Sales	Rate	Commission	
2	Fred	$25,000.00	7.00%	$1,750.00	
3	Sally	$32,700.00	9.00%	$2,943.00	
4	Amy	$48,325.00	9.00%	$4,349.25	
5	Lauren	$75,456.00	9.00%	$6,791.04	
6	Bill	$103,210.00	12.00%	$12,385.20	
7	John	$5,978.00	7.00%	$418.46	
8					

Figure F–3: Example using CSE formulas.

There are a couple of key points to mention here. First, notice the curly brackets. Excel automatically placed them around the formula when it was entered. Those brackets designate an array in Excel (more on that later). Second, Excel entered the exact same formula in each cell in the range **D2:D7**. You cannot change any of the array formulas without changing all of them, and you must press **Ctrl+Shift+Enter** if you wish to modify the array formula. This adds a level of protection for the formulas in your worksheets. Again, there will be more on this later.

Single–Cell Array Formulas

Single-cell array formulas perform multiple calculations on arrays and display the result in a single cell. In the second example in the previous section, a single-cell array formula was used to both multiply the sales figures by the rates for each author, and to add those results together to get the total payment figure, all with a single formula in cell **D9**.

| D9 | ▼ | : | × | ✓ | *fx* | {=SUM(B2:B7*C2:C7)} |

▲	A	B	C	D	E
1	Author	Sales	Rate		
2	Fred	$25,000.00	7.00%		
3	Sally	$32,700.00	9.00%		
4	Amy	$48,325.00	9.00%		
5	Lauren	$75,456.00	9.00%		
6	Bill	$103,210.00	12.00%		
7	John	$5,978.00	7.00%		
8					
9		Total Commissions Paid		$28,636.95	
10					

Figure F-4: Example using single-cell array formula.

Notice here that Excel automatically added the curly brackets around the formula, indicating it is an array formula. Also take note that the SUM function was used with the range references as arguments to complete the calculation. The array formula performed the first part of the calculation just as the aforementioned multi-cell array formula example did, and then it used the SUM function to add all of the results together. This illustrates the true power of the array formula.

You can use array formulas to save time, ensure formula accuracy, create leaner workbooks that take up less storage space and refresh calculations more quickly, use less real estate on your worksheets, and add a level of protection to your workbook calculations.

Array Formula Syntax

As is the case with any formula or function in Excel, understanding array syntax and array formula syntax lies at the core of mastering array formulas. You'll first look at array syntax and then examine how that applies to array formula syntax.

Array Syntax

As previously mentioned, arrays are similar to ranges but they exist in a computer's memory as opposed to existing in a series of worksheet cells. Although you can reference cell ranges in array formulas, you can also create arrays that exist only in memory. These arrays are known as *array constants*. An array constant is simply a series of values, logical values, or text entries stored in memory (as defined names) or entered directly into array formulas, as opposed to being entered in cells. Once created, array constants can be used in array formulas just as a constant can be used in a standard formula. There are four key points of array constant syntax:

- As with array formulas, array constants must be enclosed in curly brackets. There is an important difference between the two, though: you manually type the curly brackets to create an array constant.
- To separate entries into columns in an array constant, use commas.
- To separate entries into rows in an array constant, use semicolons.
- If you include text entries in an array constant, they must be enclosed in double quotation marks (" ").

Consider the following example:

10	15	20
12	56	32
11	98	78

The array constant equivalent of this range is **{10, 15, 20; 12, 56, 32; 11, 98, 78}**.

 Note: Keep in mind that array constants don't exist in actual, "physical" cells, so cell and range references do not apply.

So, rather than taking up worksheet space by populating the numeric values, you can simply use the array constant. Remember that you can also save an array by using a defined name so you can reuse it in multiple array formulas.

 Note: Array constants saved as defined names do not appear in the **Name Box** drop-down menu, but you can manually enter them into formulas or functions, and they do appear in the **Formula AutoComplete** drop-down menu.

Arrays in Array Formula Syntax

You create array formulas by using any formula operators or existing functions you would use to create standard formulas and functions in Excel. The key difference in the syntax of array formulas, as opposed to standard formulas and functions, is the set of curly brackets that enclose the formula. Excel automatically places brackets around a formula or function when you enter it by pressing **Ctrl +Shift+Enter**.

One other main difference is that you can include ranges and array constants as arguments in array formulas in order to perform multiple calculations using formula and function operators simultaneously, without having to copy formulas in multiple cells. Let's look at one more example to illustrate this point.

| D8 | ▼ | : | ✕ | ✓ | *fx* | {=SUM(B2:B6*C2:C6*D2:D6)} |

◢	A	B	C	D	E	F
1	Rep	Units Sold	Price	Rate		
2	Fred	12	$1,500.00	9.0%		
3	Amy	87	$1,700.00	8.0%		
4	Josephine	15	$3,265.00	12.0%		
5	Terri	65	$1,578.00	7.0%		
6	Joe	38	$9,874.00	9.0%		
7						
8		Total Commissions		$60,277.98		
9						

Figure F–5: Example of array formula syntax.

This example is slightly more complex than the first one examined. Here, the number of units each sales rep sold is being multiplied by the cost of the product each rep sells and then that number is multiplied by each sales rep's commission rate. This is all enclosed in a SUM function, so in one step, the total sales commissions the organization will have to pay out has been calculated. Let's break down the syntax:

- The curly brackets tell Excel that this is an array formula, so it can perform operations on related values from a series of arrays (in this case, ranges).
- The SUM function tells Excel to add a series of values.

- The set of parentheses enclose the arguments for the SUM function as they would for a standard SUM function.
- The arguments for the SUM function, as this is an array formula, are telling Excel to multiply the corresponding values in the various columns for each rep. For example, for Fred, the formula multiplies 12 by 1,500 and then multiplies the product of that calculation by 9 percent. For Amy, the formula multiplies 87 by 1,700, and then multiplies the product by 8 percent. This carries on for each rep, and then Excel sums all of those values to provide the total commissions paid of $60,277.98.

It is also important to remember that you can simply include array constants in array formulas, and these can be used in place of or in conjunction with range references. Let's say you need to present the information from the previous example at a sales meeting and you don't want to reveal commission rates for sales reps to the other people in the room. By using array constants, you can create the same array formula without the need to display the commission rate data in cells.

| D8 | | fx | {=SUM(B2:B6*C2:C6*{0.09;0.08;0.12;0.07;0.09})} |

	A	B	C	D	E	F	G	H
1	Rep	Units Sold	Price					
2	Fred	12	$1,500.00					
3	Amy	87	$1,700.00					
4	Josephine	15	$3,265.00					
5	Terri	65	$1,578.00					
6	Joe	38	$9,874.00					
7								
8		Total Commissions		$60,277.98				
9								

Figure F-6: Example using array constants in array formulas.

Notice here that the range reference **D2:D6** was simply replaced with the array constant **{0.09;0.08;0.12;0.07;0.09}**. This way, the data doesn't need to appear in the worksheet but the array formula performs the same calculation. Remember that you must manually type the curly brackets around array constants in array formulas. You must also press **Ctrl+Shift+Enter** to enter the formula as an array formula; again, Excel automatically places the outside curly brackets around the entire array formula.

Let's look at one more simple example of how array formulas can work on entire ranges (arrays) of data. Let's say you want to multiply one range of values by another range of values, but the values are contained in multiple rows and columns as in this worksheet.

Figure F–7: Example of array formulas and ranges of data.

Here, the array formula is multiplying the corresponding values from the range **A1:C3** and the range **E1:G3** and returning the products in the cells in **A5:C7**. The formula systematically multiplies the value in **A1** by the value in **E1** and places the result in cell **A5**. Then it does the same for **B1** and **F1** and places the result in **B5**. This carries on until all nine values are calculated and the results are returned in the associated cells. And it's all done with a single array formula.

Array Formula Rules

You must follow some pretty specific rules when working with arrays and array formulas. While some of these have been touched upon in the previous sections, here is a recap of the rules that have already been covered and a few rules that haven't been mentioned yet.

Array Formula Rules

- You must press **Ctrl+Shift+Enter** to enter an array formula. This is perhaps the most important rule you should remember about array formulas.
- Excel automatically places the curly brackets around an array formula when you press **Ctrl+Shift +Enter**. If you type them in the formula yourself, Excel treats the formula like text. Remember that all formulas must begin with an equal sign. If you begin a formula with an open curly bracket, Excel won't know you want to enter a formula.
- You can use any of the built-in functions in Excel as array formulas.

Multi-Cell Array Formula Rules

- You must first select all cells into which you wish to place a multi-cell array formula, and then enter the formula.
- You cannot edit or delete a multi-cell array formula in just one or only some of the cells containing it. You must delete or change it in all cells at once.
- You can move an entire multi-cell array formula, but you cannot move only some of the cells included in the formula.
- You cannot insert or delete rows, columns, or cells in a multi-cell array formula, but you can add rows or columns to the end of one.

Array Rules

- You must manually enter the curly brackets around array constants.
- In arrays, commas separate entries into columns and semicolons separate entries into rows.
- Arrays can contain numeric values, text, or logical values.
- In arrays, text must be enclosed in double quotation marks (" ").
- Array constants cannot contain other arrays, formulas, or functions.

- You can save array constants as defined names, and use those defined names in formulas and functions just as you would a named cell or range.

> **Access the Checklist tile on your CHOICE Course screen for reference information and job aids on How to Use Array Formulas.**

ACTIVITY F–1
Using Array Formulas

Data File

C:\091056Data\Using Array Formulas\Author Data.xlsx

Before You Begin

Excel 2016 is open.

Scenario

Company leadership is interested in knowing more about how much value they're receiving from the company's relationships with its authors. In addition to the information you've already provided, your supervisor is now asking for detailed information about income based on the number of titles each of the authors has published through Fuller and Ackerman and the average income the company has earned per contract year. Specifically, she wants to know:

- How much income has the company generated from each author per title?
- What is the average income per year under contract for all authors?

You'd like anyone viewing your workbook to be able to easily tell how you arrived at these figures, so you decide not to use the calculated totals in the **Income Earned** column to perform the calculations to answer the first question. You also decide to use array formulas to answer both questions to avoid unnecessary copying of formulas.

---

1. In Excel, open the workbook, **Author Data.xlsx**.

2. Label a column for income per title and add a new label for average income per contract year.

   a) If necessary, select cell **H1**, type *Income Per Title* and then press **Enter**.
   b) Select cell **J4**, type *Average Income/Contract Year* and then press **Enter**.
   c) If necessary, adjust the width of column **J** to accommodate the new label.

3. Use a multi-cell array formula to determine the income per title for each author.

   a) In the **Name Box**, type *h2:h94* and then press **Enter**.

    Note: Please follow these steps precisely as written. After you type the range and press **Enter**, you can simply begin typing the text in the following step. You do not need to select anything on-screen first.

   b) Type *=(n*
   c) From the pop-up menu, double-click **No_of_Books_Sold**.
   d) Type **se*
   e) From the pop-up menu, double-click **Sell_Price**.

f) Type **)/no** and, from the pop-up menu, double-click **No_of_Titles_in_Print**.

H	I	J	K
=(No_of_Books_Sold*Sell_Price)/No_of_Titles_in_Print			
		Average Sales Over $5.99	$3,213,926.04
		Average Income/Contract Year	

g) Press **Ctrl+Shift+Enter**.

h) Verify that Excel placed curly brackets around the formula and entered it into all of the selected cells.

fx {=(No_of_Books_Sold*Sell_Price)/No_of_Titles_in_Print}

i) Apply the **Currency** number format to the cells in column **H**.

4. Use a single-cell array formula to determine the overall average of income per contract year.

   a) Select cell **K4**.
   b) Enter the following formula: *=average(Income_Earned/Years_Under_Contract)*
   c) Press **Ctrl+Shift+Enter**.
   d) Verify that Excel placed curly brackets around the function and then entered it into cell **K4**.

fx {=AVERAGE(Income_Earned/Years_Under_Contract)}

Earned	Income Per Title	I	J	K
,785.63	$84,119.04		Authors Five or Fewer Years	28
,214.56	$147,586.75		Average Sales Over $5.99	$3,213,926.04
,643.50	$1,021,321.75		Average Income/Contract Year	602911.8288
,555.01	$83,323.18			

   e) Apply the **Currency** number format to cell **K4**.

5. Save and close the workbook.

Mastery Builders

Mastery Builders are provided for certain lessons as additional learning resources for this course. Mastery Builders are developed for selected lessons within a course in cases when they seem most instructionally useful as well as technically feasible. In general, mastery builders are supplemental, optional unguided practice and may or may not be performed as part of the classroom activities. Your instructor will consider setup requirements, classroom timing, and instructional needs to determine which mastery builders are appropriate for you to perform, and at what point during the class. If you do not perform the mastery builders in class, your instructor can tell you if you can perform them independently as self-study, and if there are any special setup requirements.

Mastery Builder 1-1
Working with Functions

Activity Time: 10 minutes

Data File

C:\091056Data\Working with Functions\Employee Summary.xlsx

Scenario

You are the sales manager for your organization. You are preparing a summary of employee location information and their hire dates. The company is awarding a gas grill to all employees with 20 years of service, and a telescope to those with 25 years of service. You need to figure out which employees on your list will be awarded which gift.

1. Open Excel 2016, and open the workbook **Employee Summary.xlsx**.

2. Enter a function in **B1** to insert today's date.

3. Create range names for the columns in the dataset based on the column labels.

4. Enter a function to join campus, building, and floor to create Location Code.

5. Enter a function to join First and Last Name with a space between them.

6. Enter a function to calculate the Years of Service.

7. Enter a function to calculate the award given if an employee has greater than or equal to 25 years of service (they will be awarded a telescope). If they have greater than or equal to 20 years service, they will be awarded a grill.

8. Save the workbook to the **C:\091056Data\Working with Functions** folder as *My Employee Summary.xlsx* and close the file.

Mastery Builder 2–1
Working with Lists

Activity Time: 10 minutes

Data File

C:\091056Data\Working with Lists\All Employees.xlsx

Scenario

In your role as an HR Generalist, you have a listing of all employees. This list was created in the order in which the employees were added. You want to sort the employees list to put it in order by last name. You also want to find out how many employees are from Alaska. In addition, you want a set of employees that are from either Carbon Creek or Carlin. You decide to perform an advanced filter and copy the results to another area in order to leave the original list unchanged.

---

1. Open the workbook **All Employees.xlsx**.

2. Sort the Employees list by last name.

3. Filter the list for employees living in Alaska.

4. Clear the filter from State.

5. Create a criteria area to search for employees that live in either Carbon Creek or Carlin using the asterisk (*) wildcard.

6. Perform an Advanced Filter and copy the results to cell **J4**.

7. Save the workbook to the **C:\091056Data\Working with Lists** folder as *My All Employees.xlsx* and close the file.

Mastery Builder 3-1
Analyzing Data

Activity Time: 10 minutes

Data File

C:\091056Data\Analyzing Data\European Sales.xlsx

Scenario

As the European Sales Manager, you are analyzing quarterly sales across Europe. You want to create a table from the listed data and add in totals for each country as well as for each quarter. In addition, you want to highlight the countries with the highest total sales

1. Open the workbook **European Sales.xlsx**.

2. Insert a table for the European sales data.

3. Enter a **Totals** heading after Quarter 4.

4. Enter a function that will total each country's quarterly sales.

5. Enable the Total Row option for the table and sum each quarter.

6. Apply conditional formatting to the country names when total sales for the countries are over $20,000.

7. Save the workbook to the **C:\091056Data\Analyzing Data** folder as *My European Sales.xlsx* and close the file.

Mastery Builder 4–1
Visualizing Data with Charts

Activity Time: 10 minutes

Data File

C:\091056Data\Visualizing Data with Charts\Sales Summary.xlsx

Scenario

As the sales manager preparing for the upcoming annual sales meeting, you want to create some charts to include in your discussions. You have totaled the raw sales data by region across each quarter and want to see the trend for the next two quarters. In addition, you have total sales and average sales per quarter and you think it would be a good idea to present this data on the same chart. You decide to create a dual-axis combo chart for this data.

1. Open the workbook **Sales Summary.xlsx**.

2. Verify that the Summary worksheet is selected and create a 2-D Clustered Column chart from the data in **A1:E6**, and move it to **G1**.

3. Insert a linear trendline for **Quarter4** data forecasting forward two periods.

4. Create a dual-axis combo chart from the data in **A8:E10**.

5. Set the Average/Quarter values on the Secondary Axis and move the chart to **B18**.

6. Save the workbook to the **C:\091056Data\Visualizing Data with Charts** folder as *My Sales Summary.xlsx* and close the file.

Mastery Builder 5-1
Using PivotTables and PivotCharts

Activity Time: 10 minutes

Data File

C:\091056Data\Using PivotTables and PivotCharts\Quarterly Data.xlsx

Scenario

As the sales manager preparing for the upcoming annual sales meeting, you want to be able to answer any question from the audience regarding sales performance from any region, product line, or date. In order to accomplish this task, you decide to create a PivotTable and PivotChart. To add additional flexibility, you also want to include slicers and a timeline.

---

1. Open the workbook **Quarterly Data.xlsx**.

2. Use the values on the Data worksheet to create a new PivotTable on a new worksheet.

3. Add the following fields to the PivotTable report: Region, Product Line, Line Manager, and Total Sale.

4. Move the **Line Manager** field to the **COLUMNS** area.

5. Create a 3-D Clustered Column PivotChart from the PivotTable and move the chart to I3.

6. In the bottom-right corner of the chart, select the **Collapse Entire Field** button ▬ to collapse the detail of the report.

7. Insert a timeline for the **Date** field of the PivotTable and move it to cell I18.

8. Adjust the time level on the timeline to **Quarters** and select **Q1** of 2016.

9. Insert slicers for Region and Sales Rep and move them to cells **B12** and **E12**, respectively.

10. Using the Sales Rep slicer, filter for the sales rep **Anderson**.

11. Save the workbook to the **C:\091056Data\Analyzing Data with PivotTables and PivotCharts** folder as *My Quarterly Data.xlsx* and close the file.

Glossary

array
A range of data that can be entered into a computer's memory and accessed by Excel for data analysis that does not necessarily have to exist within worksheet cells.

array constants
A series of values, logical values, or text entries that are stored in memory or entered directly into array formulas, as opposed to being entered in cells.

array formulas
A type of Excel formula that allows users to perform multiple calculations on cells in an array simultaneously.

AutoFilters
Preconfigured, common filtering options that enable Excel users to quickly remove from view all data that does not meet some specified criteria.

cell names
Meaningful names users can assign to particular cells to make it easier to both understand what specific calculations are being performed in a formula and to reuse the references for a number of purposes.

chart elements
The individual objects that can appear on charts and that convey some level of information to a viewer about the chart's data.

charts
Graphical representations of the numeric values and relationships in a dataset.

combo chart
In Excel, a chart that contains data series of differing chart types.

comparison operators
A type of Excel operator used to compare particular values to determine whether or not they meet some specified criteria.

criteria range
In terms of Excel advanced filtering and database functions, the worksheet range that contains the user-defined criteria to perform a particular operation.

Ctrl–Shift–Enter formulas
Also known as CSE formulas. An alternate name for Excel array formulas, as users must press **Ctrl+Shift+Enter** to enter an array formula.

custom AutoFilters
User-defined Excel AutoFilters.

custom sort
A user-defined sort that can be applied to either rows or columns, that can be applied to multiple rows or columns simultaneously, and that can be highly customized.

database functions

A set of Excel functions that enable users to perform calculations on ranges of data based on specific criteria.

entry

An individual row of data in a transactional dataset. An entry represents one single transaction, such as a sale.

Excel function reference

A Help article that lists all Excel functions by category and describes each in detail.

fields

The columns in a transactional dataset.

filtering

The process of removing from view any data entries that do not match some specified criteria.

forecasting

The process of using the trends that exist within past data to predict future outcomes.

level

In terms of Excel custom sorting, an independent, specific criterion by which a dataset is sorted. Users can specify multiple levels for a custom sort.

logical values

An Excel data type that expresses whether or not particular data meets some specified criteria. There are only two logical values in Excel: TRUE and FALSE.

multi-cell array formula

An array formula that performs multiple calculations on arrays and displays the results in multiple cells.

nesting

The process of using a function as an argument in another function or as part of a formula's expression.

object properties

Particular Excel object settings that enable you to control the behavior of objects on worksheets relative to the cells beneath them.

outline

An Excel feature that enables users to organize datasets into hierarchical groups of varying levels of detail that they can expand or collapse depending on how much detail they want to see.

PivotCharts

Similar to standard Excel charts, these are graphical representations of numeric values and relationships among those values. The key difference between charts and PivotCharts is that PivotCharts are linked to the data in PivotTables.

pivoting

In Excel, a form of data manipulation that can take a column of data and pivot it into a row and vice versa.

PivotTable

A dynamic Excel data object that enables users to perform data analysis by pivoting columns and rows of raw data without altering the raw data.

quick sorts

Preconfigured sorting options that enable workbook users to quickly sort data based on common criteria.

quick styles

Preconfigured table styles.

range names

Meaningful names users can assign to particular ranges to make it easier to both understand what specific calculations are being performed in a formula and to reuse the references for a number of purposes.

rule precedence

The order in which Excel evaluates and applies conditional formatting rules to cells.

shared slicers

Slicers that are connected to and that filter multiple PivotTables simultaneously. Any

PivotTables based on a common dataset can share slicers.

single-cell array formula
An array formula that performs multiple calculations on arrays and displays the result in a single cell.

slicers
Individual Excel objects used to filter the data in PivotTables.

sorting
The process of reordering worksheet data based on some defined criteria, such as alphabetically or from highest value to lowest value.

SUBTOTAL functions
A specific set of Excel functions that perform calculations on subsets of data.

Subtotals feature
An Excel feature that enables users to automatically perform SUBTOTAL function calculations on subsets of data within a particular dataset.

summary functions
An Excel feature that automatically performs SUBTOTAL function calculations in tables. Users can access this functionality from the total row down arrows in each column.

table
A dataset composed of contiguous rows and columns that Excel treats as a single, independent object.

table styles
Particular configurations of formatting options users can apply to worksheet tables.

Text pane
An element of the Excel user interface that enables users to add and edit text on SmartArt graphics.

timelines
Individual Excel objects used to filter date-related data in PivotTables.

transactional data
Data that represents each individual transaction, or event, in a series of transactions, and that is not summarized in any way, shape, or form. Transactional data does not typically contain row labels; it includes only column labels.

Index